Joanny Moulin

Ted Hughes
The Haunted Earth

A biography

CONTENTS

FOREWORD

From time to time, one of those giants will loom forth, like huge trees casting familiar shadows around them. When they disappear, decades may elapse before there comes another poet showing promises of similar force. It is as if some tutelary spirits were presiding over the apparently arbitrary choices of literary glory. All of a sudden, some imposing figure dominates the poetic scene, and will do so till his time is over. In the case of Ted Hughes, this crystallisation, the moment when it all started, was that of his meeting with another poet of similar force: Sylvia Plath whose influence on American poetry would match that of Ted Hughes on English poetry. The strange thing is that both seemed to have had from the start the profound conviction that such would be the case. It would be truer to say that poetry had chosen them rather than they had themselves decided to follow its calling. Ted Hughes was later to write that they had only done what poetry had told them to do. The Valkyrie of glory seemed to have picked them, like the falcon of love, for reasons known to the gods alone, unless it was the tragic farce of a blind, melancholy Cupid with wings as black as a crow's. From that time on, they were the toys of a greater destiny, as if together they had been possessed by spirits whose voices they did everything they could to stay tuned to and transcribe. It would be wrong to think that Sylvia Plath was simply Ted Hughes's wife, just as it would be a mistake to see him as her husband. It is in fact both very complicated and very simple: each of their poetic works is a personal response to the enigma set by the sphinx of love. Both in their own way are wrestling with the ghoul that is after them: why love? Why this irresistible attraction and impossible agreement between a man and a woman? Ted Hughes, in his poetry, never ceased to probe the relationship between the masculine and the feminine. He would even go as far, in his attempt to account for and explain it, as to invent a theology. This places him in a long tradition of English poets: Milton, Blake, and to some extent Shelley, then more recently Yeats, who all plunged into the elaboration of imaginary worlds in their efforts to penetrate the mysteries of the world in which we live. Like them, Hughes was convinced that he had something to say to the world, and he considered it his duty to write it all before leaving it. Past and present contained so much that was regrettable, that he wanted to do everything in his power to change the future. To double his chances of being heard by the generations to come, he split himself in two to produce, in parallel, a plethora of poems and tales for children. Perhaps, he found there his true public, the readers dearest to his heart. For poetry, like childhood, is slipping out of a world getting too old too fast.

I

YORKSHIRE

Eroded relief of Yorkshire. These low hills and shal-
low dales were tirelessly scraped by the glaciers, of
which they retain the unforgettable wear. The valleys
have very little depth, and seem still erasing themselves, imperceptibly yet ineluctably. The horizons, at
once too far and too near, exsude an irremediable sadness, under pale skies that steep the landscapes with
northern light, always slightly grey. The flattened
curves of the land are like those of an incommensur-
able animal sleeping, that sometimes seems to stir a
little when some sea storm sends a shiver down its
skin. On these low waves of heath and sheep pastures
lined by stone walls, where the weather meets no
hindrance whatsoever, everything has learnt to endure. To hide away as best they can from wind and
rain, houses and trees huddle in wet hollows down
which the rain runs. The earth around the churches is
saturated with tombs of all ages, until the gravestones
make a continuous pavement, on which the rare visitors have to tread. Some stones are broken or dis-
placed, yet nobody has ever presumed to bring some
derisory order to the work of time. Dust thou art, and
to dust thou shalt return. The dead return very precisely to the earth in a kind of stoic, indifferent resig-
nation of the living: a sort of ostentatious disdain of
ostentation. Rarely does even the most unassuming of
crosses adorn the graves of these severe Puritans, who
were in the past particularly receptive to the Methodist doctrine of Wesley. Over the years, rain, frost and
the continuous tread of passers-by have got the better
of the inscriptions on the stones.

In the village of Heptonstall, the Old Church of
Saint Thomas Beckett, dedicated to the saint in about

the year 1260, was strangely abandoned in the middle of the 19th century after a storm severely damaged the steeple. Indifferent to history, the parishioners preferred to seize the opportunity thus offered to build a new church. The old church was thus abandoned to the injuries of time, the roof caved in and only stone arches remained, like the ribs of some large bird. For the poet, it inevitably evoked the derelict state of Christianity of which, he thought, nothing but ghost-like vestiges survived. In the new graveyard, the site where Edith Farrar and her husband William Hughes rest together is surmounted by a vertical tombstone of gray granite on which their names are engraved. A similar stone marks the burial place of Sylvia Plath Hughes. It bears a poetic epitaph affirming that even among fierce flames the golden lotus can be planted. A few red flowers like those of the sage, evoking the salvia, and a yellow rose bush are planted in a small narrow rectangle of earth bordered with stones indicating the place of burial, around which the trodden grass testifies to frequent visits.

The desolate streets of Heptonstall are cambered cobbled lanes, with no pavements, lined with severe-looking black stone houses with stunted front gardens, bordered with low walls made of similar stones carefully joined with cement, with a paved gutter running right at the foot. To this day, the air is charged with a vague, oppressive sense of anguish which seems to leave little room for hope in this world. The rural drift of people from the land has left these rural parts of Yorkshire still more desolate than before, yet melancholy seems to be precisely what a few tourists on short day-trips from the neighbouring cities come looking for. Throughout the ages, this country has demanded of those who tried to survive on it a constant struggle as well as a tough and rugged character.

In the 18th century, during the industrial revolution, when water mills were being turned into factories, spinning mills were built on the banks of mountain streams to exploit their water power. Later, owing to the pursuit of profit and the pressures of history, these manufacturing places were transformed into steam-powered factories, for which coal was feverishly conveyed by road in a vain attempt to keep pace with the big nearby centres of Leeds, Sheffield, Manchester, Liverpool. But soon, this sudden technological outburst began to wane, as if it were but an isolated episode lost in the indifference of an immutable nature, which would not even stoop down to pastoral beauty. At Lumb, the factory chimneys have long been conquered by brush that has outgrown them. Like the old church of Heptonstall, they are slowly going back to the earth. Now that Protestantism and the diligent practice of its virtues have finally bitten the dust, it would seem the romantic critics were right to inveigh against too strict an interpretation of the Gospel which, in the end, made no difference between the hope of an afterlife and success in this world, to the point of forgetting all the emotions of the heart.

Edith Farrar, the poet's mother, came from a family that had been strongly influenced by the Methodist revival. It owed its relatively comfortable financial means to the local textile industry. In the family they liked to talk somewhat exaggeratedly of the wealth of Uncle Walter, a jovial fellow known a little pompously as "the millionaire" because he was the proprietor of one of the local factories that made velvets and Moderna blankets. Edith was 22 in May 1920 when she married, a love-match, but a little beneath her, William Henry Hughes, who was four years older than her, a carpenter by trade and a part-time professional footballer playing for the team of Hebden Bridge until the age of 30. Billy Hughes, a convinced partisan of free enterprise, ran a tobacco shop at My-tholmroyd, a West Yorkshire village. He also sold newspapers and occasionally acted as bookmaker to supplement his income. The family lived at the back of the shop, at 1 Aspinal Street, a town house with a black brick front. Edward James Hughes was born there, on August 17th, 1930 at 1:12 a. m. according to the midwife's watch; as Britain was then on summer time, it must have been exactly twelve minutes past midnight according to the sun. Ted Hughes was to keep the precise hour of his birth secret for a long time, for he liked to convince himself of the important influence of the stars, and wanted to reserve the right to exploit this knowledge to his own advantage. Those who are born under the solar sign Leo are supposed to be radiantly egocentric, but Ted Hughes was born when Cancer was ascendant so that his fortune was strongly linked to family life. Equally noteworthy was the conjunction of the sun with Neptune, a planet associated with the invention of images and symbols. Ted Hughes was later to take an active interest in astrology through his sister Olwyn, two years his elder, in order to read in the stars the signs foretelling talents and literary glory. Ted was the youngest of three children, and this was to have great influence upon the formation of his character. He would maintain throughout his life an affectionate admiration for his brother Gerald, for example, born ten years before him, who would play the part of an initiator in a way which far surpassed what typically takes place among the members of a family.

Apart from the stars and their doubtful influence, other forces work ineluctably upon a child, and prove just as decisive. Among these atmospheric influences, one must not forget the climate of Yorkshire, which gives a grim edge to things, making happiness seem decidedly out of reach. In England, particularly in these rural parts of the North, real life always seems to be elsewhere, somewhere towards the South or beyond the sea. The low horizons, the hills worn down to the rock, upon which the clouds and the rain have weighed too long, give the impression of trapping you inside a magic circle from which you will never escape. At Mytholmroyd, towards the South, moreover, the horizon is barred by the crag of Scout Rock, above which the sun hardly ever rises in winter and whose mournful steep face seems to make the laborious routine of everyday life heavier still. Over the centuries, this severe aspect of the land communicated itself to the character of the people, until the influence of the climate joined with the silence that prevailed in the social life of this rural world. Billy Hughes, the father, whom his children laconically addressed as Pa, was a man of few words. Certainly, Yorkshire men are often naturally taciturn, but, in Billy Hughes's world, a man knew how to keep silent. But there was something else too. Sometimes, this silence grew worse and became so heavy it was disquieting. Pa would stay prostrate in his armchair as if lost in thought and cry silently without saying why. Sometimes, at night he would wake up with a shout. Other people, little by little, would bring answers to the questions that the children were asking. Aunt Hilda, perhaps, who lived at number 13 Aspinal Street, or Uncle Albert, at number 19, who spent whole days carving wooden figurines to earn a few shillings and who would one day hang himself in his attic. William Henry Hughes was a veteran of World War I, he had been awarded the Distinguished Conduct Medal for the part he had played in the tragic episode of the Dardanelles; in the landing on the Gallipoli Peninsula he had witnessed the decimation of his regiment of Lancashire Fusiliers. He was among the seventeen to have escaped from the massacre. Yet in a way, he too had been killed there. He had been caught in the chest, near the heart, by a piece of shrapnel miraculously stopped by his paybook which he kept as a souvenir in a tin box, along with his Medal and a few photographs of his conscripts, among whom were the six young men from his village whose names he would recall as he ran his finger over the yellow photograph: all killed in battle. It was as if Billy Hughes had returned from the dead after having been buried alive in a shell-hole. The affection of his family, the love of Edith and of his children had given him back the force to live, but had been unable to heal the wound of memory. Why? Many years would be needed as well as the sense of his public responsibilities, before his son Ted could bring himself to wear a poppy in his button-hole on Poppy Day to commemorate the end of the First World War and honour those who died in action. For he had already paid his debt, at far too high a price, and it seemed that the wound, still festering, would never heal.

Uncle Walt, also a veteran, had served on the continent. He used to tell, for instance, how once upon a time he had felt that being observed by a big German prisoner put the evil eye on him. And no mistake, for later on the same day he had been nailed down in a shell-hole by a sniper who had caught him in the groin and grazed his temple; while he waited patiently for the sniper to let go he had imagined himself at home walking in the hills and woods around his place from Peckett to Midgley, Mytholmroyd, Redacre, Hebden, Crimsworth Dene, Schakleton Hill, Widdop, Hardcastle, Heptonstall, along the canal as far as Ewood, the homeplace of his ancestors, and on to his worsted mill, to remote places known to himself alone where he used to make camp for the night during hunting parties. So it was that the tales of old people grafted memories of the war upon the places Ted Hughes had known as a child. In the same manner, every passionate reader, every child who is fond of tales, vividly pictures to himself the remarkable scenes that he meets in books and, setting them in the places he knows well, can almost believe they actually happened to him in real life. Indeed he feels them more intensely than the scenes of ordinary life. And so his native country was full of confused presences. It was naturally favourable to dreams, inhabited as it was by memories and ghosts whose voices seemed sometimes perceptible, in the wind and the rain and in the songs of birds. It was also the country of the Brontë sisters, and the heathery moors of *Wuthering Heights* nearby were still a place of literary pilgrimage. Melancholy, that permeates space and time like a hardly visible soot, might sometimes call for inspired dreams. But this prevalent atmosphere of diffuse intuitions found a particular echo in Edith and in the women of the family. Sometimes, Ma too would cry for no apparent reason. It was hard to understand. It made no sense, perhaps, but it was so. There was no rational way of accounting for Edith's tears. She was psychic. Powers invisible to anyone but her inhabited these gloomy landscapes. Edith would often be aware of the presence at the foot of her bed of her sister Miriam who had died in adolescence; over the years, her appearance changed, so that she came to look more and more like a luminous angel. Throughout her life the ghost would appear at the foot of her bed whenever there was a death in the family. On the night when her brother Albert hanged himself she had suffered acute pains. And again, for instance, the first time the Allies landed in Normandy, she had seen a multitude of shining crosses in the sky. Ted was later to learn that William Blake, the great romantic poet who was so much to influence his own vision of the world, had been possessed of very similar gifts and he later harboured the strong conviction that he had inherited his mother's powers to which, he believed, he could gain access in his dreams.

Although he practically never spoke of it, and then only during the last years of his life, Ted felt a strong physical fascination for his mother. There was something almost atavistic in the feeling. Edith Farrar was a small-sized, round-shaped woman with a pleasant-looking face that Ted would describe as leonine; she had very dark hair that her son liked to compare to that of an Native woman, even if it was on his father's side that one of his great grandmothers, of Spanish origin, was reputed to have been "half-moorish." But it was on the Farrar side that the most historically distinguished of his ancestors were to be found. In the 16th century, one Robert Farrar, an Anglican bishop, had the glory of being burnt alive in the reign of Mary the Catholic, which won him an immortal place among the heroes of the Reformation in Foxe's *Book of Martyrs*. Then, in the 17th century, Nicholas Farrar, the protestant pastor had founded the religious community of Little Gidding commemorated by T.S. Eliot in his *Four Quartets*. Again John Farrar, Nicholas's brother, had emigrated to America to join the Virginia Company. Numbered among his descendants was Thomas Jefferson and the John Farrar who later founded the publishing house Farrar & Strauss, today Farrar, Strauss & Giroux, that published most of Ted Hughes's poems in America. Beyond these anecdotes, however, Ted liked to think that his family's roots went deep down into this Northern part of England which his anthropological studies inclined him to regard as corresponding to the frontiers of Elmet, which he saw as the last Celtic realm of the Great British Isle. In his poetic dreamland, umbilically linking Ted Hughes to his country was Ma's voice. Ma, a voluble woman mostly, never short on stories and gossip that she would recount in dialect to those who were still able to understand it, but always with the gruff accent characteristic of Yorkshire, that Ted himself would never lose.

However, long before he became conscious of these decisive influences, as far back as he could remember, Ted, as a child, played with small lead animals that were sold in the family shop at Mytholmroyd. Then, while his elder brother Gerald was busy modelling motor boats in balsa wood which he would sail on the canal and aeroplanes which really could fly, Ted would spend long hours fashioning animals out of clay. Looking back upon that period of his life, he would say that the animal which fascinated him most as a child was the jaguar, like the one he had seen one day locked up in a very small cage at Morecambe zoo during an excursion to this seaside town in Lancashire. It was this animal, the black panther, that he would most often try to model. As the boys grew older, the lead animals or those cut out of magazines and pictorials had aroused interests that they could no longer satisfy. But Banksfield Road, that cut Aspinal Street at a right angle, ran right through the village and straight into the countryside. Ted was six, maybe even less, when Gerald started to take him on his shooting expeditions. They would get silently out of bed at 4 or 5 in the morning to go roaming over the moors with their guns. Soon they launched into poaching expeditions in the brakes and woods of the Calder Valley. They would sleep under a tent and roast their booty over camp fires. Lying in wait for game is a difficult art: you have to remain silent and motionless in the twilight at the edge of a wood or behind a rise in the ground. The animals are there but remain invisible and, to have a chance of sighting them, one must learn to watch. Ted would later think that by the age of seven, Gerald's teaching had developed in him a new organ, a sort of sixth sense, so real that he used to call it his subsidiary brain.

They had to gain access to the right spot before dawn to watch, as the light of the day increased, the emergence of a world gradually revealing all its details. In the constantly moving air and the changing light, the shadows and outer shapes of things disclosed their magic under his gaze, and sometimes it was in this trancelike state of concentration that the meeting with an animal would take place. It always came unexpectedly, causing him to shiver, making his hair stand on end and his heart pound. It was always a moment of grace, a kind of revelation. The animal would stand exposed like Truth itself rising naked from some invisible well, precisely where you expected her least, but only in the eyes of the beholder, as if for him alone. He thought he was in a dream, he was not quite sure he could distinguish between what was real and what was only a dream, and the world seemed to metamorphose or to reveal itself according to how he looked at it. This was how the two boys played, with a passionate intensity never to be equalled, perhaps, in any other part of their lives. The world of their imagination seemed stronger than that of ordinary life. They were playing at being trappers for good. Gerald would give free rein to the gift he had for inventing stories; he imagined a hunter's world in which he was a North-American Native or a man from the paleolithic. For the sleepers in the tent, the sound of the wind in the trees, the songs of birds, the occasional rustle of dead leaves as an animal passed mingled with their dreams of chases and wonderful meetings with animals; at other times they became nightmares and inexplicable slaughters, at other times still, some strange enigma that it would take them years to understand.

Those shooting parties of his early youth, those memorable expeditions, those long periods of carelessness and intense day-dreaming were to be idealised later in his memory to form the perfect image of a golden age of childhood, so quick to pass away. For, when Ted had just turned eight, the family left his native village of Mytholmroyd and moved

south a little to settle in Mexborough. His father opened a tobacconist's and a newsagent's shop at 75
Main Street. No doubt it would have been easier for
Ted to surmount the pain of separation from all the
familiar places that had been the scene of his early
dreams, had he not had to learn to live far from his
elder brother. For Gerald, who was now eighteen, and
who had no inclination to go to college, had taken a
job as a game-keeper on a large estate away south in
Devon, much too far from the Yorkshire of their
young years for the free adventurous trappers' life to
go on. Ted felt that he had been abandoned. Gerald
had gone away to live his real life as a hunter since it
was now his job, but Ted had no part in it, and he was
too young to go hunting alone. Moreover, Mexborough was a small mining town, all black with the
grime of industrial pollution, whose factories dirtied
the surrounding countryside. It was a near Dickensian
caricature, of the small provincial town incorrigibly
stuck in its way, whose inhabitants, living for work
alone, have themselves been turned into machines.
The chapels and churches of the different denomina-
tions shared the same Protestant contempt for vani-
ties: they were barely distinguishable from the brick
industrial buildings. Workers going home at the end
of the day lost no time changing their clothes; they
could be seen silently hurrying along the wind-swept
streets in their dirty working overalls. The minds of
the people were gripped by a moral of hard work and
resigned frustration, by the ingrained belief that one
should scrimp and strain, such as each one would
strenuously practice upon himself, refusing to grant
any legitimacy to their own desires as if their lot was
only hard work in this world, and the bare hope of
better days in the world to come. And yet, this society
seemed quietly to radiate a peculiar energy that came
not so much from resentment as from grim endurance
and sturdy resistance to pain. These unassuming peo-

ple were independent and wilful; they took pride in self-denial and they doggedly continued to fight day after day in the face of adversity, clenching their fists and gritting their teeth. In the evening, they would go and watch a film or the news, then they would meet at the pub between men over a few pints of beer until the bell rang and the bartender announced closing time. Then, around 11 PM, they would all go home more or less quietly, often singing in the streets to ward off the following day.

The Hugheses' tobacconist's shop was undoubtedly one of the most convenient places where people could have a chat. The customers came in to buy the newspapers or tobacco but rarely missed the opportunity to exchange a few words about the weather; they could also talk about their lives and spread local gossip. Soon the backdrop where the Hughes family lived became the anteroom of local news, resounding with the rumours of intrigues and unexpected new turns that agitated the lives of the different families of the town. Small town shops are regular treasure houses, but for a child to be the son of a newsagent is a great boon indeed. Magazines, illustrated children's books, comic strips. Everyday, when he came home from school, Ted would eagerly devour the latest of all his favourite periodicals and magazines. Most in demand were *Wide World*, *Tit-Bits*, *Everybody's*, the *Reader's Digest*, *Health & Strength* and for sportsmen *Shooting Times*, *Gamekeeper*, etc. But there were also children's books, and Ted soon became a passionate reader of *Tarka the Otter* by Williamson, *The Jungle Books* by Kipling and *Hiawatha*, a long narrative poem by Longfellow based on the traditional lore of the Ojibwa that the American poet wrote in a meter derived from the Finnish saga *Kalevala*. William Hughes knew large extracts by heart that he would recite to his children.

With Gerald absent, Olwyn had the opportunity to assume her role as Ted's mentor. She herself obtained excellent results at school, particularly in English, and showed precocious gifts in verse making. It was not long before her affectionate advice produced its effects upon an intelligent and sensitive young boy, even if this had not been her initial intention. There was a mutual admiration between brother and sister, and she had the instinctive certainty that her brother was exceptional. Soon, his schoolmistresses, Miss Briggs and Miss McLeod began to praise Ted's remarkable aptitudes. At Mexborough Grammar School he won the admiration of his English teacher, John Fisher, who was to remain a friend for life. If a proof was needed that this was not the effect of his partiality, there was Miss Pauline Mayne, the supply teacher, to furnish it : her attention had once been arrested by a sentence in one of his compositions, in which Ted had sought to convey the crack of a shot in the frosty air in sonorous alliterations. "That is poetry!" she said. So that *was* poetry! There Ted was to find a lasting encouragement to marshal consonants and vowels in cadence. He was to say that these teachers had been one of the best strokes of luck of his life, but it is also true that good pupils make good teachers and, at different moments of his life, Ted was to run into such encounters which were to prove mutually invigorating. So, after hearing such encouraging comments for some time, Edith set about the task of buying an entire second hand library of good authors, chiefly the classics of English poetry. For she too was fond of poetry, particularly Wordsworth, the popular romantic poet who sang of nature and simple emotions. Moreover, Edith, who was at ease with words, liked to make up stories inspired by a children's encyclopaedia devoting long chapters to folk tales. Soon there grew around Ted, by now the only boy of the household, an atmosphere of feminine excitement, and a passionate interest for literature. It was not perhaps a literary atmosphere in the strict sense of the word, but it was a pastime enjoyed by imaginative and passionate amateurs who liked to produce texts according to their own shared tastes, irrespective of what the great authors may have done. They also practiced popular forms of literary production, just as women in those days got on with knitting and sewing without bothering in the least to keep up with the fashions, though they could easily find fashionable dress patterns in needle magazines. The poetic vocation of Ted Hughes has its source in these games for children, enlightened embroiderers and do-it-yourself men, who take their models from boys' weeklies and children's literature, comics and tales. Ted started out very early in literature, like a fiddler learning to play music by ear, with no lack of application but with no inhibitions either. Why care for great music when we enjoy playing ours?

There came a time, however, when he felt that this protective care of mother and sister was a bit too much. Olwyn's and Ma's mothering devotion could sometimes be quite stifling. In one way or another, the judgments they made upon his initiatives were always severe and their demands, no doubt well-meant, were burdensome as if whatever he did was never good enough. By the time he reached the age of eleven, Ted felt under constant pressure at home, as if he had been in a pressure cooker: some safety valve was needed. And so, when he was about twelve, he developed an aversion to ink in all its forms. Fortunately there was the world of friends: neighbours' children, school mates, most of them workers' sons. Among them Brian Seymour, Derek Robertson, and Donald Crossley, who was to leave school at the age of fourteen to work at a press in a garment factory and would later be known for his paintings of local scenery. Thus did each boy become conscious that he had his part to play in the vast world where an inexhaustible store of adventures lay in store for him. They would go fishing in the canal with a landing net made with the gauze of the old kitchen curtains. Loach are small speckled fish with whiskers, like miniature panthers that would live in the water. They disappear at the slightest noise but will soon come out of their hiding places if you know how to stay motionless. Later, one would go and buy fishing lines and hooks, from old Hemingway the one-eyed saddler who wore an eye-patch and sold fishing tackle in the workshop, where he sat all day sewing school satchels and horses' harnesses. But there were other treats too. At the top of the street leading to the station there was a flat open space where travelling circuses frequently pitched their tent, and showmen used to set up their booths and a few merry-go-rounds. And then, every year on November 5th when all over England Guys are burnt on the anniversary of the Gunpower Plot, a great bonfire was made in the field just behind the Hugheses' house to burn the effigy of Guy Fawkes, the Catholic plotter who very nearly blew up the Protestant Monarch in his Parliament in 1605. In all these festive occasions of popular merry-making, as well as all these hours of ordinary amusement, his friends retained the memory of Ted as a pleasant companion who liked to play tricks and to have fun. But above all they remembered his loud hearty laugh. A photograph of that period shows him looking like any ordinary schoolboy with his short hair and freckled face, dressed in a knitted shirt with one point of its collar sticking up; he has however very delicately touched up his image adding a little pink to the lips, a little blue to the sky and a few birds flying in it and also, remarkably, the text of a personal motto: "Twice armed is he who has his quarrel just. Thrice armed is he who gets his blow in fust. Me (Motter)."

The children had not immediately realised it but something was changing. The world was becoming darker. In 1940, when Ted was ten, Gerald left the bucolic world of rabbit hunting to join the RAF. The war was upon them and the life of the family suddenly seemed to draw closer. The anguish for the eldest son, the big brother who had to go and risk his life one did not know exactly where, silently increased and intensified the affection of the women. The ghosts of the First World War had come back and lay more heavily upon Pa's life, waking him up much too often at night. Nobody sang in the streets after dark. In the shop, when conversations were not stopped altogether, they continued in a grave tone, and people bought their newspapers with deep apprehension. In June of the same year, the first ration cards appeared: 4 oz. of bacon and ham per week, 12 oz. of sugar , 4 oz. of butter. Meat was rationed from March. In July, it was tea, the next year it would be jam and syrups. Soon eggs and milk were to be found only in powder. In no time, trade reverted to the practice of barter. People did their best to respect the instructions of Lord Woolton the Food Minister in his national campaign against waste. It was considered patriotic to space out one's baths as much as possible and not to use more than 5 inches of water at the bottom of the tub whenever possible. In everything one had to learn either to do without or to make do with the little one had in order to survive. As in all the rural parts of Europe, these restrictions meant hunting and fishing again became of vital importance—a very simple means, but practically the only one, to ensure fresh meat. Ted thus returned to the old practice as with Gerald; he would get up early, for it is at dawn after the long fast of the night that hunger pushes the fish to bite and drives animals to come out of their hiding places. It did not take him long in the grey hours before sunrise to walk to the banks of the Don or the

Dearne, two rivers which would soon give their names to the newspaper of Mexborough Grammar School: the *Don and Dearne*. A hunting territory is a secret world: its inner logic is known to the hunter alone. The poacher freely comes and goes in the grey and pink bushes which exist only in the wan twilight hours and only for him. Ted could have retraced his steps blindfolded to one or the other of these steep-hemmed clearings, where he could move in quietly, hoping to capture an animal. There were rabbits, that you could shoot or catch with a loop of wire, which would make excellent stews or pies once skinned and gutted.

But with the cruelty of a child he would shoot at all that stirred: robins, blue tits, warblers or wagtails, even grass snakes. It soon became a regular obsession and he kept notebooks to list his trophies each day. But above all he liked to skin and dismember the animals he had killed. He particularly liked their pelts. One of his friends lived on a farm; he entered into competition with the cats of the place and set a series of traps for mice. Once caught, he would skin them and prepare their pelts, scraping them with care to remove all that was likely to rot, before drying them. He kept a whole collection of them in his desk at school that he would sell for a few pence. In the woods he would also set nooses to catch martens, weasels and musk rats, the skins of which, once tanned, would fetch much higher prices. But more important than these few pence of pocket money was the prestige that these activities brought him. For they made him look like Davy Crockett, as if he had just stepped out of some adventure among North American trappers. An animal's skin—now that was impressive. Where had he got it? And there was better; he often carried tiny living creatures in his pockets, a mouse or a frog maybe. How funny it was to tell a girl to shut her eyes and to put it in her hand. His first poems and his first stories were being circulated in the same manner, out of a desire to perform, to claim attention, before being printed in the *Don & Dearne*. They were stories about cowboys and Red Indians, like "Far West", the story of Carson McReared the Terrible, or "Too Bad for Hell", that of Whisky John the Pirate. At other times they were melancholy pastorals steeped in the sombre lines of adolescence, stories of demonic incubi and succubi, or of Rabelaisian beasts with two backs, or again adventure stories in the fantastic vein, extolling thrilling assaults of irrational panic that set upon one at night in the woods. Again and again, one encounters the developing figure of a young wanderer, nocturnal and solitary, his head full of gothic reveries. But all these texts were already written in a sonorous tongue meant to produce maximum effect upon the ear. Ted always gave the impression of physically working upon the words, as if they were the plasticine of his childhood; he was kneading the English tongue as if it were a piece of clay, or hewing it as he would have done a block of granite with a chisel and hammer.

After a rapid spurt of growth in adolescence, Ted's lanky figure would often be taken for Gerald's, who came home but rarely when the army gave him leave. For there was a strange resemblance between the two brothers even if the elder's hair was much darker, having inherited — as Ted thought — the jet-black hair of their mother as well as of their Spanish great-grandmother. But both had straight hair with long locks combed back, cut high and short at the nape of the neck, in keeping with the fashion of the 1940s. Ted and Gerald were as tall and strong as their mother was short and round; but they had the same wideset eyes and large mouth. Both, like Edith, had hair forming a V shape on their forehead, as was characteristic of the Farrars. But both had taken over from the Hughes the same angular nose and prominent chin, the same V-shaped dip in the middle of their upper lip. The two brothers had also taken from their paternal grandmother the asymmetrical look in their eyes which was so particular. The right eye was unmistakably more open than the other and seemed to cast upon the world an intensely objective look, whereas the left one bore an introverted expression, the bottom of the iris touching the lower eyelashes and the top partly masked by the eyelid. There was perhaps more than a genetic coincidence in this resemblance that was at times rather disquieting, as if some unconscious pressure had more or less brought him to compensate too early for the absence of his brother who had left the family nest. For time would bring no remedy: all his life Ted would complain that he missed Gerald. It was from those years onwards that Ted was gradually to feel convinced that his mother was silently mourning for the absence of his brother as well as for the death of her sister and he came to feel more and more, whenever Ma's affection increased, that it was meant for two. She could not help but pour on her younger son the love she could not give to his brother. These things cannot be said, one hardly even dares to confess them to oneself. Many years later, he wrote to Gerald explaining that since then he had been forced to admit that he could never fill the gap in their mother's love. Though he was the only son in the household, he would never be Ma's only son. And having no other outlet for his jealousy, he would complain that his mother had only seen in him his brother's absence. Like Cain, he convinced himself that, do what he may, he would be condemned to remain the less loved of the two.

As is the case with most sportsmen, angling and hunting were his secret garden, where he would go to be alone, a necessary escape from his life at home; it enabled him to withdraw from the world of women whose desires always seemed to lie beyond what he was able to satisfy. He had to get away from the over tidy domestic interior with its severe-looking furniture, its meticulously ranged books with the portraits of old members of the family on an upright piano, a place where everything was neatly arranged in wall cupboards behind heavy doors of dark old wood. On Sunday mornings, the children went with Edith to hear the service in the Methodist Chapel where all trace of vain ostentation was painstakingly avoided, and Ted would sit bored to death on his bench. He had long since stopped listening to the sermon. Instead he would dream that he was roaming the woods like a solitary wolf; these good Protestants reminded him of a flock of sheep just shorn of their fleece, too austere even to dare to allow themselves to live. And so, since he could not do anything about it and as, despite all appearances, he was not expected to do anything in particular, it was better to go before boredom made him mad, to clear off into the woods on the sly, leave these too orderly houses, let the civilised world disappear for a time and return to his daydreams in the heart of nature, as if he were changing worlds and passing into another dimension. The solitary hunter prayed in a manner that was all his own, and his withdrawal into his inner world was lulled by the sound of the wind, the song of birds and the murmur of water; there was no such thing as silence in his ear, but the confused music of the world around him seemed to mingle with the inner voice of his thoughts. Just as an animal would sometimes creep up unawares on his senses, snatches of poetry unexpectedly came into his mind: it could be words he had picked up somewhere which had struck him as beautiful, like those small pebbles, bright coloured feathers, curious shaped pieces of wood, all the odds and ends that a child gathers in his pockets and keeps as treasures. He repeated them over and again, speaking to himself as he walked, or lying in wait for game in a bush, or perched in the high fork of a tree, toying with the words and their sounds, shifting them around, trying new combinations, like a child playing with newly discovered toys. He would remain lost in his thoughts like a child at his game, then emerged from it like someone who suddenly wakes up, and jot down his poems as one would transcribe a dream before it vanishes from the mind. For this purpose he always carried a notepad in the inside pocket of his jacket just as in his other pockets there were brass-wire snares, hooks ready fixed to the end of their lines, a few cartridges, and a box full of various baits. He liked the smell of ink and paper, appreciating the reticence of his hand — moving always a little too slow — to trace letters whose form it seemed, he could never quite manage to control. Most of the time, sometimes without being aware of it, he would talk out loud, speaking as if to another version of himself, a reflection of himself to whom he would tell his stories and explain his hunting and angling expeditions. At times it would be Gerald, or else the person who most captured his attention at the time, to the point of haunting him in his hours of solitude, and perhaps even more so in such moments. The fact remains that, when he played, the child was rarely alone: every one of his gestures was addressed to an invisible double that seemed sometimes to answer him and who understood his arts and desires without necessarily having to put them into words. It sometimes happened that the role of the partner was played by a flesh and blood person such as when he went with Uncle Walt on hunting expeditions in the Hollins Valley. Walt was the benevolent uncle on the mother's side, a friendly father figure whose face and hands were so strikingly like those of Ma. In his day dreams as a child hunter, whether he was alone or not, there were always two of him. Ted often played with John, a tall, slim boy who was much like him in appearance, for between the two of them there was a natural and spontaneous agreement, and they were like brothers between whom there was no cause for rivalry, no reason to be jealous. Since when had they known each other? Neither of them would remember precisely, nor did the question come into their heads. Their friendship must have started somewhere around 1941 when the war restrictions revived Ted's nostalgia for the life in the woods he had known with Gerald at Mytholmroyd. John Wholey, two years older than Ted, in the same form as his sister Olwyn. His father was the gamekeeper at Crookhill estate. This more or less legally entitled him to take the several acres of the park as his playground, with its large pond where they went angling for roach, perch and pike.

Essox the Pike, a legendary character in medieval imagery, is a long green fish streaked or flecked with gold, a mouth with a long beak like that of the platypus but armed with teeth like a wolf. It is a voracious fish, which likes to lie in wait in aquatic plants or under water lilies. It can remain motionless for hours as if asleep, then shoot forward with the suddenness of a released spring to dart upon his prey. It is fished with live bait, by threading a hook through the back of a small live fish which you cast near the beast. For a while, at school, the children kept three young pikes in a fish tank which they fed with fry that they caught in the streams nearby. But the passing of time tends to breed negligence and, during a brief school holiday, the children forgot to attend to the pikes; when they came back there was only one left, grown drowsy and fat. Over the years, Ted would maintain a passionate interest in this ferocious fresh-water leopard, that is said to be able to reach a fabulous size and which is best hunted out in winter when the cold plunges the small fish upon which he feeds into a deep sleep. To the excitement of hunting this miniature tiger, there is added the magical charm of winter, the smallest twigs and blades of grass sparkling with frost, the crumpled surface of the frozen water in the less sheltered places, the angler's fingers numb with cold, his breath turning to mist in the blue air at dawn and then the dramatic revelation of the bite which always comes as a surprise: the onslaught of the fish is like an electric shock running up the line and delivering a sudden discharge of energy into body and mind. Ted was later to write a poem — among the finest of his first period — which clearly attests that the experience of pike fishing was for him a revelation. For, through the effect of a truly religious sense of grace, the child found himself connected to a natural force, hitherto invisible, but whose secret presence was suddenly made manifest to him. To this fascinating discovery was added the striking impression, almost a certainty, that the aggressiveness of the pike surging from beneath the surface of water answered the accumulated desire of the angler himself. The attack of one predator was the response to the prayer of another. Each saw the same look in the other's eyes.

At the Wholeys', Ted was nearly a member of the family and he often came on Friday evenings to spend the weekend with John. At first, they played children's games such as climbing up trees, so high that they no longer dared come down, or they would throw a hedgehog into the water to see if it could swim and then, in a fit of remorse, fish it out again and put it to dry near the wood fire, wrapped up in a piece of clothing like a convalescent. But as they grew up, hunting and above all angling became for them more than a sport; they would spend long hours mounting lines, twisting nylon thread round the shaft of hooks and fastening it with a slipknot, making decoys, artificial flies with a piece of thread and the bristling barbs of feathers. In winter, to kill time, they would make casting rods for themselves, preparing the glue by boiling skins to a jelly on the kitchen stove, an operation which gave forth an infernal stench. The eyelets were fastened onto the cane by tightly rolling up around it a thread coated with cobbler's wax; this was a long operation, demanding great care for which nimble fingers were required; just the right task for Edna, Johnnie's elder sister who was one year older than him and three years older than Ted. Edna was not one of those city-bred girls who, when asked to close their eyes will scream with fright when you place a dormouse in their hand; Edna was a big girl, fully determined never to let herself be impressed by two young brats who would always be her juniors. At school, children were made to read the same books as their parents had before them. *Hiawatha* was still going strong and they recited long passages of the poem by heart while walking in the wood, or shared roles between them: Edna was dark-eyed Minnehaha, the beautiful young wife of Hiawatha, condemned by a cruel fate to a pathetic end. Imperceptibly, Edna replaced her brother in Ted's affection and they spent long hours walking together over fields and woods, talking endlessly. Sometimes they would stop abruptly and Ted would say "Wait! Listen!" and recite a poem of which Edna, all eyes, very often did not understand a single word. If, not commenting on what he had wanted to say, Edna did find it beautiful, because of the rhythm or the rhymes, then Ted would keep the poem; otherwise, if she did not like it, he would fold up the sheets and dispose of them in the crevice of a dead tree.

Over the years, Ted continued to produce farcical stories for the school magazine, set in the Far West, in Africa or in the jungle, always far removed from the dreariness of Yorkshire in the war years. But his interest in the music of words had if anything increased, and the texts he published in the school paper were written in a style rendered more obscure by his work upon words, and his poems impressed his readers mainly because of the great difficulty they found in understanding them. There was something of a wizard or a caster of spells in this budding rhymester whose magic power rested only on his capacity to produce beautiful and mysterious stories bathed in a nocturnal atmosphere upon which reigned the symbolic form of the moon and the image of the eye. For, from his early years, Ted had resolutely set about writing verse under the influence of Rudyard Kipling. He read *The Jungle Books* at an early age and he found a natural affinity that was not a figment of his imagination with Mowgli, the boy reared in the woods. But when he came to read Kipling's poems he fell under the charm of their strong regular rhythms and imposing rhymes, which seemed to radiate strong inner conviction. The remarks of his English teachers on Thomas Hardy's *The Woodlanders*, on Shelley's *Adonais*, which he had learnt by heart, or on the poetic intensity of the language in *King Lear* brought him sensuously to realise the magic power of words, one that he would practice himself in his verses as if it were an end in itself. Always an avid reader, Ted developed a passion for tales and legends that he used to collect like others do stamps and lead soldiers. This particular taste of his led him to develop a passion for William Butler Yeats, the great Irish poet, whose work is embued with the Celtic folklore of his native land. Reading Yeats' *The Wanderings of Oisin* was a deeply moving experience for the young Hughes, making him aware of the pleasing, powerful results that the combined magic of legends and versification can achieve. Whereas Kipling's verse marched in step with the accentual verse of Anglo-Saxon poetry, the voice of Yeats diffused a Celtic music, whose contours were more seductive because less definite, so that legend and poetry seemed to combine in the same enchanting world. Rhythms and rhymes seemed to open a natural path, from which imaginary worlds could emerge, and so Ted drank freely of the myths of Ireland and the magic of songs, finding infinite pleasure in their intoxicating effects.

Among the writers who marked his adolescence there was also D.H. Lawrence, author of animal poems and romantic novels who protested against the supposedly nefarious suppression that English society had brought to bear on sex. Ted Hughes had read all his novels, with the exception of *Lady Chatterley's Lover* which had some years previously been censored as immoral and which could not be found in such an out-of-the-way place as Mexborough. Among Lawrence's convictions, the faith he placed in primitive instincts and in the inner life, as well as his conception of marriage viewed as the consecration of physical as much as spiritual love, and on the whole fantasised as the only possible paradise, were those that echoed loudest in Ted Hughes. It was a new way of thinking, a romantic and carnal renewal of the Platonic myth, which conceives love as the mystical union of two beings. Without being at all conscious that this conception was linked, somehow, to the myth of the sister-soul, a generation of young Englishmen read Lawrence, then tantamount to heresy, as a way of asserting their libertarian attitude, retaining from it only a fascination for sex. But the times were not particularly well suited for a lark. The war was draining the United Kingdom, leaving it almost as exhausted as the rest of Europe; a sort of general stupefaction weighed upon everyone's mind, giving the impression that the country would never recover from the shock; it stayed numb, it seemed, like a convalescent old man. In 1945, filmed news had been shown in the cinemas about the liberation of the extermination camps and when people opened the *Picture Post* or other illustrated newspapers they were filled with horror at the sight of masses of corpses being moved away by bulldozers. A few miles further south, Liverpool and Leeds had been bombed by the Luftwaffe. In the country, even, a few stray bombs had been dropped here and there by German planes emptying their bays on the way home. For no apparent reason, it was at about this time that Uncle Albert hanged himself in his garret and,— horrible to say — it sometimes seemed, that the men just released from the armed forces were regretting the end of the war and their unavoidable return to a boring civilian life.

All the same, Britain could well be proud of her ancestral values, which had enabled her, once again, to resist invasion; the country wanted more than ever to preserve the old school traditions, which had demonstrated their value with such charity. Team sports were part of a physical training achieved the hard way, giving pride of place to manly virtues. In the competitions between schools the boys ran barefoot as in ancient Greece. At school, Edwards James Hughes was an athletic boy who particularly excelled at disc throwing, but also at archery, and very soon he was doing target practice two hours a day in order to shine in local competitions. What sport is more typically English than archery? Its practice, once compulsory, had earned medieval English archers a formidable reputation: it was moreover a solitary sport admirably suited to Ted's temperament, quiet and even-tempered, as well as to his steady hand, and cold right eye seemingly forged to take sure aim at the target. Physically, he was the typical Englishman, he took after the yeoman of old or after a rustic John Bull with his tall slim figure, his broad-shoulders, his long legs that gave him a sauntering air while he moved fast in long strides; his large broad hands, his deep voice like that of a giant and the thick locks of dark air falling over half his typically English face. In class as well as in sports, Hughes was a promising pupil; in 1948, Mexborough Grammar School decided to enter him for a Cambridge scholarship, for since the Education

Act of 1944 children from modest families could aspire to higher education if they obtained a scholarship. For a Grammar School in the North in those years it was, on the whole, a rare event, but Ted Hughes did credit to his masters and won an Open Exhibition to Pembroke College, Cambridge University. He did not go up to Cambridge immediately, though, for there were two years' compulsory national service first which he would do as a telegraph engineer in the RAF.

While he was waiting to be drafted, Ted afforded himself a few months of well-deserved holiday. Apart from a school-leavers journey to Switzerland with the pupils of his form when they had visited the lake of Geneva and then the Jungfrau with its famous rack railway, Ted was again reading great authors: Yeats, as always, Shakespeare, of course, Milton, but also the Romantics; —Blake, Wordsworth, Coleridge, Shelley, Keats — and the devout Catholic Hopkins, and also the more ancient Spenser and his *Faerie Queene*. But, at eighteen, one can't be serious all the time, and so there would be picnics and short bicycle trips into Derbyshire to show the countryside to beautiful Alice Wilson who had lived in a city all her life. It was a time for flirting, falling in love a little, although, in the end, it was Johnnie Wholey, Alice's pen-friend during his military service, whom she would later marry, no doubt because he had known how to pen beautiful answers to her letters. There was also Edna, when she could escape from her nurses' training school. Ted and Edna had resumed their literary walks in woods and fields and she would stifle a yawn when Ted read to her from Greek authors in translation, stretched on the ground with his head resting romantically in her lap. Between these interludes, however, Edna lived in a much more practical world, carrying on with her training at the nurses' school. One day, she came back from town with a real boy-friend. John and Ted gave him a friendly welcome and made haste to initiate him into fishing and hunting. One may well imagine Edna's surprise, when very soon afterwards, she received a letter from Ted seriously questioning her judgment: she must be mad to have become infatuated with a type who did not know how to use a gun or a fishing rod. In the end, Edna would marry her Stanley, a city boy. On their wedding day, her father stopped the car when it drew level with a tall beanpole walking along the road: it was Ted going on fast to attend the marriage ceremony, and so Edna entered the village sitting between Ted and her father. However, Ted was asked to alight at a discreet place so as to respect etiquette. Returning from her honeymoon she found a poem from Ted in praise of the bride and the bridegroom. But the marriage would not last. Her second marriage was a happy one and her second husband was more to the taste of the poet, who even declared that, this time, she had made a good choice. Ted Hughes indeed liked to exert his power of seduction and derived pleasure from the fascination he exerted on people, as well as from the hold he knew he was able to establish over his readers.

Childhood is all too short and Ted was seeing it end with regret. The end of the war had widened the gap between brothers and sister even more. Gerald had decided to stay for a while in the RAF after his time to complete his training as a technical engineer, and Olwyn left for Paris to learn French. On October 27th, 1949, Ted was drafted into the RAF; he would do his military service as a technician in the ground staff of the Signals Corps, stationed at West Kirby in Cheshire. Very few must have been the new recruits called up for national service who had not found a pen-friend with whom they could exchange letters to while away the time. For Ted, it would be Edna, for they had fallen into the habit of writing to each other ever since she had gone away to train as a nurse. From his forced residence in Barracks D 35, Hughes E.J., regimental number 2449573 AC2, squadron A, 5th section RT, continued, in his letters, to court her just for the fun of it. Occasionally, he risk an innuendo. He would also complain of the days of bad weather, of the slow pace of time. Was any colour worse than RAF blue? At Christmas he would kiss her hands and carve their two names into the bark of a yew tree with moons and stars and leopards. But now, Ted was barely recognisable, with his head shaven except for a tuft of hair on top so that, in his own words, he resembled a wooden post that had been pounded so much that the fibres of the wood had been flattened out at the top. He watched the falling rain, sometimes the hail or the snow. The misty landscape seemed to dissolve in boredom and mud; even the sun looked drenched and cold.

As spells of bad weather followed each other in quick succession, Ted had plenty of free time for reading. He went on with his reading of Shakespeare but he also read Rilke who, in his *Letter To A Young Poet*, explained that one should decide on poetry as a career only if one could not do otherwise. Did this apply to him? Certainly it did. He had never imagined himself doing anything else. He also read, in English translation, the work of the Swiss thinker Carl Gustav Jung and he took a passionate interest in his science of myths and symbols. Myths seemed to be psychological equivalents of the voyages of exploration in unchartered, faraway lands, that he had been so fond of as a child. He also read a book that his teacher, John Fisher, had given him as a parting present when he had left school: it was *The White Goddess* by Robert Graves, published in 1948, the year Ted Hughes completed his studies at the grammar school. Graves belonged to his father's generation. He had fought in the Great War and had taken part in the

battle of the Somme in 1916, where he had been gravely wounded and given up for dead. He came back
from the war very critical of English society and of its
virile imperial manners, a point of view that he had
developed in *Goodbye to All That*, a 1929 memoir of
the First World War. *The White Goddess*, a long essay
subtitled "A Historical Grammar of the Poetic Myth,"
revived the Romantic belief in poetry which, contrary
to philosophy, held in poor esteem, was viewed as an
indispensable activity, essential to the good health of
human societies. In the course of a long demonstration backed up by examples taken from different religions and cultures across the globe from time immemorial, Graves challenged the legitimacy of the
patriarchal structures of Western Civilisations. His
preference went to a type of civilisation that was
based upon a female deity whose creative force lay in
its destructive power. He conceived poetry as necessarily in conflict with Christianity, just as the Cult of
Astaroth had been in direct opposition to that of Jehovah. Thus poetry, in his opinion, had its roots in the
matriarchal phase of human history, and no one could
be authentically a poet if he had not first fallen in love
with the white goddess, an ancestral deity who, most
of the time, takes the form of a slender young woman
with a pallid face. She endlessly metamorphoses into
various animals and imaginary entities, and the forms
she can take are as innumerable as her names. But
everything Graves wrote about, the constant quest for
a mysterious encounter, the tracking down of animals,
resulting in a surprising moment of emotion, words
and their music which seemed always to come without warning and this so particular feeling, a mixture
of horror and exaltation — was it not what Ted
Hughes had always known? The intensely personal,
intimate experience, was it not precisely the same
thing as the magic of words which had fascinated him
all these years? The myths and legends explored by

Graves to support his theory, perhaps more in the Celtic world than in the sphere of Greco-Roman mythology, was it not what had filled him with enthusiasm when he had read the poems of W.B. Yeats? In the vacuous intellectual atmosphere inspired by the boredom of military service, where the mindless routine of a soldier's life in a exclusively masculine environment was a crude caricature of patriarchal and Judeo-Christian English society, Ted Hughes found in Graves an authoritative voice which confirmed his most secret thoughts.

The rain never let up and the land on which the military camp was based was a little below sea-level. With each downpour, men and beasts took on a strange appearance. Supply vehicles would get bogged down and the privates spent long hours floundering in the mud in pouring rain, busying themselves with winches, miners' bars and iron plates to pull lorries free of the quagmire. The rest of the time they would ward off with catapults a herd of angry bulls determined to conquer their vital space. In a quieter period, Ted had taken a liking to a hedgehog, which he had found one day behind some cardboard boxes. In time, the hedgehog became more and more a symbol of nostalgia and of an insatiable desire. It was in such a mood, one night, at three in the morning, when he was on duty, looking at the clouds drifting across the moon and listening to the wind, that a poem came fully-fledged to his mind, as if dictated by some inner voice — "O lady..." It is a simple, melancholy evocation of an inaccessible feminine ideal, as in Verlaine's dream, a woman who seems dead and yet unmistakably present, borne along in the sea and the wind, in the moon and the stars. The poet, whose heart is literally broken after that immemorial meeting, cannot contemplate ever losing her: her loss would be his death. Later, Hughes came to realise that this was the first of his poems that stood a chance of lasting and that deserved to be published. But seven years would elapse before he would be inspired to compose another poem that he would allow himself to consider of equal value. Ted Hughes was eighteen when he composed this "Song"; he would be twenty-five when he next produced a poem that he considered good enough to be kept.

But he would only realise it a long time afterwards and it was his sister Olwyn, to whom he had sent a copy of the poem in a letter, who would enable him to recover the manuscript. The text had been preserved in a bundle of typed sheets sewn into a copybook. On the cover there is a photograph of Ted Hughes cut out of a newspaper and fixed with yellow bands of sellotape. The poem figures at the end of the book as an epilogue under the title: "Invocation to the nearest Muse and tuning of musical instruments." The most important text in this paginated document of sixteen pages is a long ode written for Gerald's birthday. It is followed in the text by five long stanzas of an epithalamium that Ted had composed with no great enthusiasm in honour of Edna Wholey's marriage to her first husband, Stanley. The poems of that period are far from being unforgettable. It seems that the voice of their author will never have done breaking. The style is rendered not so much obscure as blurred by tortured syntax and hesitant images groping for meaning. His manner of approaching poetry is reminiscent of that of the letter-writer or of the diarist. If letter-writing is a literary genre in its own right, then Ted Hughes' letters may be remembered among the treasures of English literature. Furthermore, they prove a fertile soil from which his greatest poetry would grow. After all, a true letter-writer performs a sort of conjurer's trick, for the signs, the words and the sentences that his hand traces on the page seem to maintain the presence of his absent addressee. His fountain pen is a magic wand writing with sympathetic ink. His art is white magic. If being in love means wanting to interfere in somebody's private life, then the letters of Ted Hughes are always love letters, in one way or another. For this reason his published poems produce the effect (so characteristic of his manner) of seeming at once to radiate a contagious force of conviction and to take you, with real empathy, into the heart of the subjects they deal with. During this period of his life, however, the poems he used to join to his letters were like small presents intended to tighten his links of affection with the persons he loved. For example, "For Olwyn, every night" is a prayer or a charm through which a brother bestows his blessing on his sister at the hour when sleep is seeping into her tired head, like beneficent darkness settling in a room as daylight fails. Among the unpublished poems of this category, there is also the interminable "Ode upon his departure to Australia," in which Ted tried to get used to the idea that his elder brother had left England for good. For Gerald wanted to make the best of the aeronautical knowledge he had acquired in the RAF, but in England he had found nothing better than a job in the Nottingham Constabulary. So he yielded to the siren call of the Australian government who, wishing to encourage the development of this former Dominion of the Crown, now a free independent sovereign member of the Commonwealth, was offering young Englishmen a quality of life that made them dream of exile. Ted would never totally recover from this separation; to the end he wanted to believe that it would be only temporary. And to the end of his life Gerald would remain a privileged correspondent. His long letters were full of circumstantial descriptions of everyday life down to the smallest details, of analyses of personal sentiments, but teemed also with questions and requests. There is, in the true letter-writer, beside the pleasure of introspection, an autobiographical urge, a desire to remake his life afresh and without delay. But, above all, such a need to write letters is a sort of graphomania, a physical passion for the very act of putting pen to paper, the resistance of the sheet scratched by the running pen, the smell of ink, the movements of the tendons in the hand and the muscles in the arm. Moreover, there was the contact with copy-paper, pink and green and yellow and blue, which made a particular rustling sound, so thin that you could slip several sheets into the envelop without having to pay anything extra. Ted covered them from end to end in a hand that was both ample and close. He did the same with the prepaid sky-blue air-mail letters, all of the same prescribed form and size on the model of letters of old, consisting of a single sheet to be folded along the dotted line close to a rectangular border of blue and red lozenges. Ted went from end to end, covering the entire sheet as if lack of space alone would make him stop writing once he had placed the three letters of his name: "Ted". In moments of greatest empathy, he would not turn the sheet from right to left but from bottom up and go down on the back: his two hands would then be lifted together with pen and paper, without disjoining the two more than was necessary, as if he wanted to deny that the sheet had an edge.

II

CAMBRIDGE, FROM PEMBROKE TO SAINT BOTOLPH

Ted was never to live again in the family house at Mexborough; he would only come back for short visits when on leave from military service. On such rare occasions he found Olwyn, Gerald and his young wife Joan there. Such stays were barely long enough for fishing expeditions and various outings, making it all the more important to immortalise these moments spent together in photographs. Apparently, the family had never been so united as during these days when everybody seemed to be smiling. In October 1951, when Ted went up to Cambridge, it was more than a year since his parents had left Mexborough to return to West Yorkshire where William Hughes was now a tobacconist and a bookmaker at Hebden Bridge, not far from Todmorden, only miles from Mytholmroyd. They had bought a house at the edge of the village, called the Beacon. It is a square-shaped building, like the New Jerusalem in Saint John's vision, an imposing cubic affair of black stone with two rows of sash windows at the front and a rain-water pipe running down in the middle. The upper frames of the windows are decorated with coloured lozenges and rectangles of stained glass. On one side, two narrow windows let in a sparse light. The fields come right up to the back of the house which is built at the far end of the village. Its four-sided slate roof is surmounted in the centre by a chimney containing four cylindrical flues. It is flanked on either side by lean-to buildings and surrounded by a low wall. It is a large ungainly house bravely turning its back to the north-westerly gales; at the front are its windows and its door, with a large entrance porch sheltered by a two-sided roof, an indispensable additional protection in those rainy regions. Hughes's parents had moved from Mytholmroyd to Mexborough at the time when Gerald had gone to Devonshire. Now, their return to West Yorkshire, not far from the place where their children were born, was taking place when their elder son was leaving England for good and Ted was going up to Cambridge.

At Pembroke, his rooms were in the first courtyard on the left once through the great wooden door of the gatehouse. Ted was then twenty-one, he wore an impressive moustache which did not suit him, but in the end his brother's constant teasing him got the better of him and he shaved it. With his black tie, black shoes, corduroy jacket bought at the ex-factory price from Walt Farrar's which he dyed black himself, he looked like a country giant walking with nonchalance, and, it seemed, obliged to lower his head to go through the doorways of ancestral Cambridge whose stone walls and ancient panelled ceilings always give the impression that they have been built on a slightly reduced scale. According to the immemorial custom of the place, every gentleman admitted into the elite of the nation had a servant calling him "Sir" coming each morning to bring him water to shave, attend to his washing up and make his bed. That was Cambridge; congeries of bicycles parked near the college gates, cyclists wearing opera-hats with ornamental tufts speeding along, stiff as a post, their gowns flapping in the wind. The Petty Curry shops, Heffer's, the famous bookshop, and Fitzbillies, the cake shop on Trumpington Street, opposite Pembroke. There were ancient houses like those one finds in the heart of old England, with their wooden frames showing on the outside, and their upper stories jutting out over the streets. The smallest of the round cobblestones of the pavements inspires a feeling of respect in every newcomer to this town as he thinks of all the great men who have walked upon them. Pembroke College, founded in the 14th century, is among the three oldest colleges in town. Its monastic buildings, arranged around a large courtyard, are made of stone, the brickwork in some of them signalling the most recent parts, with their different cloisters, flying buttresses, bay windows, classical capitals, corbelled constructions, gables, paterae, bas-reliefs, slate roofs, arched windows in the high-ceiling rooms of the chapel, the refectory and the library. The latter looks indeed very much like a church with its neo-gothic spire built in the sort of medieval style dear to Alfred Waterhouse. Discipline was easily maintained owing to the prefect and his two bulldogs, and meals were taken at fixed hours. The gates closed on the stroke of 10. For students who failed to come in on time there was a fine of two pence, or four pence after 11 o'clock. After midnight they had to climb over the gate unseen or prepare an explanation for their tutor on the following morning. Wearing a gown was absolutely compulsory but, as well established tradition would have it, a strict attendance of lectures was not, and the hours spent studying in the libraries were regarded as just as profitable. Hughes often went to Trinity College Library too, the work of Sir Christopher Wren, the neo-classical architect, who had built Pembroke College chapel in the same style; in both buildings, the same stately conception of art, typical of the end of the 17th century, is to be found, the same classical, well-polished wooden furniture stands on floors paved with alternating black and white lozenges and lofty stuccoed ceilings as white as whipped cream.

The Cam, an indolent river of the flat region of East Anglia, leisurely meanders through the town, bearing punts, long flat-bottomed boats moved with a pole like gondolas. From Silver Street Bridge, you can see Mathematics Bridge on one side, linking Queen's College, and on the other, going through

Granta Place you come into the Coe marshes, a large green area right in the middle of town where cattle can be seen grazing. Even in the sullen days right after the war, Cambridge continued ingenuously to pretend it was a little earthly paradise where the intellectual elite of a generation seemed to have gathered, as becomes well-bred dilettantes. The teaching was given under the guidance of a tutor whom each student went to meet in his rooms. The first tutor to supervise Hughes's studies was a certain Mottram, a poet of sorts; with him tutorials were occasions for passionate exchanges that often extended well beyond the assigned time. Then came Hodgart; he too willingly recognised Hughes's talent but came soon to regret his lack of regularity in handing in weekly essays. There are so many exciting things to do in Cambridge when you are twenty. Hughes spent no end of time at the archery club, training assiduously to maintain good results in competitions. He prided himself on being able to hit a target no bigger than a rat from a distance of thirty yards, and he would rise early to go shooting rabbits with his bow and arrows in the surrounding countryside. There was a mouse in his room that he heard scurrying when it ventured out at night to nibble at his supplies of biscuits. In the room above, one of his fellow students used to make a racket at night and Ted would avenge himself by playing Beethoven's Ninth Symphony at full blast on his gramophone until well into the night. He developed a passion for Beethoven whom he considered as the model of the creative artist because, he said, the full force of his music is already present in the first bars, ready to be unfolded in the rest of the piece. In his eyes, Beethoven's music was a perfect model of creative efficiency, a paragon of the unconstrained imaginative faculty capable of hitting the appropriate expression like an arrow on its target. It was about that time that Ted had discovered the pleasure there is in making quick boldly drawn sketches. He had also managed to obtain a copy of the death mask of the great composer. The poet Peter Redgrove, two years younger than Ted Hughes, used to relate how Ted, who had learnt that the great man was short in stature, would bend down and lower his knees when he went to meet his visitors, with the mask over his face coming level with their chests, and, shouting to be heard over the sound of the music, announced that he was really no taller and that such was his particular way of walking. It was meant as a test: those who took his behaviour for a ludicrous prank were deemed superficial, whereas those who shared his enthusiasm were judged worthy of consideration.

In February 1952, when King George VI died, his daughter Elizabeth became queen of England: she was twenty-six. Ted Hughes, who was four years younger, then reflected that the Englishmen of her reign were the first Elizabethans since Shakespeare wrote *Hamlet*. He saw it as a sure sign that the grandeur of Albion was going to be revived, and relied on the authority of obscure books of antiquated lore to predict to friends and acquaintances alike that England would enjoy sixty years of unprecedented wealth and prosperity. She would possibly still go through difficult times until 1960 but, owing to her dominions she would then become more powerful than ever. Till the advent of these glorious times, Hughes clearly entrusted his future to the tigers of inspiration rather than to the horses of instruction, and obviously he was intent less on becoming a scholar than a poet. Indeed, it had not taken him long to acquire this reputation for he availed himself of every opportunity to assume the character of a poet, behaving with studied eccentricity. It appeared in various guises: the intensity of feeling he would put in his silences, the inflections of his voice or the expression in his eyes; the boorish humour that he affected was further reinforced by his shaggy hair falling over his face. Soon, after his sister Olwyn had enlightened him in astrology, he was able to enrich his image with a touch of mystery, handing out personal horoscopes. All this soon attracted around him in no time a circle of friends. But in Cambridge, in the first years of their stay in particular, a great part of the students' energy is side-tracked into the pubs. Ted and his tribe met mainly at the Anchor, where they used to sing around a few beers, songs of Irish rebels mainly, such as *The Wearing of the Green* or *Sir Patrick Spens*, which Ted sang particularly well.

One of his favourite pastimes was to denigrate the people they disliked, whom they called "crumbs". It is noteworthy that Ted and his friends had in common been exposed to the snobbery of the higher social classes. It was only a decade since new laws had made it possible for children of the lower middle class and, to a lesser extent, for those of the working class, to win scholarships enabling them to enter the holy of holies for the trainee elite. It did not take intelligent young men long to realise that, if they had undoubtedly been admitted to Cambridge, they did not really belong. Among this group of friends who more or less shared a certain social bitterness, some were Irish like Terence McCaughey, a future Gaelic professor at Trinity College, Dublin, some were Scottish left-wingers like Colin White and Keir Hardie, or Americans like Lucas Meyers, Bertram Wyatt-Brown or Harold Bloom later to become a prominent figure at Yale. There was also Daniel Weissbort, the son of a wealthy and learned tailor who had left Poland for the United Kingdom only in 1920. In short, England remained a class-conscious society in which social barriers were no less rigid for being sometimes invisible, and though they were brilliant, and in certain cases even wealthy, these young men did not belong to the gilded set of King's College or to the Bloomsbury

Club of London. And, as a result, they felt slightly angry and resentful. In all ages and in all places, such resentment does affect those who are confronted with social realities for the first time in their lives, but Cambridge, and Oxford as well, continued to be a sort of breeding ground for celebrity which does not necessarily correspond to social background or intellectual excellence. There was, for instance, a way of making use of Oxbridge which consisted in getting sent down, preferably after causing a great stir. That was part of the game. Such was the case of a certain Mark Boxer, a Cambridge resident when Ted Hughes was there, for a time the editor of the literary magazine *Granta*. With no great merit on his part he managed to have himself turned out by publishing a poem in which God rhymed with sod. Boxer, who liked to say that since society happened to have a top the only thing that mattered was to be there, enjoyed his first hour of glory when his peers symbolically offered him a burial ceremony; he was borne in triumph down King's Parade in a rented hearse at the head of a long procession. It was not altogether devoid of style. But Ted would never have been involved in anything of the sort. He was certainly not devoid of humour, but his provincial and middle-class education seemed to have given him a quiet reserve in his manners. Hughes absolutely lacked the easy demonstrativeness of the clown, and his personal charm was of the sombre sort. He was not a bad boy, either, and there was very little of the Byronic hero about his character. He was a mysterious and secretive young man with no talent for comedy, always wrapped in a sort of romantic gloom. Because of his high stature and his harsh Yorkshire accent he was often compared with Heathcliffe, the most savage character in Emily Brontë's famous novel. He would recite by heart inspired and visionary poems by Blake or Hopkins, in an impassioned tone of voice, so low that you could feel its vibrations.

In those years it was well thought of to display an interest in William Blake, the forerunner of English Romanticism and the enemy of the movement of rationalism and materialism of the 18th century Enlightenment. Nor was it mundane, in the 1950s, to continue to admire Gerard Manley Hopkins, an Anglican who had been received in the Catholic Church and, going one step further against English decencies, had joined the hereditary foe by becoming a Jesuit. Hopkins's poems, which were published one generation after his death, had been at the centre of a debate that had given rise in England to two distinct conceptions of modernism. Hopkins had been very much admired by Yeats, the great Irish poet, himself a spiritual inheritor of Blake, and the young Hughes had admired Yeats's esoteric poems, full of mythological and legendary lore. But Hopkins did not receive the same admiration from that high priest of English modernism T.S. Eliot, an American who had become an English citizen and a member of the Anglican Church. A short time before, he had been close to Ezra Pound, who had acted as a sort of midwife in the birth of *The Waste Land*, a long poem which became one of the outstanding literary monuments of an epoch that perceived the Western world as sadly deprived of spirituality. Now, Hopkins had himself been active in favour of the Oxford Movement which, around Cardinal Newman in the middle of the 19th century had recommended the return of the Anglican Church to the Catholic fold. Central to their convictions was the idea that the Reformation, by setting afloat the rationalist spirit, had made a mistake diverting man from the pursuit of holiness and opening the way to sterile materialism. Blake, in his time, followed the same line, yet, in the mid 20th century, these ideas were regarded by most as old romantic lucubrations that were definitely outdated. T.S. Eliot very quickly reached his zenith in the 1920s, then engaged in a publisher's career with Faber & Faber where he exercised a conservative influence of considerable effect upon the London literary world. In the 1930s, a new generation succeeded him in this role, centred around W.H. Auden: Louis MacNeice, Stephen Spender, Christopher Isherwood, and Cecil Day Lewis writing what was known as "pylon poetry". Their distinguishing hallmark was a poetry steeped in the events of everyday life in an urban and industrial environment, materialistic and modishly leftist. But in 1938 Auden had gone to live in the United States. His complaint was that "poetry makes nothing happen" and is powerless when it comes to changing life, and he felt discouraged and bitter with the "low and dishonest decade" of the 1930s, to which his literary fame would remain attached. Then came the Second World War, followed by the Cold War, with their numbing effect upon the mind of the nation, having somewhat cooled the socialist enthusiasm of the thirties. The discovery of an ancestral savagery still lying deep in the psyche of western man that no philosophy had been able to eradicate had left a rankling sense of guilt in the nations of Europe, notwithstanding the need to direct their energies into reconstruction. A pessimistic atmosphere undoubtedly prevailed on the literary scene. Continuing the long English tradition of utopias, Aldous Huxley had published his successful *Brave New World* in the early thirties. 1948 saw the publication of George Orwell's *1984*, a novel of anticipation in which he envisaged the inescapable victory of totalitarianism in a not too distant future. In his 1952 fable *Lord of the Flies*, William Golding had shaken the complacency of the victorious nations by showing what degree of barbarity decent English boys could reach if left to their own devices in the heart of nature. Poetry took its tone from what was known, for lack of a better word, as "The Movement". Donald Davie, it seemed, saw no hope of salvation outside a return to neoclassicism and tended towards an exquisite perfectionism. Philip Larkin was the most brilliant illustration of a poetic model which consisted in giving polished form to what appeared to be flat conversational exchanges between well-bred people, even though they sometimes lapsed into coarse outbursts with a clearly calculated literary effect. The general tone was one of bitter disappointment, the point of view conservative, illustrating the English taste for compromise. The posture was a resigned stoical attitude verging on depression.

The prevailing mood seemed dominated by rigid standards of social behaviour weighing heavily upon the young, creating a sort of irreverent irritation. Hughes would later explain that the return to peace, heavily fraught with the insidious dangers of the Cold War and the violence surrounding decolonisation had the terrible effect, sometimes, of awakening a vague nostalgia for the war in English minds, so widespread was the feeling of frustration weighing upon the return to normalcy. It became fashionable to launch into callous acts of shocking behaviour to defy etiquette. It was considered good form to dispense with what were regarded as the out-of-date and oppressive rules of English good manners. Transgression was becoming an enjoyable sport. the Reverend Meredith Dewey, for instance, Dean of Pembroke, was reputed to invite students to tea in his lodgings where he would engage them in coarse conversation, for it was fashionable at the time to distance yourself from the manners of a gentleman, deemed antiquated and hypocritical. Ted Hughes, for his part, was anything but a dandy: his clothes were unclean, his hair was greasy and he had dandruff on his jacket while his face bore the marks of great nervous tension, as he had developed a tic of twisting his mouth to one side when he spoke. Class-consciousness was the root of the problem, for it was inverted snobbery which consisted, somehow, in confronting such upper-class dandies as Evelyn Waugh had described in *Brideshead Revisited*, sporting their bow-ties, their waistcoats of rich brocade and other inaccessible eccentricities. But this reaction, reinforced by the opening of universities to lower classes was further exacerbated, at the time, by the subterranean build-up of forces preparing the explosion of the swinging sixties. In the fifties, Cambridge was like a boiling cauldron seething with activity. Politics was as always one of the most active centres of student life. At the Socialist Club, Stephen Spender, whose reputation as a poet dated back to the thirties and who had been a key figure of the Auden generation, was launching the cultural magazine *Encounter*, but these were people with whom Ted Hughes did not mix. He was more naturally drawn towards another tradition. So much so, for instance, that Ted Hughes never met Tom Gunn at Cambridge, for Gunn (with whom he later associated in a publishing venture) was at the time a member of the socialist group and gravitated therefore in altogether different circles. Hughes, for his part, preferred to frequent the English Club where he could hear poetry readings and lectures by poets such as George Barker, today a little forgotten, or Dylan Thomas, the neo-romantic Welsh bard who liked to declaim his verse in a dramatic voice vaguely reminiscent of the tone in which Malraux used to deliver his speeches.

Totally engrossed in his love of poetry and in his desire to nurture his admiration of poets of the past as well as of the present, Hughes was rather surprised to discover that all was not for the best in the best of all possible worlds, when he got only a pass at the end of the first year. His teachers had not been overly impressed by the use he had made of his science of astrology in an essay on the importance of the notion of horror in English literature. Though he had joined a text of fiction of his own composition to the pieces of writing he had to produce for his masters at the end of the year, it had all been in vain. There seemed to be some sort of misapprehension between himself and his teachers. There was not the same current of sympathy as there had been with John Fisher at the Mexborough Grammar School. All in all, he was led to believe that this was some sort of misunderstanding. In a way, Hughes had been unlucky to come to study literature in Cambridge in those years when New Criticism reigned supreme. One dominant figure was F. R. Leavis, the author of *The Great Tradition*; at Downing College he practised a type of literary criticism radically opposed to the buoyant historical approach that was in favour at King's. To give a firm institutional anchorage to his passion for sounding and anatomising poems, he had launched the review *Scrutiny* in 1932 which continued until the end of the sixties. In his opinion, the virtue of a good poem did not derive from any associational values but from its own, independent, masterly internal organisation. A century and a half before, William Wordsworth had sounded the revolt against such narrow-minded rationalism, making "intellect" resoundingly rhyme with "dissect", and it was barely twenty years since Ezra Pound had declared that he would pay no attention to the poetic opinions of anyone who was not himself a recognised poet. But at Cambridge at that time, coldly intellectual masters were submitting poems to a careful, methodical post-mortem examination, in the firm belief, apparently, that there was no fundamental difference between a machine and a living text. Their conception of literary studies had also been influenced by I. A. Richards, himself a pure product of Cambridge, and a recognised literary critic since the publication of his *Principles of Literary Criticism* before the war. This very "scientific" approach to literature, tending towards a mathematical and mechanical ideal, found a very favourable practical application in poetry, whose generously tendered ready-made rules of prosody were ideally suited to the construction of small intellectual contraptions, which are to poetry what decoy-birds are to waterfowl. The best-known celebrant of this cerebral practice was probably William Empson, whose productions are a good example of the type of texts that Hughes would range in the category "lists of clues for crossword puzzles." In Ted Hughes's generation, this Cambridge School found its spiritual heir in the person of J. H. Prynne, the famous librarian of Gonville and Gaius, an upholder of a style of poetry issued in confidential editions, bearing a certain likeness to the virtually unreadable modernist productions of the American school of "Language". Moreover, at Cambridge, this sort of aesthetics with strong ideological implications had a theoretical foundation in the philosophy of Wittgenstein, the author of *Tractatus Logico-Philologicus*, still teaching at Trinity College in 1947, where he had formerly been the disciple of Bertrand Russell, the socialist philosopher.

Though he did not yet have the necessary maturity to fully comprehend the reasons of his malaise, Ted Hughes felt in such a historical context as much at home as a bull in a china shop; he soon declared that the Cambridge of the time was a pretty deadly institution for anyone who had not set out to become a scholar or a gentleman. The essays that he failed to hand in to his teachers on time, the difficulties he had to fit in the conventional mould and to come out with what was expected of him, his aversion to literary studies as they were being practiced, were all symptomatic of his total, deep-seated disagreement with the prevailing ideology. He soon became conscious that the atmosphere was inimical to his genius, and having been at first intimidated and afraid, he came to feel an intense dislike for it. In fact, with each passing day he felt that he was going to be inescapably confronted with a choice amounting to a dilemma, for it became clearer and clearer that if he really wanted to be a poet, it would have to be in spite of the University, by dint of sustained resistance to what was taught there. He knew perfectly well what he ought to have done in order to excel; he simply could not bring himself to do it. Try as he may to write essays according to the rules, his page would stay blank, he would put it off indefinitely, find a thousand other things to do, go to sleep too early, get up too late. Anxiety would take hold of him. And then, there were his dreams, strangely alike, coming at regular intervals. One night, when he was lying in bed asleep, he had had the feeling that a creature had come into the room, there, just above his armchair. He could see its two green eyes shining in the dark. In his dream, if a dream it was, he got out of bed to see what it was; he drew closer, then he saw and cried out all at once: "A Leopard!" In silence, the animal placed his two hands on his shoulders and slowly pushed him back. Ted woke up, chilled to the bones; he had fallen backwards into his leather armchair and found himself with his legs slung over the arms of the chair. Was it not the jaguar or the panther that he had modelled so often in clay as a child? Surely not. Another time, when he had fallen asleep over his blank page, unable to bring himself to write his essay on Samuel Johnson, the 18th century lexicographer and biographer who esteemed the Metaphysical poets were too difficult, he was once again visited by an apparition. This time it was a fox, an abnormally large one, the size of a wolf, standing erect on its hind legs like a man. His whole body looked as if it had been grazed, flayed even or rather badly burned. The animal drew near, raised one paw which looked like a bloodied human hand, laid it on his blank page, and said "enough of this, you are destroying us", then disappeared, leaving a shining humid trace.

It would take years for this dream to find its way into a poem describing the lurid encounter. Hughes would call it "The Thought-Fox"; it was the first poem since "Song" (the poem that had come to him as a poetic gift one night during his military service), that he would deem worthy to be kept. In this simple poem, a dual vision of the world is coming into existence, based on the simultaneous experience of its two dimensions: on the one hand, the outer world of things materialised by the tick-tock of a clock in a room at night, the mechanical world of physicians. But, beneath its surface, the inner world manifests itself, the world of spirits emerging from the silence upon the senses of those who can listen, the sense of something welling up from some obscure depth to confront the poet's eye and become one with it, leaving no other trace of its coming than the poem, whose letters and words are like the fresh footprints in the snow left by some mysterious animal. The writing technique is masterfully controlled, totally different from the spontaneous outpouring of "Song". The clarity of his expression is matched by the strength of the conviction with which the poet chooses to place his faith in poetry writing, and it seems to radiate such inner certainty and wilfulness that the reader is carried along and forced to concur. Between these two poems a poetic vocation had come into being. It was the immediate outcome of the dreams that were soon to inspire this new poem, but for the time being, they were giving a practical shape to a deep moral crisis: Ted Hughes had resolved to turn his back on the study of English literature as practiced at the University, and to make a fresh start in social anthropology and archaeology.

By switching onto this new course of studies midway, Hughes was compromising his chances of getting an Honours degree at the end of his three years at the University. But, for the time being, it did not worry him too much. In his letters to his brother, he was forming the project of running a hotel — he would buy a house in Cambridge and rent rooms to students: human pigs, when all was said and done, were the best investment that a farmer could imagine. Of course, he did not have the first penny to buy the doormat, but he was confident that with a Cambridge degree he would have no difficulties getting a job that would help him to his feet. Another solution would be to join Gerald in Australia, and to live on the product of their hunting activity. But for the moment, the important thing was to free himself from what he viewed as a totalitarian ideology that was detrimental to his talent as a creative author. The disciplines to which he turned, the new social sciences derived from the historical studies that were academic developments of the preceding century, were more in keeping with the spirit of Cambridge, which traditionally had a stronger leaning towards the sciences than Oxford. Archaeology and anthropology are, by definition, concerned with the past, but they were, moreover, generally regarded as quite mature disciplines because they benefited from the prestige of at least one famous pioneer: the Scotsman, Sir John Frazer, a former student of Cambridge and Glasgow Universities and a Cambridge resident for the major part of his life, though he was at the same time professor of social anthropology at Liverpool University. By the turn of the twentieth century he had acquired a solid reputation with the publication of *The Golden Bough*, which he defined himself as a comparative study of religions. The works of Frazer prefigured those of the French historian of religions Levy-Bruhl, in particular his research on the *Primitive Soul*. The theses put forward in *Totemism and Exogamy* had greatly influenced those of Freud in *Totem and Taboo*, to soon be made obsolete by the work of Levi-Strauss in *The Elementary Structures of Kinship*. This epoch-making book, first published in Paris in 1949, was not available in English until the end of the 1950s. Structuralism would meet with lasting resistance in England, as did the works of Freud which, for historical reasons, would never be fully accepted in the English-speaking world, which tended to favour Jung. But behind these tensions, largely unexpressed, as it is often the case in England for all that concerns the world of ideas, there lurked an ideological conflict of the same nature as the one that alienated Ted Hughes from literary studies according to current diktats. Frazer's *Golden Bough*, a huge synthesis of modern and ancient religions, had opened new roads between history and philosophy, which aimed at occupying the space left vacant by the slow process of de-Christianisation that had been started by the "noble elucidation of truth" at work in the 18th century in England, and continued in the 19th century with Darwin's theory of evolution, and pushed one stage further by Bertrand Russel's agnosticism. Now the religious or metaphysical issue, that is the question of the possible survival of a spiritual dimension in whatever form, had been the dominant theme ceaselessly revisited by poets since the Romantics at least, in fact since the Reformation, in other words since the birth of modern England. It was so much the case indeed that, to a large extent, poetry might be said to have been one of the rare places, perhaps the last one still extant, where spiritual needs could be satisfied. But poetry, in the true sense of the term, as distinct from crosswords and *bouts-rimés*, poetry was becoming extinct. With this sort of reasoning Ted Hughes found himself perforce involved in what Blake, two centuries before, had called a spiritual fight. The battle, an ancient conflict, was still going on — it was an unavoidable fact and no poet, no man of letters it seemed, could avoid choosing his camp. In the eyes of the literary exegetes of *Scrutiny*, of the Freudian socialists of Bloomsbury or, on the continent, in such an exotic country as France where, since the beginning of the century, Church and State had turned their backs on each other, it could possibly be viewed as a rearguard action come too late to succeed, condemned to failure by the onward march of history, in spite of the harsh lucubrations of a Malraux prophesying in the desert that the 21st century, if anything, would be religious. But in England, things did not look so clear-cut: a young queen, hardly twenty years of age, had just succeeded to the throne, thus becoming the supreme head of the Church of England, Pope Elizabeth in her realm. The appointment of bishops and archbishops lay in her royal hands, with all due deference to philosophers whom she could always raise to the peerage — if they did not already belong to it like the Third Earl Russell, to reward them for their distinguished efforts on behalf of English culture.

Besides, in the field of literature from which he had turned away so as better to come back to it one day, Hughes was not alone, far from it. There existed a culture of opposition to the conception of literature such as it existed at the University, focussed around literary figureheads like W.B. Yeats, D.H. Lawrence or Dylan Thomas, the Welsh bard who died the very year Hughes decided to abandon his course of English literature. Above all there was the model of Robert Graves who had, without a doubt, known how to preserve his creative genius; here was a poet and a novelist who was also engaged in theorising a different approach to literature. Did Graves not propose to do for literature what Frazer had achieved in the field of religions? It would be something in the vein of the research work by Auerbach, a German scholar engaged in comparative studies, who had been forced to flee nazi Germany and who, in the post-war years, had published *Mimesis*, study highlighting recurring motifs in European literature. Graves was engaged in a work of great scope on the different mythologies and their importance in the field of literature and of ideas. In Graves's works, Hughes also found the model of a polemical discourse arguing the case of poetry against its contenders and liquidators. He dated back the spread of the scientific spirit, which blamed the myths for want of trying to understand their function to Socrates; it was the same spirit which drove Plato to exclude poets from his *Republic*. Robert Graves was nearing sixty when Ted Hughes had the opportunity to meet him at Cambridge, where he had been invited to give the Clark Lectures at Trinity College in 1954. He was then in the most brilliant phase of his career, the crown of which would be his appointment to the chair of poetry at Oxford in 1961. Hughes found in him his literary champion; he had read his work as soon as it came out, on leaving the grammar school. The authority of the great man would bring to him the security he needed to allow his chosen plan to come to fruition. Graves's work opened up the treasures of ancient myths, a whole repertoire of imaginations and metamorphoses; they would provide him with the building blocks of a poetic tongue made of proverbs, tales, legends, nursery rhymes, dialect words and simple rhymes. He felt that a methodical study of the vocabulary and syntax of this sort of idiom which must be close to the tongue of true poets, would enable him to communicate with his dreams, and to converse in some way with the strange creatures which inhabited his visions.

The change of orientation in his studies brought relief, as if the anxiety of the emotional crisis he had gone through had suddenly been released; he gave free rein to his intellectual curiosity in those years when Cambridge witnessed the development of the Society of Psychological Research, which showed a great interest in paranormal phenomena. Unsurprisingly, it did not fail to capture the attention of an astrologer who wanted moreover to become an apprentice sorcerer. At that time also, in the Gog Magog hills, a few miles south-east of Cambridge, archaeological excavations had brought to light the remains of a bronze age settlement, bringing additional evidence, is was said, of the existence of a Gaelic moon goddess. These hills were also, perhaps, the mystic location of the true Troy for, according to a heroic hypothesis, the Trojans could well have been the true ancestors of the English, and Spenser, in the days of Queen Elizabeth I, in imitation of Virgil had already supported this claim, giving to London the name of Troynovant in his *Faërie Queene*. Was it possible, moreover, that Gog and Magog evoked by Ezechiel, and by Saint John in the book of Revelation, had a historic link with England? Once emancipated from its too strictly scientific limits, archaeology opened a vast field to the imagination. Archaeology and anthropology are admittedly scientific disciplines, but Hughes saw them mainly as sources of inspiration: they were for him, in Larkin's phrase, a "myth kitty". He sought in them the confirmation of his day dreams, but also images and bits of legend which for him retained a mysterious and fascinating power. If the works of Robert Graves exerted an undeniable influence on men of letters avid for antimodern forms, they were not really recognised by anthropologists and historians of religions and ideas. Nevertheless, the reticence of the University, far from being a check on Hughes's enthusiasm, confirmed his belief, as if justifying the severe judgment he passed upon Western society, where a scientific spirit and the fake God of Reformed Christianity, too cerebral, too exclusively masculine held sway. Along with a myth kitty, Hughes had found in Graves an ideology that confirmed him in his belief that he was right to dispute the validity of most of the dominant ideas of the time in England. Among the first-rate authors with whom Hughes had spontaneously felt at home was D.H. Lawrence. Like him, he had rebelled against the pressure which, according to him, society brought to bear upon an individual, the damaging sexual repression that characterised it, the systematic destruction of nature for the benefit of an industrial Moloch which knew no other value than money. In Graves and Lawrence, Hughes found the same sort of critical ideology, hostile to the modern world; he himself belonged to this family of romantic Cassandras, he shared with them the same lyrical gift of spinning an engaging conservative lament, a vision of the world which was not devoid of paranoia. He would court failure the better to support his theories. Unknown to him, this mental attitude, which was the belated effect of his Protestant education, inclined Hughes to look among the incidents of his life for proofs of his special calling. By choosing to be a poet he was placing himself on the side of those that the philosophical spirit of Socrates had always wanted to expel from the city and, as a consequence, since a poet was always a reprobate of sorts, the incomprehension of the University came as confirmation of his poetic vocation. Without his ever acknowledging it, academic success would have boded ill for him.

During this third year at the University, Hughes consciously distanced himself from ordinary social life and he noticed that, at some deep level, a reorientation of his psychic energy was taking place. He had had a strong feeling, amounting to a deep-seated physical certainty, that the efforts he made to fit into the mould were destroying him. It was not only a matter of literary opinion; above all, it concerned his mode of life. The pressure to conform, the inescapable demands of social life, were draining him of his strength until he felt he was constantly straining to fit into an absurd and hysterical system. The continuous and silent pressure was exhausting him, transforming him, forcing him to go in a direction that seemed opposed to his most vital interest, obliging him, in a word, to do what he did not want to do, to live what he did not want to live. In short, his freedom was at stake. Hughes would rather remain a hungry solitary wolf than become a well-fed dog with the mark of a collar round his neck. For this reason, he sought to follow his own inclination, striving to live according to his own desire, and so he came to realise that this anti-method enabled him to recapture his strength, and restore his inner self. Eating when he was hungry, sleeping when he felt sleepy, by these means he felt that, provided he could be patient enough, he would slowly be able to retrieve his basic self again, repossess himself of his soul. He had discovered a secret. The sound and fury of the world around him was of no real importance, and it was a mistake to follow each of its movements as if one's life depended on it. Therefore, he must discipline himself, concentrate on what was for him of real value, interesting himself in the outside world only on special occasions that he would choose himself. Hughes was discovering the virtues of withdrawing into an inner self, the joys one gets in an ivory tower, the taste there is in the simple pleasure of meditating upon the quiver of ink in an inkpot.

To cultivate his creative powers, and perhaps also to follow the Nietzschean ideal of a Socrates turned musician to obey the voice telling him to learn the arts, Hughes rented a piano and tried his best to teach himself to play. But, in many ways, music for the musician is the opposite of what it is for the music-lover. Hughes did not make the progress he expected: he would be overcome with apathy, give in to boredom, become listless. In an attempt to fight this surprising fatigue, he would dose himself up between meals with food complements that he would mix himself by whipping eggs, for instance, in a pint of warm milk with a large handful of brown sugar. He would buy meat and grill it on the fire in his room, which would attract some people on the scrounge who tried to cheer him up for a while. Or else he would go to bed twice a day in order to try and recover his strength, getting up at 2 or 3 a. m. to work, sing, play and draw; he had covered one of the walls in his room with huge leopards, green and red; then going back to bed towards 7, he would sleep till 9 or 10. He held that your first sleep is always the most beneficial, and so he hoped by such means to make double his profits. Besides, he thought that it was during the second sleep that you had the most beautiful dreams. What pleased him most in this way of life was that it gave him the impression of living two lives, one during the day and one at night and, of course, it was the latter that he liked best. The silence of the night seemed to be all his own, rich in latent possibilities; thus he reinvented a poetic version of the hunting expeditions of his childhood, when he would rise from bed before dawn to roam the hills on the alert for any chance meeting with wild game. And now, although he did not move from his room, the long night hours were pregnant with the same mysterious waiting, as full of intellectual adventures in which everything seemed likely to happen. In these heavily loaded hours on the reverse side of waking life, on the hidden face of the world, poetry visited him again. Had Wordsworth not said that poetry was strong emotion recollected in tranquillity? It was during a night like this that he had remembered the dreams of the green-eyed leopard and of the fox with bloody marks. In the silence of the night, with the deceitful noises of the world washed away, just as in the daytime the light of the sun causes the stars to fade away though they are still there, he felt the teasing presence of inspiration at the tip of his pen. The poem seemed to present itself of its own free will, so to speak, at times leaving traces of its coming on the page. Writing, he thought, was like catching animals. You had to know how to place yourself in the right frame of mind; all you had to do was compose yourself. It was a form of prayer. You had to let silence come upon you so that you could listen to your inner voice and stop the outer noise. Hughes would explain how it could be done, some years later, in a series of radio programs on education aimed at teaching children to develop their own creative faculties.

In the poems written during these years, very few of which Hughes would judge good enough to be published, the portrait of the poet as sleepwalker recurs over and over again. In such poems as "Song of the Sorry Lovers" or the "Woman with Such High Heels That She Looked Dangerous", the night is always the setting for a violent meeting. It is also the metaphor of an essential anonymity, and if Hughes published poems in Cambridge in periodicals like *Granta* as he had done before in the grammar school paper at Mexborough, he did so at first under a pen name. It is a frequent practice with poets at their debuts, but there was also, in Hughes's case, the desire to let the poem produce its own effect, undisturbed by any association with anyone in particular. For instance, he would have some poems, like "Scene Without An Act" in *Granta*, published under the pseudonym Daniel Hearing, thus placing his writing under the double sign of the prophet Daniel and of a technique of writing based on hearing. On other occasions, as for instance for the poems he published in *Chequers*, a second-rate students' review, he would sign Peter Crew, good-humorously, if somewhat irreverently poking fun at the New Testament scene: what did Peter crow to the damsel outside the palace when the cock crew? The noun "crew" may also be relevant here for at the time

Hughes was adopting a satanic attitude, and it would not have displeased him if his name had been manifold, for he dreamt of imitating the Portuguese poet Fernando Pessoa, an author who had published his work under several assumed names. By this means he could have written simultaneously both in different styles and under different masks. Later, in an interview to the *Paris Review* at a time when he already knew the weight of celebrity, he said he was convinced that a poet had lost part of his freedom once he had been published. To be in print was to enter a system which poetry was the exact opposite of; it meant being labelled, pigeonholed, pinned down like Gulliver in Lilliput; it meant being brought back into the petty society of mankind with all its constraints, instead of staying, like Orpheus in a legendary past, Saint Francis of Assisi or Saint Kevin of Glendalough, withdrawn in solitude among the free world of animals. For Hughes poetry was never primarily a matter of worldly vanity, but rather the quest of a power akin to magic, drawing the best part of its strength from secrecy.

The fact remains that one writes chiefly in order to be read, and it was at Cambridge that his reputation as a poet first developed. Hughes still moved in the circle of friends who used to meet at The Anchor to chat, sing and read poems. New figures had since joined the set, like Lucas Meyers, an American who had arrived to study at Cambridge two year after Hughes, and who also gave up English to take up anthropology. Luke, who would remain one of Ted's closest friends, also entertained poetic ambitions. The poems he wrote were strongly influenced by Hart Crane and Wallace Stevens, whose American style brought a welcome gust of wind from overseas into stuffy English traditions. Ted and he enjoyed writing poems or doggerel verse on themes they used to set each other, mostly of a comic or erotic character.

Ted's gown was beginning to get badly torn from climbing over railings while regaining his rooms after midnight at Pembroke. The group now met more often at The Mill, a pub in a narrow street of that name behind *Granta*, which served a cheap but particularly strong Merrydown cider. Another poet in the making, who was promised to certain fame, was Peter Redgrove, who had just founded the review *Delta*, whose ambition was to rival in importance with *Granta*, considered far too snobbish. Among the members of the editorial staff there was a certain Philip Hobsbaum, a student from Downing College, like Lucas Meyers. He had by then started to gather in his rooms a few chosen poets who came to read and discuss their poems. He was later to develop this practice, forming around him what came to be known as "The Group", first in London, where Hughes would continue to pay short calls for a while, then in Belfast where Seamus Heaney attracted attention by his rare and discreet participations. Hobsbaum indeed belonged to the species of authors who thrive in coteries and know how to push themselves forward. He seemed to have a special gift for establishing contacts and a rare talent for publicity. He was obviously a critic who was going to count in the future, indeed he was already engaged in promoting the work of some of the rising generation, which contained names with unequal claims to immortality, such as Edward Lucie-Smith and Peter Redgrove, but also David Ward or Christopher Levenson, and soon there would be Martin Bell or Peter Porter. The only problem for Hughes was that Hobsbaum was a student of F. R. Leavis's and a partisan of his vivisectionist's methods; and what was more he disliked intensely any type of poetry resembling that of Yeats or Hopkins. In spite of such differences, however, Hughes one day gave him a bundle of his poems to see if he might perhaps publish them in *Delta*, doing it so off-handedly that it was clear he did not entertain great hopes of ever seeing them published there. Indeed, had he wanted his poems to be refused he would not have acted differently; he had thrown the batch on the table in the pub, between two glasses of beer, perfunctorily, as he rose to go to the gents. As was to be expected, Hobsbaum refused them, an error of judgment that he was to regret in later years when literary history was to prove him wrong. Two years after this scene, however, *Delta* published "The Woman With Such High Heels" in its fifth issue; once again, however, even in this allegedly new publication, the dictates of modernism weighed heavily — as they would often do — upon Hughes's relationships with the literary establishment of his generation.

The poems that Hughes managed to have published in Cambridge's literary magazines were accepted with great difficulty. None had yet been published in Cambridge when he received his upper second-class degree in July 1954. With bitter disappointment he then realised that his university studies had no economic value, and his sonorous but useless Cambridge title was for him like the hypocritical smile of society politely shutting the door in his face. What was he to do? How was he to explain the fact to his parents? How could Ma, proud as she was of her son with a Cambridge degree, possibly understand? Gerald was in Australia with his wife Joan. Olwyn was in Paris working as an au pair girl. Ted then thought of a brilliant method to make the family's fortune. He may, it is true, have taken the idea from Evelyn Waugh's novel *A Handful of Dust*. He would set up a mink farm and before it started to bring in money, he would live a Spartan life, poaching to keep body and soul together while continuing to write poems. The idea was excellent. He wrote about it to Gerald. He worked out that it could earn £12,000 in four years. All that was needed to start the farm was a few cages and fifteen minks which could be fed on giblets that he would collect from the neighbourhood butchers. The only problem was the labour force, but Gerald and Joan could come back from Australia, Olwyn from France, the family would be again reunited and in a few years at most they would be rich. Gerald could then go back to Australia, if he wished, and buy hotels, for instance. Uncle Walt himself, the millionaire, would be green with envy. But Gerald turned a deaf ear to the whole project and went on reading his letters with a smile, as he would do for the many other plans, each more flamboyant than the one before, that kept germinating in Ted's mind over the years. Meanwhile, however, something had to be done for Ted: Uncle Walt proposed he come as his chauffeur during a journey on the continent in his big car. He hoped to get him interested in his firm, for he would have liked his nephew, who was intelligent — though too much intelligence might be a problem — to succeed him in his textile factory. And so, he took him to the battlefields of the Somme, to see where he had been wounded. While he went on talking about the war, he did not forget his objective of recruiting a bright mind for his business; they stopped at the best hotels, ate in the best restaurants, drank the best claret, to the extent that from that time onward claret would remain for Ted the supreme sign of affluence. As for the idea of ending at the head of a velvet factory in his native Yorkshire, there was no question that Ted would ever bring himself round to the idea. Of course, the position would have made him financially comfortable — even wealthy — it would also have left him enough leisure time to write poetry or for any other hobby of his choice, but he already had the intuition that poetry would be no amateurish thing for him; on the contrary the opportunity to gorge himself must yield to poetry. Perhaps, too, he confusedly felt that he needed a certain amount of poverty to preserve the force of his vocation, which might otherwise have been nothing but the passing fancy of an adolescent. At that time, Hughes already considered a poet's career as a sacred calling and he obscurely felt he had been born for it, as nothing else really interested him. In the most essential sense of the word, he wanted to devote his life to poetry.

Meanwhile, and in the hope that better days would come, he took a temporary job at London Zoo in Regent's Park, doing the washing up. However, some months previously a certain Daniel Hearing had succeeded at last in getting one of his poems published in *Granta*: "The Little Boys and the Seasons". But Ted, for the moment, spent his days washing up, standing in front of a window through which he could see a jaguar left in transit in a cage far too small for him. The animal reminded him of another jaguar that he had seen as a child at Morecambe Zoo, in Lancashire, and that he had so often played at modeling out of plasticine. This jaguar would never again be absent from his memory, and at different periods of his life he would draw him in different attitudes, mouth wide open or standing on his hind legs, half hidden behind town buildings. Seeing this other jaguar at Regent's Park gave him the idea of writing a poem that would be the equivalent in words of the plasticine jaguar of his early childhood. This was the beginning of a long period of work which would last for over two years before it reached its final stage. It was now the winter of 1954, and he was lodging in the unheated apartment of a girl, a trained nurse. Ted liked to relate the strange adventure that had happened to him one day when he was working at his poem in the leather coat that Walt had worn during the offensive on the Somme. While he was trying to find words to describe the funny grin that jaguars and other big cats have when they are baring their teeth, twisting their mouths on one side to simulate a bite, the image of a shepherd dog asleep in the sun had come into his head: a fly alights on the nose of the dog which, reluctant to rouse itself from sleep, tries to catch the fly by contorting its mouth on one side. Then working up the image to a higher pitch of intensity, he imagines that the fly gets into one of the dog's nostrils, increasing the dog's irritation to an unbearable degree. It was as he was engaged in this description that something extraordinary happened: a large-size bluebottle started to fly across the room in which it had been so cold for so many months that no insect could move its wings. The fly flew straight at him and into his nose; he caught it and pressed it in his volume of Shakespeare, a thick red book that was always close at hand. It is not easy to decide the part that dream had played in this story; Hughes would often mention similar episodes of his life in which he liked to see the proof that his poetic activity was akin to magic.

This magic could sometimes bring him some money when one of his poems was awarded a prize in a newspaper competition. He was living very precariously from day to day, and very often under a tent. Once he thought of going to sea on a fishing boat for the winter season on the North Sea, but on second thoughts changed his mind, for fear that Ma would worry to death. After doing the washing up at the zoo, he became for a time a night warden in a factory, and in these large buildings where the slightest noise became a booming sound, he whiled away the time writing a poem that he called "Money, my Enemy". His only aim was to stay in a job long enough to save the money to go and live in Cambridge until it ran out. There he would continue to see those of his friends who still gathered at The Anchor, which had tables outside along the river Cam with its ducks and punters. Apart from a few Americans and some other foreigners, the people he met there were mostly from Ireland, Scotland and the North of England. There was Harold Bloom, always spruce and smart, who never tired of reciting long poems, there was Daniel Weissbort who played the piano. As they all loved songs a Jazz group was formed, in keeping with the mood of the time, with the trombone player Michael Boddy and Joe Lyde, a protestant from Ulster well-known for his insolence. Among a number of would-be poets, one would have met a Welsh Catholic, Dan Huws, reputed for his ferocious criticism. And there was still his friend Lucas Meyer, who had come from Tennessee to study English literature and anthropology in Cambridge. He, too, was a keen reader of Graves, although his teacher Edmund Leach had warned him that *The White Goddess* had little credit with social scientists. A close friend of Ted Hughes's, he too sought a metaphysical truth that could take over from Christianity. Ted lodged for a time in Lucas's rooms in Cambridge where he had a camp bed, but his clandestine presence was reported to the authorities and he was forced to leave. Still, Lucas Meyers hastened to place an announcement in *Varsity* and found free accommodation at Mrs Hitchcock's, the widow of Saint Botolph's vicar; the reciprocal arrangement was that he should see to it that the Aga kitchen range and the Sentry stove did not go out at the vicarage in Tennison Road, in exchange for the use of a shed at the bottom of the garden, a small shelter of no more than fifty square feet, whose door opened only halfway and which had once been used as a hen-house. Ted slept there only two nights before pitching his tent in the garden. He would later good-humorously complain that his green velvet jacket had always kept the smell of hen droppings. For a time the place even became a poets' paradise: one could sleep under the trees, lulled to sleep by the song of birds and awakened by the light of the sun filtering through the leaves. But a woman on the scene complicated the matter. Blond hair that seemed much too long for a college of men seen in Dan Huws's bed at Pembroke created a scandal, and the culprit, confounded and sent down for a term, came to join Hughes and Meyers with his sweetheart. This was courting disaster; the whole lot was asked to leave the vicar's garden. Hughes, who was no longer a resident, was forbidden to come within three miles of Saint Mary's Church, a decision that was both so ridiculous and difficult to enforce that he chose to ignore it. And the next term, they all came back to Saint Botolph's in the wake of Lucas Meyers, to whom Mrs Hitchcock had now let her drawing-room. With no declared intention on their part, the vicarage became a centre of literary dissent, where black clothes and blue gauloises were de rigueur. The blond Helga Kobuszewski could be met there on occasions, soon to become Mrs Huws, along with Bertram Wyatt-Brown and David Ross, a Jungian psychoanalyst who was the editor for a time with Lucas Meyers of a fortnightly periodical of literary criticism called *Broadsheet*. It was a small set of people under the diffuse influence of Robert Graves, and although they might at times denounce the insufficiently scientific quality of his research, they felt the spell of his ideas strongly. Some of them, like Hughes and Myers, had been studying anthropology, which predisposed them in favour of ancient cults and pagan mythologies. They also took a passionate interest in shamanism, a primitive religion which is still practised today in Siberia or among Native Americans. The interest for this form of religion was due in great part to Mircea Eliade, soon to be appointed professor at Chicago University. In the 1940s he had been cultural attaché in the Romanian embassy in London, and in those years he had made a name for himself with his *Treatise on the History of Religions*. The members of the group dreamt of occult powers and of magic skills. They tried hypnosis with some success, and also levitation, with slightly less convincing results.

Something that was also in great favour among students was the game called Ouija. The best Ouija boards were those that you made yourself; all that was needed was a perfectly smooth piece of wood on which were written the letters of the alphabet and the figures from 0 to 9, sometimes a moon and a sun and, most important of all, a question mark and the words Yes and No. The name derived from a probable French and German origin: *oui / ja*. Two players sat face to face, balancing the board with an upturned glass on it on their knees. One player would ask questions and the other note down the answers given by the glass moving more or less at random on the board. Their intention was thus to practise the art of divination or to bring the spirit of some dead person to write his message as surely as he would have spoken it the course of a spiritualist's séance, even to attempt by this means to compose a novel. It was a variant of automatic writing, so much in favour among the surrealists.

Hard pressed by economic necessities, Ted had found a temporary job in a rose garden at Walworth in Hertfordshire. He still slept under a tent, and got up at dawn feeling the pinch of cold and hunger. He would write to Ma, urging her to send him a blanket, two pairs of socks (thick ones), a knife, a fork, his RAF tin plate, a biscuit tin that she could fill with filches of bacon, kidney beans, lard, chocolate, etc. But he was becoming more and more aware that he would have to go to the bother of finding a respectable job if he did not want Ma to worry herself to death on his account. His sister Olwyn, who had found a job as a bilingual secretary for NATO in France, kept pestering him with letters whose reproachful tone made him uneasy. He thought of applying for a job as an English teacher in Madrid where the cost of living was lower than in England. But he had also heard that in Hungary one could live on even less money than in Spain. Was it really so? Still another solution would be to go and join Gerald in Australia and earn his living there as a schoolmaster. In November 1954 "The Jaguar" appeared in the 7th issue of *Chequers* with some other texts by Ted Hughes and by Daniel Huws, whose surnames caused some people to assume that both were Welsh. Ted was then in London, where he had taken up lodgings in a rather decrepit bachelor's flat at18 Rugby Street, rented by Dan in the district of Bloomsbury. He attended some of the meetings held in Philip Hobsbaum's bed-sitter near Edgware Road, and once scandalised the landlady by frying black pudding on the stove while singing ballads with his girlfriend of the moment, Rosemary Joseph, a very shy girl who probably inspired the poem "Secretary". At the same time, he was also keeping on form with amatory partners, some nurses at Addenbrookes Hospital among whom there was a certain Christine. His six-and-a-half foot stature, deep "Russian" voice, scruffy appearance and loutish manners seemed to exert an irrepressible appeal on the fairer sex. For he had the cruel look of one devoid of scruples, as fascinating a figure, one might say, as Heathcliffe in *Wuthering Heights*, or as Jack Palance in *Shane*. Ted was clearly rather proud of his many successes with women, and he was generous with advice on the proper way to behave with them; to his mind, you should little by little establish such relationships as to cause the poor dears to fall into your power without realising it.

In London, during the literary evenings got up by Hobsbaum, Hughes sometimes read some poems by Hopkins with such emotional intensity that to uncultivated ears they might have passed for his own. This unique voice of his was admired by all his friends, so that Ted was soon spending hours recording long stretches of *Sir Gawain and the Green Knight*, the anonymous 14th century verse romance on the tape-recorder of his friend Peter Redgrove. Redgrove made use of the recording to get him a job at the BBC. But Hughes, right from the start, made a deplorable impression in Auntie's studios. He was really too badly dressed and too gruff in his behaviour not to be seen as an exhibit of bad taste: with his fierce general demeanour and his stony stare he was plainly a ladies' fright. This immediate allergic reaction was indeed mutual, and Hughes would declare that never in his life had he seen anything so disgraceful as these television people. As it was indeed sadly evident that he lacked the knack of making money out of his Cambridge education by treading the ordinary path of the worldly wise, a job was found for him in an office. He became a reader in the Pinewood studios of Arthur Rank at Iver Heath, near Heathrow, where he would spend his time reading novels and theatre plays to see if scenarios might not be extracted from them. But, predictably, few of these masterpieces he deemed good enough to deserve a report on their filmic potentials. In any case, he soon realised that the typewriter had a harmful effect upon his style. It was as if his writing were inexplicably in danger as soon as he could no longer control the unfolding verbal thread with the run of his pen, because too complex an apparatus was intruding inopportunely between his brains and his words. But this was not the worst of it: he came to realise that having to read such a lot of bad literature was literally polluting his mind and was appreciably contaminating his mental faculties. It was vital, he felt, that he should ascend to some higher place and take a deep breath before returning with pinched nose to his pearl-diver's chores. Thus, from time to time he would take out of the top left drawer of his desk his one-volume edition, bound in red, of the Complete Works of Shakespeare on Indian paper, and so attained the glory of being dismissed for reading Shakespeare.

Poor England! It was the last straw. Despairing of finding his proper place in the English society of the time, Ted Hughes decided on the spot to go to Australia, like Gerald, at the expense of the host country. Having gone through all the red tape involved in having his name entered on a waiting list, he believed that any moment, in a month or a year, he would be given the green light to sail. He found a girl sufficiently in love to be willing to go with him should it so happen, and he thought about marrying her, even, at the last minute. She was a nurse, entirely devoted to him, and everybody found that she resembled him. Her name was Shirley. Ted had gone as far as to take her with him to his native Yorkshire and to introduce her to his parents and his sister. Things were turning out, it seemed, as if he would settle down and follow in the steps of his brother Gerald. But if Ted had gone so far as to make the choice of emigrating, it was as a last resort, because he could see no promising prospects for him in England. To linger on at the University doing useless studies was, he though, to deceive oneself, and he had nothing but scorn for the hidebound conservatism of English society with its segregated social strata. If he was not naive to the point of believing that Australia was a paradise, at least he thought that it would somehow be possible to make a place for himself in the sun. But time was drawing on, and he felt sure that if he had told Ma of his Australian projects she would no doubt have fallen ill. And so, he sometimes went to visit his parents in their house at the Beacon, in Heptonstall, that big black cube on the bare back of a hill, in the middle of the rainy, windswept undulations of West Yorkshire and the Pennines. One day of ruffling weather, one of those stormy days when you feel strangely sick at heart, when it no longer seems even possible to believe that what you see is real, Ted was looking out of the window at a football match being played in the gale on the sports field of Slack. The world outside, as if torn from its mooring by the raging wind, seemed even more unreal when seen from inside a home whose shelter, necessarily precarious, seemed unreasonably threatened by the howling of the wind under the rafters and the patter of sleet-like rain against the window pane. To his archaeologist's eyes, the human figures and their edifices, and even the large expanse of history, all the huge outrageous turmoil of the world and its wars in which his father William had lost much of his capacity for enjoying life, everything, in short, appeared derisory, as if already swiped away by some brutal force. These few minutes of melancholy meditation would later flower into the poem "Wind", and they would continue to cling to his memory, like those things in the mind which one keeps revisiting without knowing why, in hours of solitude. It would also inspire him to write "Football at Slack", a poem in which the ball, ceaselessly deflected and carried away by the gale, seems to be the toy of some mischievous occult force making fun of human endeavours.

A sullen melancholy mixed with exasperated boredom continued to be the dominant mood of a country still haunted by ghosts in uniforms. Too open a display of vitality, and all forms of energy that seemed bent on expressing themselves freely aroused suspicion. It was as if a word higher than another, or an opinion too frankly expressed, risked opening the door enough to let in fascism. The cold war was exerting a numbing influence on people's minds. The only possible future seemed strictly limited to a material world in which all trace of unconventional spirituality seemed in danger, sooner or later, of being whisked over the ravine into some barbarous madness; it was utterly out of place in a gentlemen's country. The England of the 1950s was definitely not favourable to primitivism. More time would be needed before the paintings of Francis Bacon could come into being, followed by pop art, the drumbeats of pop music and the howlings of rock'n roll. For the moment, public taste went no further than jazz, all very neat and proper. The poets of the Movement held pride of place with their conversational flatness, their small-minded belief that the "myth kitty" was a Pandora's box, and the soporific tone of their exquisitely self-rejecting witticisms. The younger generation were dragged down with boredom, with no visible chance of being successful in their economic or artistic careers. A strong wind was needed to bring fresh air and dispel this musty atmosphere. Hughes was adrift; the poetry he had the ambition to write stood little chance of going down well in England at the time. It would indeed be Australia, where he could be with Gerald. He wrote, asking him to send a list of the things he wanted. The gun? The fishing rod? The small metal spinning rod, those for pike? What was that Italian perfume that Joan liked so much? While waiting for the boat, Ted spent much time in pubs frequented by poets where he would sometimes meet colourful personages sporting the sad, disillusioned look that is the paradoxical charm of confidential artists. In London, he often went to The Lamb, the Conduit Street pub, in Holborn. There, over a few pints of beer, he would meet literary figures of the previous generation who would have deserved to be better known — the deaf poet David Wright, and also George Barker, John Heath-Stubbs, and William Sidney Graham — in an outdated Victorian décor of old dark wood furniture, leather-covered benches and sepia photographs. But Cambridge was where you had to be to meet the turbulent young groups of students whose periodicals where being scoured in preference to others by old literary students of the University on the look-out for promising talents for publishing houses. The impatient young men gravitating towards Saint Botolph's shared a common anarchistic exasperation with English society, also tinged with different sorts of interests for occult knowledge, the belief in the superiority of what is primitive derived from anthropology, and an outspoken insolence that served as a trademark. Before time would disperse them all, they wanted to leave some trace of their youthful years. Keats, one must always remember, the poet who was most to be admired among the romantics, had already flowered into canonical glory when he died of tuberculosis at the age of 26; once he had gone beyond that early age, every budding poet was a dead Keats. As Hughes would say: we are all dead Keatses. It was then that, as a last resort, David Ross, a member of their group, obtained from his father, a well-to-do city banker, the money necessary to the publication of the first number of a poetry review they would call the *Saint Botolph's Review*. The most poetically minded of all these poets gave each a few texts. They were David Ross, Daniel Weissbort, his brother George, Lucas Meyers, and Ted Hughes himself contributed four poems. They took the results to a printer, and groups of good friends were set up to peddle the review in the streets of Cambridge. A special evening was got up to set the thing afloat on February 26th, 1956. On notepaper headed "Pembroke College" Hughes busied himself drawing the horoscopes of Keats and of Marlowe, then he eventually nerved himself to examine whether the stars would be propitious to him on that date. He foresaw a disaster. Astrology was not a science for him; but like tarot, or reading the future in coffee dregs or tea leaves, it was simply an age-old rudimentary technique useful to help you discover and develop your own intuitions, an old wives' trick to set your mind working as in a waking dream. In the Middle Ages, odd practices like this had been common in Europe, putting a bit of magic in men's lives, but the spirit of Protestantism and the development of rational thought had weaned people from them, as from so many idiotic toys and useless amusements. Had Chaucer himself, the great English poet of the 14th century, and a serious astrologer himself, cast such a horoscope, he would no doubt have prudently stayed at home on that day, but all that horoscopy was perhaps nothing but pure twaddle and out-of-date ideas, certainly not enough to make you stay away from such a festive occasion.

A room had been rented on the second floor of the Women Students' Union, in Falcon Yard, behind Petty Curry, and a piano had been installed. When the big day arrived, they all gathered there, all of them dressed in black, with the friends of their friends who had been rounded up for the occasion. The jazz band, composed of a group of cronies from Saint Botolph's vicarage, from The Mill and The Anchor, did their best to galvanise the crowd, with Daniel Weissbort playing the piano, Michael Boddy the trombone and Joe Lyde the trumpet. The common practice on such occasions was to arrive already slightly tipsy before the evening actually began. People danced to the sound of jazz music in a free and easy bohemian style. Many dark and furtive looks had the satanic glint that is the sign of impatient ambitions. Ted Hughes was there. He had defied the judgment of the stars and come along with his girlfriend Shirley. You could not miss his towering figure, slightly stooping when addressing this or that woman, gazing intently into her eyes through the lock of hair that kept falling down across his face, holding his head on one side and watching the company over his shoulder from time to time, playing the part of Byronic poet and seducer. The music got louder and louder, faster and faster. Luke Meyers distinguished himself by his frenzied way of dancing the jitterbug, but the magnetic centre attracting everyone's attention was a young woman dressed in red and black. She danced rather badly but radiated a strong physical presence that no one could fail to notice. Tall as a fashion model, blazing red shoes, full pulpy lips set off by bright red lipstick, a nearly simian way that she had of moving her fingers when she talked, and listening intently to her addressee with a disgruntled air, lowering the corners of her mouth in a little grimace of excessive concentration that was truly disturbing. She was an American come on a Fulbright scholarship to study at the Newnham College for women. Her name was Sylvia Plath. She was known because of a photograph of her in a polka dot bikini that had appeared in *Varsity*: 5 feet and 7 inches high for a weight of 10 stone, tall and broad-shouldered, with a voracious appetite. But her face was not really beautiful; her nose was too big and her complexion wax-like. She was biting her lips and the tip of her tongue was showing a little too much when she talked. She was indeed too perfect a caricature of the American woman for the guarded taste of the English students of those days. She dressed too showily, talked too loudly, and made ill-advised efforts to attract sympathy by giving vent to impulsive remarks when she met somebody for the first time. Her general behaviour met with ill-concealed disdain tempered with a very banal feeling of jealousy on the part of these young Englishmen who seemed destined to become less rich and less fully-grown than this fine and brilliant creature. Above all, she had retained from her education at Smith College, the private Women's University at Northampton, Massachusetts, and then from the success she had known among the very smart ladies of the editorial staff of *Vogue*, an idea of self-promotion derived from advertising that offended the feelings of those straight young people of Cambridge. And yet she had worked hard at trying to improve her appearance to lessen the infamous cultural differences between the two countries, leaving in America the Marilyn-style platinum blond hair dye and the glamorous outfits of a pleasure-loving princess. For old Europe, she had adopted a light brown colour for her hair and quieter clothes, calculated to make her look more like a serious student. But she was also a product of the American campus where the young people deemed it sane, almost hygienic, to go the limit on the back seats of sedan cars when out on a date. And so, to the embarrassment of some Englishmen who lacked the frankness and honesty to live a happy life to the full, she did not conceal her pronounced taste for what she called "athletic sex". Somewhat flustered by the end of an affair that was drawing out with one Richard Sassoon, she had vowed of late, as if to avenge herself, to accept the advances of whoever happened to make them. Just now, she was going out with a certain David Hamisch Stewart, a Canadian who had come to study English at Queen's College. In order to put themselves in the mood of the evening, the two had been downing whiskies in a bar on King's Parade. What is more, despite appearances, which are not, it is true, often to be trusted, Sylvia Plath prided herself on being a poet, as everybody else did, in a way, but in her case very much so. Recently, one of her poems called "Three Caryatids", which had appeared in the magazine *Chequers*, had been slated in *Broadsheet* by Dan Huws, the Welsh friend of Ted Hughes. Huws claimed to see nothing but humbug in these contrived verses of hers, and he concluded his onslaught with a remark that was frankly sexist; perhaps he was wrong, he said, to criticise her so much, for after all she might well be good-looking. If for nothing else, Sylvia had come along that evening to settle some accounts. She had bought an issue of the *Saint Botolph's Review* and had learnt all the poems by heart. The reckless Dan Huws had just had a bad time of it. Then she had turned to Lucas Meyers and had recited one of his poems. As soon as she entered the room, Ted and

Sylvia had eyes for no one but each other. Sylvia kept asking who this tall, sombre-looking man was, but no one wanted to reply, as if her question did not call for an answer. And then, all of a sudden, he was there, standing in front of her, looking straight into her eyes with a strange little grin as he pronounced her name: Sylvia Plath. His name? Ted Hughes. Then she started to recite, at the top of her voice to cover the sound of the music, "When Two Men Meet for the First Time", a poem of Ted Hughes's later called "Law in the Country of the Cats", in which he poked fun at Rousseau's ideal of universal brotherhood and maintained that on their first meeting two men necessarily detest each other like death. Ah! She liked it? With no further ado, he dragged her into another room, closed the door on them and set about pouring her another drink that she drained on the spot. They talked to each other, at the top of their voices, as if in a high wind. Sylvia kept tapping with her feet on the ground. Then Ted kissed her on the mouth, tore the red band from her hair and pulled off her ear-rings. Then, when he kissed her again in the neck, she set her teeth into his cheek. There upon, he turned on his heels and walked back home with his trophies in his pocket and a visibly jealous Shirley. Later on, with all the drinking that had been going on, the party started to get out of control. David Ross boxed the ears of a man who had called on him to make him a poem since he said that he was a poet. Some window panes were broken. Sylvia accompanied one Hamish to his rooms. They had to climb over the railings in spite of their inebriated state. Her tight dress got torn and she cut her hands on the spikes without feeling any pain on the moment. They made love and she went back home in the early morning. She felt as if a high wind was blowing behind her eyes, and she was in no condition to write her essay on Racine's *Phaedra*. So she plunged into her diary, for what was the use of a life without constraints if not for the sake of keeping a journal?

The *Saint Botolph's Review* was never to issue another number. Its launching party turned out to be its farewell evening. Meyers's tutor asked him to leave Saint Botolph's vicarage because of a certain hullabaloo that took place on February 25th, 1956 at the Women Students' Union in Falcon Yard. Some time later, Hughes received an ultimatum from the Australian authorities and he asked to be able to defer sailing for nine months. He was back in Cambridge at the beginning of March where he sought lodgings in Meyers's rooms by discreetly singing an Irish republican song under his windows. He got Sylvia Plath's address through Bertram Wyatt-Brown, Luke's cousin, and they went out together at night, trying to wake her up by throwing clods of earth against her window panes. They would learn later that it was the wrong window and that she had gone out with a man. They came back another time and realised they had again targeted the wrong window. In yet another of their commando attacks at Whitstead, they ended up waking another resident who went to fetch Plath but could not wake her up. Hughes had left for London asking Meyers to slip Plath his address and to do his best to provide free accommodation for her in London if she went there, which Myers agreed to do much against his will. Ted Hughes felt that he was falling in love and tried in vain to fight back. Sylvia Plath admitted in her diary that she was madly in love with him, but she refused to go to bed with somebody who was, they told her, the greatest seducer in Cambridge. She was afraid to be the talk and laughing stock of scandal-mongering friends, and so she went on filling up notebooks and writing to Richard Sassoon who was studying French at the Sorbonne. Richard was a distant cousin of Siegfried Sassoon who had become famous for his poems as well as by his military valour during World War I, together with Wilfred Owen and a few other War Poets. Sylvia had met Richard in New York. They had engaged in an exuberant enough love affair, rich in nights of love-making, spankings and other merry sexual games. In Europe, they had gone together on a scooter trip along the Riviera. Then life, imperceptibly, caused them to drift apart. Richard was in fact using his letters to Sylvia as first versions of the papers he had to write for the creative writing classes he attended. Sylvia gradually came to suspect the joyous insincerity of a lover whom she had thought she could control at will, and she had started to write in her journal of using these writings, and perhaps even Richard's letters as well, as material for a novel. Their journey in the South of France on a scooter had already provided her with the matter of a short story that she had tried to publish on her return to Cambridge. But, above all things, tall Sylvia hated the idea of Richard being so much smaller than she was. She dreamt of a man who would lift her up and carry her away in his arms, but she was regularly visited by the same nightmare: she found herself married to a diminutive husband, which gave her the sensation of being penetrated by some buzzing catatonic insect that obliged her to lay thousands of little eggs. And so it was with a relief one can well imagine that she met Ted Hughes, a giant of a man, who, of all the men she had ever met, seemed the only one capable of measuring up to her expectations. Playing on words, she liked to say that he was the only one huge enough for her.

And yet she continued to write to Richard, saying that the poems she wrote were all for him. Still with him in mind, she composed "Pursuit", a poem in which she feels she is being chased by a panther. The inspiration for this poem had come to her and had consumed a whole day of her time, in a long outburst of irrepressible desire. She would class every man in terms of sexual compatibility; three of them made the grade. They were, in ascending order, Sassoon, Meyers, and Hughes. The last one was an ideal figure of a man, but she seriously doubted if she could ever manage to get at him. She finally decided on a three-week visit to Paris in the hope of seeing Richard who had stopped answering her letters. She stayed in London on her way to Paris and took a room in a hotel through the recommendation of Luke, who had invited her to dinner in his Barton Road apartment. Meyers had agreed to play the go-between somewhat reluctantly. On the evening of March 23rd, 1956 he met Sylvia Plath again with Michael Body at The Lamb, the poets' pub of Conduit Street. It was on that occasion that Plath learnt, in the course of a desultory conversation, that Ted Hughes lived in a flat not very far from this place, at number 18 Rugby Street, and that you had to rap on the front door with the knocker twice and Hughes would throw you the key. The place where he lived was a tiny bed-sitter with no running water, the communal bathroom being three stories below, in a decrepit 18th century building. Ted Hughes worked sitting at a joiner's bench which served him as a table, and the legend has it that it was there that he had finished composing "The Thought-Fox" in remembrance of the Cambridge nocturnal apparitions that had definitely set the seal upon his poetic vocation. When Sylvia Plath came to visit him, one of his cheeks still bore the round-shaped mark of her teeth. She too bore marks on her temples and a scar under her right eye. She told him why. She told him how, in August 1953, she had crawled into the basement of her mother's house where she thought nobody would find her and swallowed a whole bottle of sedative tablets. She had remained there unconscious for two days before her brother had at last found her. She had vomited up the tablets and scraped her face on the ground so badly that it had left a lasting scar under her eye. The smaller marks on her temples had been left by the electrodes applied there when they had tried to cure her from depression by electro-concussive treatment in Boston hospital. As they talked, the night fell and time went on its course. Luke Meyers and Michael Boddy, after a long wait outside on the pavement finally decided to go up. On entering the flat, they heard Sylvia and Ted talking quietly in soft voices. They were sitting on chairs, face to face, Sylvia with her legs tucked under her and Ted with his knees pressed against her chair. Later Ted would say that an interior voice had warned him at the time to keep safe from this strange girl. Yet he had followed her away into her hotel room where they had made love furiously, for such was their style, making a night of it, a "holocaust" night as Sylvia Plath would soon describe it in her journal. For Ted's ideas concerning sex were absolute and nearly religious. He would expose them in various poems, the first of which is "Bride And Groom Lie Hidden For Three Days", a sort of carnal version of the old Platonic myth of the ideal communion of souls: the lovers are meticulously engaged in a mutual reassembling of their dismembered bodies, each amorously refitting the other's body like two dismantled machines, with enchanted cries of sensuous delight, "like two god of mud".

The following morning, while Ted, in Luke's company, was ravenously eating sausages in his insalubrious Rugby Street flat, Sylvia was in the train, heading for Paris on the track of Richard, trying to revive the memories of the last Christmas that she spent with him and other American students in dutiful admiration of Notre-Dame, la Comédie Française, Montmartre, the gaudy prostitutes of Pigalle, while time went so pleasantly as they sat at café tables. Then, again the Côte d'Azur with Richard, the Matisse Chapel in Vence, like a winter resurgence of the days of wind and sunlight too quickly gone, which had already yielded such a nice short story. But at number 4, rue du Vivier, after questioning the concierge, it appeared Richard was nowhere to be found. Never mind! Sylvia was not the sort of woman to let such a situation get her down and she resolved to seize the opportunity of enjoying herself in gay Paris. She decided to spend her time in cafés, desultorily drawing sketches of what happened to be there: a vase full of flowers, a shoe, bottles on a shelf and, since in Paris everyone was drawing, she slept with a journalist who happened to be drawing at the same terrace as herself. Life was beautiful. She bumped into Gary Haupt, another American student who, not so very long ago, had held her hand when she was having a speck of dust removed from her eye at Addenbrookes Hospital in Cambridge. In a word, she was so happy here, in France, that she toyed for a time with the idea of not returning to England. Paris was full of opportunities, throbbing with avant-garde energy and breathing the fresh air of fashion. She had also gone up into a room of the Hotel du Béarn with an irresolute young man, called Tony, who had approached her in the street and then stupidly changed his mind and failed to deliver. And so, what else was there to do? For an American in Paris, the American Express Office is a place of strategic importance. She went there to send a postcard to her mother and another one to Ted reproducing *The Snake Charmer* by Le Douanier Rousseau. She also met Gordon Lameyer, another friend that she had known for a long time, a person of leisure and independent means like herself. She decided on the spot to accompany him on a European tour via Munich, Venice and Rome. But these two *enfants terribles* were no sooner on board the train that they started to quarrel and it ended in a separation in Rome, five days later, when Gordon elegantly got rid of Sylvia by buying her a return ticket to London. Stopping in

Paris on her way back she had found a letter from Ted sent care of the American Express. No doubt, it was Ted with whom she was madly in love and she wrote to her mother that he was the strongest of men, with a voice like God's thunder itself, truly the only one cut out big enough to be her match. On April 13th, as soon as she arrived in England, she made haste to throw herself into the arms of *her* Ted. They were to have a wonderful life, they were to have many children and make plenty of poems, they were to have a marvellous globe-trotters' existence, like D.H. Lawrence and his wife Frieda. Australia? Good-bye to all that.

III

SYLVIA, OR NEW ENGLAND

In April 1956 Ted Hughes was lodging in a garret in Cambridge, at the top of Alexander House, a restaurant run by the Volunteer Women's Service. Sleeping on a mattress laid on the floor, he shared the room with a woman who had just left her husband, but he was apparently too much in love with Sylvia to have the heart to console her. Moreover, he was said to have resisted the advances of a pretty plumb girl, gap-toothed, like Chaucer's Wife of Bath, which is a sign of good fortune. In short, there was evidence everywhere that he was badly smitten and no longer himself. His friends were worried, and tried by every conceivable means to bring him back to his senses. But all to no avail: he had not found it funny to be told that Ellen Chase and Eleanor Duckett, two American friends of Sylvia's who had come over to visit Cambridge, had pederasts' voices. He was certainly ready to admit there was something ludicrous about them but he was uncertain as to the sort of admiration Sylvia had for these women who were able to make "fabulous money" with their writings. He had even appeared sincerely hurt to learn that Plath had described her Paris holiday in *Varsity*, an American undergraduates' magazine, in terms so ridiculously enthusiastic that — in the eyes of Meyers, the critical American — she must have fallen into a trap set by some publisher who had encouraged her to write such an outré text. It was obviously destined to be read as a caricature — involuntarily comical — of an exaggeratedly American style, energetically positive, effusive and superficial, which seemed bound by some sort of moral obligation to express a boisterous *joie de vivre* at any cost. But Ted, who looked on Sylvia's with a lover's eyes, did not see things in that light. Of course, he was obliged to admit to himself that love had him in its grasp and he was still feebly trying, at this stage, to keep his head by taking exercises, which seemed, furthermore, to be the necessary condition for his writing good poetry, another being abundantly out-pouring himself in prose. All the same, what she had told him about her attempted suicide kept worrying him. She was born on October 9th, 1932 and when he prepared her horoscope along with those of Virginia Woolf and of Nietzsche, again and again he would fall upon aspects of the heavens that were strongly indicative of suicide. But ever since reading some of her poems he had been convinced of the presence of a genius of sorts. Very soon, he sensed a change in his own writing, a continent of new possibilities seemed to lie open before him. More effectively than Austra-lia could have done, the Americanness of Sylvia res-cued him from the ingrained English insularity that had been insidiously stifling him for too long. As far as his mental make-up was concerned, he had just discovered America and he kept reciting to himself, as if in a dream, the lines from John Donne's very erotic Nineteenth Elegy: "O my America! my new-found land!"

As for Sylvia, she had an enormous admiration for his poems and for his abundant fertility of mind. His strongly alliterative lines reawakened in her the echoes of his big voice and made her think of the rushes of a strong wind in the riggings of a ship. Her desire for him, the pleasure she had in loving him, sent silent cries of happiness into her head, giving her a formidable assurance. The hours she spent with him were more intense, as if they were being lived at full speed all the time. He took her into woods and fields and he seemed to know all the secrets of nature and of the lives of animals. In April, she composed an "Ode for Ted" in which he figured as a sort of Orpheus or another God Pan. Green corn seemed magically to sprout under his feet. He gave animals their names as they came out of thickets. At a sign of his hand, birds would build their nests, she was grateful to be the Eve of this new Adam. From the pockets of his faithful corduroy jacket he would draw horoscopes which he taught her to prepare and interpret, but also trout freshly caught or fish eggs that he showed her how to cook and which they would eat eagerly with a sort of animal greed. She wrote to her mother to send out her cookery book by return of post. In May, she discovered punting on the Cam when Ted took her for a long trip on one of the flat-bottomed gondolas, showing her how to move it along with a long pole. There was no other boat on the river. They were alone in the world, like two pioneers. She wrote warning her mother that she might be surprised by Ted's appearance, adding by way of advice to prepare her for the shock, that she should picture in her mind a tall Huckleberry Finn stepping straight out of one of Mark Twain's novels. Her life with him was nothing but discovery and spontaneity. She formed a romantic image of him: that of the ideal American, the very type of the new natural man shorn of all artificially accumulated bookish knowledge, but full of instinct with a deep, organic, intuitive understanding of the world. Indeed he was so obviously the best man in the world, such a treasure of a man that she began sending out letters to American magazines containing samples of his poems that she had typed out herself like a good fairy, because she wanted to prepare the ground for Ted by bringing the American establishment to the right pitch of expectancy when she would at last come back to America with her wonderful poet. When he was writing at full throttle, his poems, she said, were dynamite. And so, she set about stirring a lot of advance publicity for him and, in order to improve his social skills, she took him out for an evening organised for Fulbright students, all shaggy and unkempt in his old suit, shiny with wear, and she introduced him for whatever use it might have to the U.S. Ambassador and the Duke of Edinburgh, from whom he drew a smile and a sigh when he told him he was chaperoning Sylvia.

As a matter of fact, he had never proposed to her; it was she who first alluded to marriage as a good idea and he had answered that he rather agreed to the idea, in fact. Why not? But Sylvia, above all things, made him swear that their marriage should be kept absolutely secret, even from his closest friends and from the members of his family, under the fallacious pretext that in the event of the marriage coming to be known she would be in danger of losing her scholarship. In actual fact, it was because she wanted to have two marriages: a small one, very romantic and secret in England at once, and a grand marriage in the States the year after, in the Unitarian Church at Wellesley with all her friends and her family who would be told that they'd only been officially engaged in England. And thus, a ceremony of sorts was organised within a very restricted circle: her mother Aurelia Plath and her brother were the only persons she would let into the secret. While Aurelia was in Boston catching a plane to London, Sylvia and Ted hurried to get a marriage licence bearing the seal of the Bishop of Canterbury, which did much to impress the future bride. To do so it was necessary for Ted to contact the clergyman of the parish where he lived. He instinctively picked him out in the street and followed him as far as his house to check that he was right. Sylvia was overcome with admiration upon learning that the man of God lived right in front of the house of Charles Dickens. They spent their last shillings on decent clothes for Ted and on gold wedding rings. Then, on the eve of the great day, Ted had a dream, a distant resurgence of the fishing expeditions for pike in the pond of Johnnie Wesley's father and of the cannibal young pike that had devoured one another in the school aquarium: he was angling in the bottomless moat of some ancient monastery when a mysterious force rose from the darkness in the form of an eye which slowly fixed its stare on him. And already the dream had gone into the first draft of a poem. On the morning, a heavy rain was falling which did not let up all day. Ted gave Sylvia a pink rose to match the pink ribbon in her hair and the pink jersey dress that her mother had brought her. On 16 June 1956 at about 1:30 p. m. Edward James Hughes, age 25, writer, and Sylvia Plath, 23, student, recited the marriage vows according to the rites of the Anglican Church and were married by the Reverend Mercer Wilson, in the presence of his curate Richard Burnston and of Aurelia Plath in the parish church of Saint George the Martyr in Holborn. Sylvia wept with joy.

Out of consideration, perhaps, for the German origins of the Plaths, he invited his mother-in-law to Schmidt's, a good German restaurant reputed for its moderate prices. Then the three of them went to France because Sylvia was very anxious to show her mother Paris before she returned to the States. They would then spend their honeymoon in Spain. In Sylvia's eyes, Paris was still the town known by the American writers of the first half of the century, and she thought she was breathing the same air as Francis Scott Fitzgerald, Ernest Hemingway, Gertrude Stein or Ezra Pound. But for Ted, who had already visited Paris with his uncle Walt, the World War I veteran whose mind was still full of the dreadful tales of his experience, Paris was haunted by the ghosts of German occupation and the memory of the fight for its liberation, kept alive by the bullet marks still visible on some of the façades. Oh! but this is not French Paris, Sylvia would explain to him. Besides, the only language you could hear was English. And in point of fact, who of all people did they meet on the Pont Neuf but the inevitable Luke Meyers, who just happened to be loitering there. Meyers felt a little out of place to find himself with these two newly-weds on their honeymoon, floating along in happiness while Sylvia dreamed aloud, wondering what Jean Cocteau could be doing just then. They were living inside a novel with no end, punctuated by poems. The two of them wanted to write as they lived, trusting in one and the same spontaneous movement. Firmly resolved to earn his living as a writer since, once and for all, he had decided that to live was for him to write, Ted set about churning out an interminable story, composed of a series of fables for children, comical suppositions about how animals have become what they are. He modelled his style on that of Jonathan Swift in *Gulliver's Travels* but inclined towards an ever greater simplicity. As soon as he had composed one, he would read it aloud to Sylvia who sometimes burst out laughing and sometimes broke into a flood of tears, and sometimes did both; he wanted to see the encouraging responses as signs that these tales would make his fortune. He imagined that he was selling them to Walt Disney at a fabulous price, so that, through the sole magic of his pen, he was becoming richer than Uncle Walt himself.

On July 4th, Independence Day in America, they were still in Paris; on July 14th, Bastille Day in France, Ted and Sylvia arrived in Spain, on the Costa Bianca, in Benidorm which had not yet been submerged by mass tourism. Sylvia's habit of going on her travels with an impressive wardrobe packed in heavy Samsonite suitcases was an encumbrance on their way, but they finally reached their destination at the end of a long journey by train via Madrid and Alicante, during which they resisted the suffocating heat with copious gulps of red wine squirted into their mouths from goatskin gourds passed on by workers much amused by the sight of Ted Hughes struggling with his small dictionary. The day after, like the true Englishman he remained to the last, Ted was as red as a lobster and Sylvia was so ill for having drunk foul water at the Señora Mangada's that he had to hypnotise her to send her to sleep and put an end to her complaints. When Sylvia insisted that Ted should buy a linen suit for summer and a few colourful shirts, the scanty state of their purse obliged them to lose no time in finding cheaper lodgings and to adopt habits of strict economy where every penny would have to do the work of four. The only luxury they indulged in was white coffee for Sylvia and milk and brandy for Ted. But they decided that for the moment they could not afford to send manuscripts to the States, considering the cost of Spanish air-mail postage. However, *The Nation*, a New-York magazine, had just accepted Ted's poem "The Witch" and there were other signs that, perhaps, success was not too far ahead. Their honeymoon proper was in Paris. Ted and Sylvia had not come to Spain on a tourists' holiday. In the letters that he wrote to his parents to attempt to obtain their forgiveness — if that was possible — for getting married without telling them, he explained that he planned to go to Madrid at the beginning of the Autumn term in order to find a job as an English teacher. To this end, he was already taking lessons in Spanish with a woman to whom he taught English in return, adding, however, that his progress was slow, for he found the local Catalan accent a near insurmountable obstacle. For the future, still faithful to his original idea of being a globe-trotting writer, he contemplated teaching English in Spain for a year, then going to the U.S. to teach literature in a University, before coming back to Europe to teach English, say, in Italy and so on, in different countries of the world, here one year, elsewhere the next. There was nothing particularly quixotic or even unworkable in this project for which they prepared with thorough conscientiousness. At 59 Tomas Ortunio, Benidorm, Province of Alicante, Spain, Ted and Sylvia worked on either side of the dining room table. They would write all morning, from 8:30 to midday; from 8 to 10 in the evening was devoted to the study of languages. Ted was learning Spanish and Sylvia was translating "*Le Rouge et le Noire*", still hesitating here and there on the agreement of adjectives, but with great courage and tenacity. This left them a few hours for a siesta, for going to bathe and for simple meals of fish and bread washed down by wine with a few almonds they had gathered from the trees themselves, and for playing at being God with the ants. In her diary, Sylvia described at great length the table on which they worked. On Ted's side were disordered sheets covered with his firm handwriting and drawings of animals, all in blue ink, on the backs of the reports he had typed for the Pinewood studios. His red Shakespeare was by the side of an anthology of Spanish poetry and a cookery book open at the page of the rabbit stew where Sylvia had left it. Crumpled sheets lay everywhere. He cleared them up at intervals and threw them away into an old crate on the floor that served as a waste paper basket. Nothing was organised, everything lay in disorder, while his inkpot, always open, stood perilously poised on top of a pile of sheets. On Sylvia's side, books lay either open with passages carefully underscored, or else were neatly shut. Notebooks and sketchbooks, conscientiously covered, were tidily piled up and aligned and the bottle of black ink scrupulously closed by the side of her portable Olivetti type-writer and her indispensable *Roget's Thesaurus* in which she continually buried herself in search of the right word. On a corner of the table lay her sunglasses inside a white case decorated with a red starfish which she prized very much in memory of the summer of 1953 when she had been guest editor of the American magazine *Mademoiselle*.

If Sylvia was most of the time an enthusiastic admirer of her husband's literary prowess, she did not refrain, however, from exerting her critical judgment on his texts but, most of the time, the passages she condemned were those he did not find very satisfying himself. For his part, he recommended to her the same exercises of concentration that he imposed upon himself. Before sitting at his table to write, he went diligently through special periods of relaxation, concentrating his attention upon different points of his spine. After this rather athletic preparation, the formation of an adequate verbal texture was induced by exercises of accurate description to mutually reinforce a sense of what exists and the verbal imitation attempting to render it. Ted guided Sylvia in these exercises, inviting her to adopt the same intellectual approach in her writing by concentrating on the accuracy of the description. Indeed the look he cast upon the world had the visual precision of a photographer's, whereas Sylvia's vision was always more hastily perceived and slightly out of focus. Once, they went to a *corrida*, the rule being for each to make as precise and accurate a description of the bullfight as possible. Each went into all the minutiae as if they were addressing readers who had not the slightest idea of the thing. Both made the obvious remark that the bull instinctively charged the cape, never the bullfighter; the only danger being that there was a risk of the bull accidentally catching the man with his horn. Everything went on as if the men in the arena were really invisible for the bull. One picador who worked with the point of his pick to make the bull lower his head accidentally fell onto the horns of the animal. They took the bull away from the fallen man who got up to his feet, staggered away to the edge of the arena and fell again face down upon the ground. When the men picked him up, the holes made in his body by the horns could be seen. No! definitely no! Sylvia did not like Spain and her final verdict was that there was necessarily a lack of intellectual stimulation in a country where the weather was so hot. Some time later, Ted wrote the poem "You Hated Spain", looking back on their experience in Spain, where he himself, on the contrary, felt so good, expressing the blunt presence of what is essentially real, stripped of self-deceit and hypocrisy. She felt constantly slapped in the face by this Goyaesque atmosphere trespassing onto real life; the true face of the South, heavily made-up but unblushing and totally without shame, the gushing blood of life and death, all that went radically against the grain for her. It was the very opposite of the false representation of the world secreted like a protective shell by her education, that of a too optimistic young American woman in white bobby-socks. Could it be possible that Spain stood for the essence of what Sylvia wanted above all to keep away from?

Before the end of July an angry argument suddenly broke out between them to their common surprise. Sylvia had immediately gone into her sulks. Ted went out and walked in the night. But as she was afraid to stay alone, she went out in search of him; later they sat side by side for long hours in the cruel and beautiful moonlight of Spain. It was the first clash of tempers in a long series to come. In August, they were back in Paris where Sylvia introduced Ted to her brother Warren who happened to have just then crossed the Atlantic. Then they went on to Yorkshire to see Hughes's parents at Heptonstall, where they had to face the sad and sombre mood of Edith who was durably hurt that her son should not have thought to invite her to his marriage, and should now bring into her house, as a matter of course, such a perfectly strange daughter-in-law. Moreover, had not Ted said that he wanted to find a job as an English teacher in Spain?

But his wife obviously had very different projects for them in store. She had one more year to do in Cambridge for which she was given quite a comfortable grant. Then they would leave for the U.S., for the simple ceremony of their second marriage and the grandiose party that was to follow it. Ted agreed to it all, moreover, and Sylvia yearned to cook for him, in a real American kitchen, so certain was she to supplant the over simple stews of his mum's that Ted loved, the few simple recipes that this small roundish woman routinely prepared. She would herself be teaching at Smith's but, so she explained to her mother, something else would have to be found for Ted, for she knew all too well how the college was full of uncontrollable young women and she was green with jealousy at the mere thought of surrendering Ted to the hysterical admiration of such a coven of girls who were in the habit, as she knew all too well, of throwing themselves indiscriminately at all male teachers, were they one-legged or worn-out old men.

At the Beacon, Ted's parents' home in Heptonstall, she received a cheque for 50 dollars from *The Atlantic Monthly* that had agreed to publish "Pursuit", a poem in which she depicts herself as a masochistic female Severin being chased by a panther, an allegory of her suicidal impulse. Ted Hughes learned that the BBC wanted to audition him for a series of readings of his poems on the radio. Sylvia was also engaged on Radio 3 by the Scottish poet George MacBeth who later declared that on that occasion he had been surprised to hear Sylvia Plath allude to her predilection for violent subjects and tell him, moreover, that she could see that he, too, had a concentration camp in his head. But, as summer drew to its end, everyone did their best to put up with Sylvia's fits of temper. Ted would take her on long walks to the secret places of his childhood, and she took advantage of these last days of fine weather to air her Olivetti, posing on one occasion for a photograph, sitting astride a stone wall on which she had climbed to type her notes. She was perpetually taking notes intended for a short story entitled "All the Dear Dead", in which she made an indiscreet use of her reflections on Ted's family. There was Uncle Albert's suicide, Uncle Walt's mentally handicapped son, Ted's father William Hughes was pictured under the guise of Clifford Meehan, an old man, creaking with arthritis and hopelessly trapped in his war memories, whose relics, yellowing with age, he kept in a cardboard box at the bottom of a linen cupboard. Edith was portrayed under the name of Nellie Meehan, a character endowed with an inordinate propensity for gossip, hopelessly devoid of any talent for cooking. The author polished her off before the end of the story. Of course, all this was literature, but there was often an unbridgeable gap between the face that Sylvia presented to people around her and the deeper feelings that found expression in her literary creations. On her good days, she was the model wife. At dusk, Ted would take her hunting for rabbits in woods that reminded her of a fairy tale. One day, they all embarked in Uncle Walt's car on a literary pilgrimage on the trail of the Brontë sisters heading for Top Withins, supposed to have provided the setting for *Wuthering Heights*. Sylvia had drawn a rough sketch of the place and was completing a drawing, as she intended to write a little article on this memorable excursion. Olwyn, Ted's elder sister, had come back from Paris for a few days' holiday and to meet her sister-in-law who was greatly impressed by her beauty and her amber-brown eyes, while she, for her part, was disconcerted by Sylvia's taste for showy clothes. Very soon, a mutual aversion grew up between the two women, the sister's affection being just as possessive as the wife's love. Olwyn was soon to make the remark that Sylvia wanted to swallow Ted whole.

Their relationship, uneasy from the start, seemed to confirm — at least as far as the feminine half of humanity was concerned — the observation that Ted had made, not so very long ago, in his poem "Law in the Country of the Cats", that when two men meet for the first time, their first impulse is certainly not to fall into each other's arms. It was the end of summer. Following their inclination of the moment, the newlyweds went out to imitate the wood-owl's call and wait for an answer, and made love by moonlight, or stayed inside the house by the fireside, looking out the window at the moon and the stars, then retired together to read in bed enjoying long spells of silent happiness.

The new year was soon to start in Cambridge and Sylvia made ready to return to her college. After inquiring of Dorothea Krook and of Miss Morris, her tutor, at Newnham College, it soon became apparent that the necessity of keeping their marriage secret on pain of losing her scholarship was naturally unfounded. There would be no difficulties for completing her studies, whatever her marital status. She would even be allowed to reside elsewhere, and her college room would be allotted to another student if she chose no longer to reside there. Sylvia thus returned to Cambridge, and Ted, who was penniless, had to stay for a while at his parents'. The weeks dragged by since they had been parted and Sylvia felt, without the shadow of a doubt, that her husband was the indispensable other half of herself. They wrote to each other daily, remarkably vacuous letters full of inane endearments: lovelovelovelovelovelovelove! There was also an episode in London where they had arranged to meet. Sylvia, in her eagerness to shorten the separation, sent a last minute letter telling Ted that she would meet him at a certain stop before the coach terminal. But Ted did not receive the letter which had been sent too late and, impatient to meet her, he asked the driver to let him get off before they came to the terminal, but in yet another place. The long and the short of it was that they missed each other. Not finding her Ted at the appointed place, Sylvia soon burst into tears, then jumped into a taxi and for the half-hour of the drive she kept pestering the driver to take her instantaneously to Charing Cross Station where she could at last throw herself, body and soul, into the arms of her beautiful husband. At that time she admitted quite willingly that she was living for Ted alone.

Nonetheless there was some heartening news. Cambridge the immovable was still as they had left it. Ted's tribe was still meeting at The Anchor and the network of old boys was working as ever, as Ted and Sylvia's engagements with the BBC, obtained through the Hobsbaum Group and Peter Redgrove, went to show. At the pub, Ted's friends adapted the words of an old song for him, the lament of a woman whose son had his leg taken off by a French cannon ball during a war: "I'd rather have my Ted as he used to be, than Sylvia Plath and her rich Mummy!" Yet in some respects he was the same old Ted; on October 27th, for the birthday of his beloved, he gave her a pack of tarot cards so that she could exert her powers of clairvoyance, for he was convinced she was a spirit medium just as he thought that he was one himself. As soon as they had enough money, he would buy her a crystal ball. Meanwhile, they took up the dangerous hobby of the Ouija board again. Sylvia lent her voice to the spirits while Ted jotted down their messages. Nothing was easier for them than to communicate with a spirit, soon to be familiar, which they called Pan. But the messages they got were never good. The questions they asked boiled down in the end to asking if they would be famous one day, and the answers Sylvia obtained invariably made her break into a flood of tears: glory was inevitable, said the spirits, but it would destroy them. Then, they tried to exploit the predictive science of Pan to achieve shorter-term objectives, less charged with emotion: winning a few pounds in football pools or greyhound races for instance.

They found a furnished ground floor flat at 55 Eltisley Avenue, in the western part of Cambridge. It was in a typical street lined with semi-detached brick houses with bow-windows. Ted moved in alone at the beginning of November, and Sylvia joined him in the middle of the month. He did not tell her how upset he had been to find a blood stain on the pillow on arrival. It gave him the impression that the place was haunted by the ghosts of previous occupants and he tried to dispel them by tacking a poster of the goddess Isis to the wall. That being done, he set to work resolutely. He took a job in a secondary school to teach children who had failed their eleven-plus exam. Half the pupils in his class barely knew their alphabet. Ted was hard put to believe that they knew so little and he was sad at the thought that in a few years, when they left school at the age of fourteen or fifteen, they would have become allergic to learning, quick to forget the little they had acquired and dramatically lacking in self-confidence. Hughes had been engaged as an English teacher but he also taught physical training and dramatic art. The headmaster left him free to teach them what he liked, provided he did his best to give them some smattering of general education, and instil into them a modicum of energy and enthusiasm. To that effect he chose to speak to them of the Russian revolution, the rise of fascism in Europe, and of what had happened to the Jews during the Second World War. As far as teaching was concerned, Ted Hughes was the very opposite of a dilettante. Indeed he had a vocation for teaching and, perhaps even had too high an idea of what a teacher can achieve; throughout his life, he never ceased to take a passionate interest in how best to educate young minds through the powers of speech. He would spend long hours preparing his lessons and marking his pupils' home-work. He would get up early and cycle to school to start teaching at 8. But he soon realised that teaching requires and exhausts the same energy that being a writer demands.

Nevertheless, during this short period of his life, he managed to plan his time methodically, which enabled him to do his work efficiently. As a result, he had the acute sensation of being intensely alive. He showed confidence in his poetic powers and his writing proceeded apace. Sylvia admired his poems and, at this date, she was resolved to devote to him all the enthusiasm and the ambition of which she was capable. Ted in the role of teacher reminded her of her father Otto Plath, who had left his native Prussia at the age of 16, and in his own way, by dint of virtue, had proved the truth of the American dream by becoming a University professor at Boston. He was a renowned entomologist, a specialist of bees, drones and other social insects. Sylvia had never managed to get over the shock of his death. She had never been able to accept the disappearance from her life of this impressive father, who had abandoned them so incomprehensibly, her mother Aurelia, her brother Warren and herself, by dying suddenly as the result of a simple domestic accident. When she was not yet eight years old, she had been heard to say that on this account she would no longer speak to God. In such an intensely emotional context, only a genius of a husband could make up for the unjust loss of such a brilliant father; not only was the daughter forever inconsolable, but throughout her formative years it was onto her that her Austrian mother transferred the unrelenting social and professional ambitions of Professor Otto Plath, to be achieved through an ethos of hard work, suffering not the slightest failing. Her letters to her mother during November 1956 show that she was conscientiously engaged in building an image of Ted as the perfect teacher. Indeed Ted, as he set about gathering documents on the Russian revolution and nazi Germany in a desperate attempt to motivate pupils who had failed to gain access to a secondary education, came somehow to fill the gap tragically left open at the centre of her life by the death of her father. And therefore Ted had to assume the roles, not only of lover and husband, but of father and son as well, for she enjoyed above all things being able to mother him. Like a vigilant mother looking carefully after the education of her son, Sylvia, in the traditional role of the devoted wife acting as private secretary to her husband, could sometimes spend as much as two hours a day typing the stories that he dictated to her. She also typed up his handwritten texts on several sheets of India paper with interpolated carbon paper, before sending them off to magazines and newspapers mainly in the U.S. She bulldozed publishers into taking his texts, trying as much as possible not to let him see the fits of rage and despair in which she was plunged when she received a rejection letter, but breaking into demonstrative joy at the slightest sign of encouragement. When she met with no success the first time round, she would start raving and ranting at the stupid publishers who were unable to recognised genius when it stared them in the face, sending back the same poems to the same people but in a different order and with a different presentation. Sylvia was determined, strong-willed, tenacious. She threw herself heart and soul into her work as literary agent, keeping a detailed record of her activity in a very professional way, drawing up lists on her typewriter of titles of his poems in an abbreviated form, followed by lines of initial letters standing for the periodicals to which she had sent them, each group separated from the next by a colon. When she received a favourable answer, she circled the initials with a red pencil, indicating by hand how many poems each of these publications had accepted. It was a regular family enterprise; Ted in charge of the production, Sylvia handling the distribution. Ted was devoting every scrap of spare time to writing. When he was not writing poems or tales for children, he would write letters to his sister, or to his brother, or to some other correspondent, sometimes abandoning it to take it up later, from one day onto the next, even, always filling up the sheet from end to end, leaving no space uncovered. Writing, in whichever form, had become for him a quasi-vital necessity; he realised more and more clearly that he was unhappy when he stopped writing for a while, as if some secret and unexplained necessity urged him constantly to scribble on and on. Was it a sort of mania? The favourable positions of the stars, about whose influence he regularly inquired, seemed to correspond, most of the time, to his creative periods during which he seemed particularly capable of writing poems that he considered likely to have an after-life in book form. His appreciation of a good poem was based on instinct alone and it owed nothing to fashion or to personal vanity. In most cases, these favourable intuitions were confirmed by those of Sylvia. In November, always on the look-out for new opportunities to develop and activate their network of relationships, Sylvia attended a social gathering. Chatting people up at the party, she explained to a certain John Press, a representative of the British Council, that she was engaged in promoting the writings of Ted Hughes. He gave her a brochure issued by the Poetry Center of the Young Men's and Young Women's Hebrew Association in New York, which was sponsoring a competition intended to reward the best first collection of poems of an author. The jury was composed of people of repute: Marianne Moore, the great poetess of New-England, and two glories of British poetry in the 1930s, W.H. Auden and Stephen Spender, who had left England to pursue their careers in a climate more friendly to their art. The winner was not to receive money, but a contract with Harper's, the New-York publishing house. Sylvia immediately set about meticulously typing forty of Ted's best poems; they then put their heads together to arrange them in the best possible order, before sending them to try their luck overseas, giving the collection itself the title of the poem which they thought the best: *The Hawk in the Rain*. The poem had already appeared in *Chequers*; it was a rewriting of Hopkins's famous poem "The Windhover", where the poet, trudging along in a ploughed field, admires, high up in the sky, the nearly motionless eye of the hawk effortlessly domineering the landscape.

While his helpful wife was busy promoting his writings and as soon as teaching gave him some respite Ted Hughes toyed easily with words, most of the time lying in the narrow bed of their modest flat at 55 Eltisley Street. His method consisted wholly in being tuned in to what his unconscious dictated but without ever lapsing into the incoherence of the surrealists. For spirits always addressed Ted Hughes in an orderly way. It was in that relaxed attitude that he wrote "Thrushes", a poem that extols the immediacy of animals' presence in the world, whereas human beings, cut off from the heart of nature by language in a way that is characteristic of the species, waste their time beating about the bush. Hughes even went so far as to compare Mozart's genius to the infallible instinct of predators, those animals that, it seemed to him, had a direct access to sublime truth. He also wrote "Pibroch", "Slylarks" or "Gnat Psalm" among a certain number of other poems which would take their place in his second collection of verse. But the remarkable thing was that Ted Hughes always carefully avoided speaking about himself, expressing his own sentiments or making use of certain episodes of his private life in his writings. He seemed to be averse to any lyrical expression of his own thoughts and sentiments. This peculiarity set him apart from most poets of his generation, beginning with Sylvia Plath herself who would be listed by literary history along with her contemporaries the American poets Robert Lowel and Anne Sexton as "confessionalist" poets, because they liked above all to expatiate at great length about themselves. As a worthy spiritual daughter of Hemingway, Scott Fitzgerald and Salinger, Sylvia Plath seemed to have no other literary project than to alchemically transmute her life into literature, making her literary career nothing other than an individual quest for immortality at all cost. And so it was that her love-story with Ted Hughes, necessarily marvellous for that very reason, was for her like a novel that was being written every day, even every hour. Just as the past events of her life had been short stories dictated to her by Destiny, she intended from the outset to turn the story of her marriage into a novel for which she was already trying to find a suitable title. It could be called, she thought, "Leopard Hill", "The Fox Menagerie" or, why not, "The Girl in the Mirror", but her happiest find, the one she preferred above all others, was "Falcon Yard", after the place in Cambridge where the party took place which had been set to launch the Saint Botolph's review and occasioned her memorable encounter with Ted Hughes. For the moment, she wrote regularly to her mother Aurelia; her letters had a preservative character, for in them as well as in her diary, she described what took place in her life day by day, or nearly hour by hour: the sound of Ted's footsteps when he came back from work, his slightest movements as he was writing or reading by her side. She noted down her life in the very time of its unfolding. Then, all these precious manuscripts — texts and sketches — were sent to the States to be compiled by Mum and passed on to Mrs. Olive Higgins Prouty, a successful popular novelist who devoted part of her fortune to the funding of a scholarship that enabled Sylvia to complete her studies at Smith College, a private university whose purpose was to give young women of merit the benefits of a higher education of quality. It had also been Mrs. Prouty who paid the bill to the McLean Hospital of Boston where Sylvia had been treated for deep depression following her attempted suicide in 1953. She had then started psychotherapy sessions with Dr. Ruth Beuscher, a Freudian analyst whom she had stopped consulting when she came to Europe, but who was to play a role of primary importance as one in the trio of her spiritual counsellors.

It is hard to say whether this sustained correspondence was the cause or the effect of the homesickness which invaded her in England, a country that still looked as if it would never recover from the terrible emotional shock of the war. As time went on, her prejudice against the English character increased. The Suez crisis seemed to her a perfect illustration of British arrogance and conceit. The snobbishness, the inane materialism seemed to her the very opposite of what should have been done in the circumstances. In short, England was, to her eyes, an old moribund country. Its literary circles were sterile and corrupt, and she wished with all her heart to remove Ted from them as soon as possible, if only to keep his genius alive. Day after day, America looked more and more like a Promised Land. Here, everything was old and dirty, lacking in the modern conveniences she considered as basic essentials. While she liked to wash and deodorise her body to such an extent that her London acquaintances used to say that she had no odour, she had to share a bathroom with a Canadian couple living on the floor above. At regular intervals, she was taken by a frantic desire to clean and she cleaned down the flat with impressive energy before steeping herself for a long time in the bath. It was incredible, she said, how cleanliness was soothing to her soul. And yet she also developed an obsessive liking for the virile effluvia of her husband and she saw this difference of attitude on her part as nothing other than the pungent illustration of the fact that the sexes were naturally complementary to one another.

Everything pointed to the fact that she was biding her time, waiting for the favourable moment to execute a female ruse to repatriate the couple to New England. Then it would be easy to find university sinecures for both of them, which were, she was convinced, the primrose path to happiness. But it was also increasingly evident that both Ted and Sylvia were developing a reciprocal Pygmalion complex; each of them was passionately bent on transforming the other according to their own desires. Ted was striving to develop in Sylvia her supposed gifts as a spirit medium, for he considered that her obsessive need for a body of rules to regulate her life — a disastrous consequence of her education — was hampering her creative power; at the same time he had appointed himself her teacher to help her take the degree in English literature which he had himself renounced. He synthesised data for her from various sources about certain authors on the syllabus and made her learn by heart one poem every day. Both went to bed regularly at ten in the evening and got up at six and they worked for two hours before Ted left for school. In such drastic conditions, the pressure cooker needed periodically to let out steam; they would break into violent quarrels from time to time, before resuming their old routine. Sylvia conscientiously planned their time, even fixing the day on which they were to wash their hair; Saturday afternoon, after lunch, was reserved for lovemaking. Unable to overcome the blank page syndrome, she had for the moment set herself the task of sparing no effort to help her husband achieve literary success. A non-negligible part of the enterprise consisted in feeding him well. In the first place, having a poor opinion of her mother-in-law's cooking, she believed she could supplant her, on this account, in her son's affections; she also found that, along with cleaning the flat and washing herself, cooking had a soothing effect on her nerves. In no time her Teddy had grown as fat as a dormouse and would soon weigh well over fifteen stone.

But a persistent shadow was darkening this perfect picture of connubial happiness, which was a little too conventional to be entirely genuine. It was the worrying tendency that Sylvia had of exaggerating the slightest difficulty and giving way to panic as soon as the smallest hitch disturbed the routine of their so meticulously planned everyday life. Her diffuse feeling of anxiety then suddenly crystallised over trifles. One moment she could no longer bear the sight of a small clay statue of herself, the work of a first-year fellow-student at Smith College. Having long carried it around with apparently no problem, she could suddenly no longer bear its sight; I was like those figurines that sorcerers use to cast spells over people. The question was then how to get rid of it without the risk of awakening its evil power. They could neither keep it nor destroy it. Ted then thought of taking it into the meadows outside Cambridge. After climbing into a tree, he could wedge it tightly between two branches. The head could thus repose safely in the green peace of nature, its eyes resting on the grazing cattle; ivy would grow around it and turn it into a perennial monument. Sylvia would go and visit it from time to time, in a future thus freed from the spell that its presence was casting upon her, while she would always be assured of keeping a link with her past. Or perhaps Pan, the Ouija spirit that was their familiar, in one magic stroke of luck, could liberate them from the lot common to the average run of mortals, to which, it seemed to them, they belonged so little, by making them win a fortune at the lottery. Thus being able to walk about in the sun without a care in the world, they would be free to make poems and children, secure in their future. More and more clearly every day, America presented the same dream that Sylvia was convinced she could bring Ted to adhere to, thanks to the growing recognition that his poems met there. Ted, for his part, dreamt of angling. Despite a gang of treacherous eels he found inimical, he managed to catch grand-father pike, a fish so big that he had to struggle hard in order to land him without the help of his brother Gerald or of his friend Johnny. He interpreted this dream as a confirmation that his meeting Sylvia and his marrying her had been a stroke of luck; he thought he had observed that after every dream of the sort he would learn the next day that he had sold a poem.

Early in the morning of February 23rd, 1957, as Ted was doing up his tie and Sylvia was preparing the coffee, the postman brought a telegram: "Our congratulations that *Hawk in the Rain* judged winning volume Poetry Center First Publication. Award letter will follow." They stood agape for a long time, fearing to believe their eyes, then they started running and jumping about, yelling with joy like two sea-lions, so certain they were that this was the first indubitable sign that fame had come at last and would never leave them. Of course the book would be a bestseller, the first of a long series. Sylvia's return to the USA was to be triumphal, on the arm of a husband bathed in the glory of his recent success. Ah! the great literary stars of the jury — Marianne Moore, W.H. Auden and Stephen Spender — had known how to recognise a work of genius that those puny, pusillanimous editors had refused to publish when it was theirs for the taking. Sylvia did not doubt for a moment that they were on the threshold of a great career and that they would leave behind them plenty of great books and beautiful children. However, as this first success was a tangible proof that they were heading in the right direction, both of them redoubled their efforts. But would Sylvia meet success in her turn? Sylvia was torn between the need to cram for a first class honours degree at the end of the year and the intellectual concentration that she had to achieve in her work as a serious writer, for she was well aware of her recurring tendency to neglect both her literary and academic work to plunge body and soul into cooking and pastry, making apple tarts and stewed beef, as well as reading Virginia Woolf's journal. She consoled herself with the thought that even the greatest authors had seen their manuscripts turned down by ill-advised editors; Virginia herself had had to work off disappointment by cleaning down her kitchen. Sylvia did not let up being angry with those editors who had the cheek to refuse certain poems of Ted who was, without a doubt, the great poet of his generation, very professional at his job as a poet, the new Yeats, the new Eliot; even when they eventually deigned to take one, they did so for the wrong reason. Sylvia saw in Ted her alter ego, her masculine counterpart, even if they would occasionally fight like ragamuffins for the most absurd pretexts — when Ted, for example, had insisted, against all reason, that it might be a good idea to procure oneself the benefit of two years in prison to read and reread a bad book from beginning to end, and so come to know intimately what there was exactly that was bad in it. Sylvia meanwhile maintained with tooth and nail that it would undoubtedly be better to have nothing to read at all than to read, were it only once, a bad book from beginning to end. Bad literature, indeed, was the occasion of many heated debates between them. Sylvia had a sort of instinct amounting to a sixth sense. It was a pitiless little voice within her, that was prompt to declare her own literary production utterly worthless. It was good or it was bad, and when she judged it bad it was irredeemable. To her eyes, her style was never subtle enough, never structured enough, and so, day after day, she would sit before her blank page with a feeling of growing despair, and by hardening her judgment further increased the paralysis she was inflicting upon herself. It was all too clear: she was left high and dry, utterly sterile while poems seemed to come to Ted just as naturally as leaves to trees. Sylvia was building up plans to write the rough draft for a novel comprising a certain number of pages before May, then to go over each chapter very carefully, paying special attention to the style; yet she felt obscurely that this old idea of separating the substance from the form would only end in destroying all spontaneity. Moreover, she saw herself as being doomed, compulsively driven to forever speak of herself, imprisoned in the moods of her heroine, condemned to the eternal "she thought", "she said", as if she were totally unable to imagine anything that she had not lived. No matter. She would doggedly stick to writing her three pages a day against all odds and then, later on, during the summer vacation she would write it all again, very systematically.

Before they left for the New World, Sylvia had only to finish her studies in Cambridge and close her account with Old England, attending to the last details of a plan which was to bring Ted to fall in love with an America that she herself personified. At the beginning of March, her mother wrote saying that her wedding present would be the rental of a cottage by the sea at Cape Cod. Ted liked fishing; as such he was a true American at heart and not only by his marriage. In this quiet place they would have plenty of time to write. Ted would go out fishing and she would be gloriously happy in the glare of a neat and tidy kitchen, complete with refrigerator and all modern appliances. Ted did not seem to be aware of the deliberate thoroughness with which his wife and her self-appointed literary agent were drawing plans for his future. He was then plunged deep in the works of Schopenhauer and a life of Leopardi, thinking only of preserving his energy for himself in order to marshal it all, if possible, into his writing. Ideally, he would have liked to concentrate on writing poetry at the highest level he was capable of, and then devote the rest of his time to the production of children's books. His mind was teeming with all sorts of ideas, even for theatre plays, mostly in a fantastic or surrealistic vein. Since his poems had begun to be recognised, his interest in teaching had gradually faded and writing was now uppermost in his mind. In the letters and the telephone calls he received from the people at Harper's, and from those of the New York Poetry Center, he marvelled at the politeness and generosity, the warm attention — or so it seemed — that make the charm of American social manners. How different it was from the cold, distant style of his countrymen. The difference was so striking that he wondered why he had not left England sooner. The promising future lying in wait for him contrasted with the nagging recollection that he still owed Uncle Walt a few pounds from the sum he had borrowed for their journey to Spain. The profit he made from the sale of his books — 10 cents for each volume sold — did not amount to much. There was still no living to be made out of literary glory. And he reflected that it was much more profitable to sell his poems one by one to various newspapers and magazines than to sign a contract, prestigious though it might sound, with the greatest publishers. The ones that Sylvia had managed to sell, and which had simultaneously appeared in the pages of *Poetry*, *The Spectator*, *The Nation*, the *Times Literary Supplement*, of *The New Yorker*, of *The London Magazine*, of *The New Statesman*, and even of *Harper's Magazine* were doing much more to better their daily fare. The change, however, was real, and it was nowhere more visible than in the fact that when he was again invited to the BBC, it was to read his own poems. In April, he read "The Martyrdom of Bishop Farrar". Besides, though he was under contract with Harper's, he was perfectly free to negotiate the publication of his book in the United Kingdom with any publisher of his choice. Ted and Sylvia had therefore chosen to try their luck with the great London publishing house Faber & Faber, the fief, at that time, of the great modernist poet T.S. Eliot. At the beginning of May, an answer came from Faber & Faber through one of their commercial attachés, saying that Mr. Eliot desired to let Mr. Hughes know that he had personally much appreciated his poems and that he offered him his congratulations. And so, in the most natural of ways, Ted Hughes entered the great London publishing house on Queen Square, the very square on which stood the parish church of Saint George the Martyr in Holborn, where, less than a year before, he had married Sylvia Plath.

In order to keep a full record of the events which were crowding upon them, Sylvia bought a large-size copy-book in which she stored for their grandchildren all the important letters which were the first landmarks of Ted's poetic career. Sitting for her exam while suffering from writer's cramp (that Ted thought was due to spending too much time at her typewriter, until the muscles of her arm were no longer used to holding a pen), she distinctly felt that an unreasonable prejudice was growing within her against the impossible Englishness of England, hand in hand with an impatience to see her native America. What a terrible year! She had spared no pains, exerting herself lavishly, always to the limits of her capacities, so that Mrs. Prouty once asked her to write a little poem for her that would not be so intense as those she was wont to send, and she would caution her that she might burn herself out like an electric bulb submitted to an excessive voltage. Ted and Sylvia were counting down the days separating them from their departure for the Promised Land. At last, on 20 June 1957, they embarked on the *HMS Queen Elizabeth*. Ted had a £50 note in his pocket and the proof of *The Hawk in the Rain* bearing a dedicatory inscription "to Sylvia" which so filled her with pride that a quiver of joy ran down her spine every time she read it.

But America, they say, is a land of contrasts. In New-York, the customs officers found a copy of *Lady Chatterley's Lover* in Sylvia's luggage and they asked her if she really intended to teach "that" in the United States. Too much taken aback to find anything to say in return, she burst into tears. But Ted, as one would expect, was much impressed by the Big Apple, which made him think of some gigantic Martian city. And, as he was soon to explain in a letter to Gerald, these Americans thought nothing of giving you one half of all they possessed, for on their arrival a friend of Sylvia's had offered them a much needed shower and had dressed Ted in new clothes from head to foot before treating them to a meal in a good restaurant. Ted felt embarrassed to be put under such great obligation, but he was also uneasy to be the object of so much friendly and disinterested generosity that expected nothing in return, and he was annoyed with himself for being culturally afflicted with such mean and paltry thoughts which seemed utterly out of place in the circumstances. Then there was the big garden-party, a long-standing project to celebrate their marriage, under the marquee erected in the garden next to Aurelia's house at Wellesley, Massachusetts. Then, at last, they had found themselves alone for a second honeymoon, in the large cottage on Cape Cod, at Eastham, the Old Naucett, where some of the Pilgrim Fathers from the Mayflower had come to settle on their arrival in America. Sylvia's brother, Warren, drove them there with their two English bikes firmly fastened on the roof of his car. And so it was in the steps of its first settlers that Ted and Sylvia began rediscovering America. The place promised to be a summer's paradise for two writers free to start afresh in comfort on an experience they had already gone through in Spartan conditions in Benidorm. But Ted would soon learn that the children's tales that he had started composing in Spain in such an enthusiastic and self-confident mood were being rejected by the American publisher Houghton Mifflin in indignant terms: these texts were simply considered unacceptable for they were full of monstrous beasts instead of animals which might have been frightening without being morally reprehensible. Ted Hughes would have to learn to conform to the imperatives of the children's book market. Fortunately, some good news arrived that was a compensation for this disappointment: *The Hawk in the Rain* had been proclaimed "Book of the Year" by the Poetry Book Society, an organisation founded by T.S. Eliot to help promote contemporary poetry in England. It was summertime, and the two resumed their old writing routine, broken by trips to the beach on their bikes. Now and then boredom would steal upon them and sometimes panic caught them up, as when the tide was on the ebb and they had to be towed to safety by a motor-boat which happened to be near. Their dreams were of books and children in profusion, but in July, when Sylvia thought she was pregnant, she was suddenly seized by panic and they had rushed in the pouring rain to see a doctor, and nothing but a blood test could put an end to her alarm. Literary creation was to be given priority over the creation of the flesh. To write, and write again every day. Good or bad. Something of use could always come of it. Sylvia doggedly pursued the writing of her novel *Falcon Yard* based on the faithful record of her meeting with Ted. The central image was that of a hawk, the metaphor of love that strikes once for all, perched on the fist of a knight in the company of his lady, smiling to each other as they ride on their horses. To write, to write, doing everything she could to get rid of all trivial non-essentials while feeding the slightest details of her everyday life into her book as grist to her writing.

And soon, it was the beginning of the Autumn term. They moved now to Northampton; in that New England state many towns bear the names of English towns, including Cambridge, where Harvard University is, with another 55 Eltisley Avenue. In Northampton, where Sylvia was to teach English at Smith College, they took up residence at 337 Elm Street. It was there that a telegram from Harper's announced the publication of *The Hawk in the Rain*, and the Hampshire library sent two bottles of American champagne. Soon they would find much pleasure in reading the reviews, which they found ridiculous but which were favourable on the whole, apart from the inevitable reservations from two or three grumpy English critics. In the *New Statesman*, Edwin Muir went even so far as to say that Hughes's "Jaguar" was better than Rilke's "Panther". Mrs. Prouty invited them one evening, and in her drawing-room where an ant-hill in a terrarium occupied pride of place, at once totally won over by Ted's personal charm, she went on repeating that he must go on TV. At the end of the year, they arrived in advance and fairly exhausted at Aurelia's house for the New Year's festivities; Sylvia was suffering from pneumonia and Ted was still hobbling a little after breaking his fifth metatarsus while rising too suddenly from an armchair unaware that one of his feet had gone to sleep. This was indicative of severe strain. The few months he had spent on the other side of the Atlantic had plunged him into a depression that the hyper-energy-boosting American food was unable to cure. Ted had the disagreeable feeling that he was cut off from the real world, as if life in America were entirely sterilised and wrapped in cellophane. Everything seemed more or less artificial and he often had the idea that Americans were made of plastic, precisely perhaps because they ate only pre-packaged stuff, canned food, all sorts of strange mixtures, but no produce direct from the earth. Everything around him seemed to come straight from glossy travel agency brochures. He felt tired and drained, his head full of sand like the head of Rousseau as imagined by Shelley in *The Triumph of Life*. Moreover, Sylvia complained ceaselessly of being unable to write. Ted accused teaching: it was just not compatible with writing because it required the very same psychological qualities that are indispensable to literary creation. He sought to develop more efficient ways to plunge her into a hypnotic sleep, first as a means of relaxation or to relieve some pain or other, and maybe soon to enable her to overcome the blank page syndrome by suggesting, under the influence of hypnosis, that she might prepare poems and short stories and program their writing at a specific time. He was convinced that hypnosis was the best remedy when you wanted to stop smoking or drinking; he cited the examples of Napoleon and Strindberg in support of his thesis that all great men — each in his particular way — were capable of hypnotising themselves in order to accomplish their own will, whereas the majority of human beings, living under the influence of radio and television and any other expression of the general opinion, were dragged down towards a state of ordinary mediocrity.

And indeed, for a few months Ted himself had been suffering from the same inability to write. His life seemed as sad as an empty house. His letters to Gerald and to his friend Luke sounded like requests for help and those he got from them were the only events that could rescue him for a time from the all-embracing boredom threatening to engulf him on all sides. The main cause of his malaise was the pressure that the conformist atmosphere of provincial America brought to bear upon him, where people assessed your worth according to your ability to make money. In such a social context, Ted Hughes did not cut much of a figure, and was rather considered a loser who did nothing but write poems all day long. The wife of the poet Paul Roche, with whom he was working on an adaptation of Seneca's *Oedipus*, managed to slight him: what was there, indeed, to be proud of in the fact of winning a literary prize? Didn't they have the obligation of finding a new winner every year? He had just won £300 in the Guinness Poetry competition. So what? During dinners among friends he would often bury himself in complete silence which put a damper on the evening; it was an intolerable departure from the taut obligation of playing the role that was expected of one in society. The people from Smith, that is to say Sylvia's circle of acquaintances, more or less connected with the University, struck him as particularly unbearable. He did, however, meet certain people with whom, it seemed, he could start being friends, like the poet W.S. Merwin, who had been the private teacher of Robert Graves's children in Mallorca. Merwin and his wife Dido understood the nature of Sylvia and Ted's malaise perfectly and they encouraged them to live by their pen. There was also the draughtsman, Leonard Baskin, the son of a rabbi who had been much affected by the memory of the camps, and whose religious education in the mystical Jewish tradition had given him a vision of the world that accorded well with that of Ted Hughes. Ted felt more and more that the core of his dissatisfaction had metaphysical roots, for the ennui which threatened to paralyse his genius in puritan America reminded him of the boredom that used to overcome him during the Sunday services at home as a child.

In January 1958, partly to increase their income and partly because people around him pressed him to do so, Ted Hughes took a job for one term at Amherst, University of Massachusetts, teaching literature and creative writing. He had, by now, lost all his illusions regarding the teaching profession. He went on teaching for lack of anything better, but he regarded any teaching activity as being thoroughly incompatible with his poetic vocation. He taught a medley of Milton, Goethe, Dostoevsky, Keats, Molière, Wordsworth, Yeats, Thoreau, along with the art of literary composition, to two classes of stonily indifferent young people. They belonged to a generation, he thought, brought up on television, fed on commercial forms of art, made utterly stupid by mechanical industry, which had rendered them definitely irresponsive to any sort of teaching. For what they seemed to fear above all things was to have to study by themselves, as if they had been brought up in such a way that any effort of concentration had become impossible for them. It seemed to him that the famous American way of life was irreducibly opposed to the life of the mind, averse to solitude and hostile to any attempt at personal reflection. And he saw these as the sign of a sombre age to come. America seemed to him to be doomed by an excess of civilisation. Food was good and salaries were high, but this hectic materialism, he had no doubt, was suicidal. Modern life, whose throbbing heart was indisputably the USA, seemed to him to be related to hypnosis. People were individually deprived of their freedom to think and behave by an ideological filter that settled between them and the outside world, so that without being aware of it they found themselves enslaved by totalitarian prejudices. Objective reality, as conceived by the overwhelming majority of his contemporaries, was, it seemed, the only reality. All inner life seemed to be foreclosed, and all spiritual life was reduced to nothing but a pre-established liturgical newspeak, making all mystical or visionary form of expression impossible. Hughes was beginning more and more clearly to articulate a critique of Reformed Christianity, which he viewed as the prelude to this regrettable modernity. During the Middle Ages, a sort of visionary thinking had existed among people, but this had gradually been destroyed by the spirit of the Reformation, the forerunner of the spirit of the Enlightenment which had led to the American revolution. This visionary cast of mind was a form of waking dream which had once enabled everybody to have free access to the perpetually changing world of myths and legends. Creative imagination was now assumed exclusively by poets, who were too often considered as virtually mad by other people. The inner world, however, was his hunting ground, and he explored it in search of his poems as he had done as a child in the forests at night in search of game. He was quite conscious that the constraints of social life were running counter to his quest for poetic inspiration. It did not do to write a poem from time to time on such and such a subject, for no sooner had what he called his deeper mind set to work than he had to interrupt his effort to start again afresh another time. Poetry was a serious matter; it consisted for him in immersing himself into the depths of his soul. Amateurism meant superficiality. He could not but produce awkward and clumsy poetry this way, nothing more than the warm-up exercises necessary to accede to true poetry. Such a conception of literary creation was hardly compatible with the exigencies of social life, which in America more than anywhere else were constantly reminding him of the necessity to conform. Advertising, the problems of the day and other languages of fashion brought a continual pressure to bear upon each individual person.

In a word, Hughes was somehow at odds with the intellectual and spiritual climate of New England. And the snow-storm through which he drove across

Massachusetts from Boston to Cambridge to read some of his poems at Harvard was a perfect metaphor of the coldness of the relationship. During the long drive, the two poets had counted all the Volkswagen Beetles they had met on the road, as much to while away the time on their journey as to fend off the feeling of fear and nervousness at the thought of appearing in front of the Harvard audience, and also to calm Sylvia's nerves as she implored Ted not to exceed 60 miles an hour. The streets of Cambridge were full of slush that reached up to their ankles. Ted did his best, in his introductory speech, to rouse the sympathies of his audience. There were about a hundred stern-looking people. Among a few more or less familiar faces he had spotted Mrs. Prouty, Sylvia's millionaire mentor. The public was never what one had a right to expect. For whom did one write? The critics were certainly not worthy of consideration. To take their opinion into account would have been a mistake. Ted Hughes made it a strict rule to ignore them altogether. The only readers of his poems that he would consider as important were the five or six best writers of his day, augmented by the few rare people who were firmly determined to read nothing but what was best. As for the clique of critics and prolific scribblers who, in London or elsewhere, spent their time reading précis writing rather than genuine literature, he had nothing but scorn for them. He claimed to have a sure instinct for judging the quality of a poem. For him, a poem was bad or it was good; it was a rigid absolute. No amount of work could possibly improve a bad poem. For poems are given. They are like all other creatures, exceptionally compact with genius, rarely remarkable and most of the time second rate. His experience as an author, as well as the impressions he got from his reading, confirmed him in the opinion that poetry is a sort of observatory of the hidden face of the mind. More and more, he looked upon poems simply and solely as imperfect and fragmentary images of the secret activity of the soul, to which one may sometimes gain access in dreams and which goes on continually in the recess of the conscious life of the mind. In the library, he consulted the *Journal of the Psychological Research Society* in which he found spectacular descriptions of hypnosis cases, of automatic writing, of dual personality and other similar phenomena. He was also much surprised to read that, in a right-handed person, it is the left lobe of the brain that controls all the intellectual and conscious functions, whereas the right lobe is the seat of unconscious activities. Hughes had often observed in himself, but also in many other people, that the right eye looked quite different from the left one and he now found in these scientific descriptions of the brain a confirmation of his dual vision of the world, according to which two worlds coexisted, the world of things and the world of spirits.

It was along these lines that Ted analysed Sylvia's mental state. He felt sure that the difficulties she experienced in her writing were due to her inability to gain access to her deepest feelings. He considered that the American ideology in which she had been brought up was responsible for the block, and he saw in this personal drama the illustration of what Freud had diagnosed on the larger scale of society as the "discontent of civilisation". Because of this near total incapacity to write from which she had been suffering for such a long time, Sylvia had become depressed and short-tempered. But as the same causes could not but produce the same effects, the same ailment also affected Ted himself, though to a lesser degree, and he began to fear that inspiration might desert him in the long run. Their life in common was corroded by a latent feeling of anxiety which would occasionally flare up in a sort of panic. Sylvia complained that Ted was constantly asking her what she was thinking, what she was going to do next. Conscious that they were both slowly sinking into a depressive state, they tried to react and organise their lives in a way that would be more beneficial to their talents. By turns, one of them would stay in bed to rest and read for a whole day, while the other cooked and attended to the other's needs. But one day, towards the end of the University year, as Sylvia came to meet Ted on his way back from his last class, she saw him coming along the path of Paradise Pond, completely engrossed in conversation with one of his students. She got the feeling that the girl had slunk away on seeing her. Ted wiped the complacent smile off his face, looking rather sheepish, an attitude which turned his wife's suspicions into certainties. The emotional upheaval triggered by this outburst of jealousy was to last for days, weeks, during which in page after page of her diary Sylvia kept berating Ted for his supposed infidelity. If it was not actually the case, it felt just the same. Admittedly he had dedicated his first book to her, but to whom was he going to dedicate the next? To his navel? To his penis? Most certainly her name was Shirley. She could smell it. He was past praying for. No shampoo, no soap in the world could ever clean it up. The tension between them reached such a high pitch that they once more came to blows. Sylvia hurled a glass at Ted's head with all her strength but instead of breaking, it rebounded back and caught her full on the brow. The Pyrex glass remained intact, but Sylvia saw stars. The crisis eventually found a sexual outlet, but Ted emerged from it badly scratched and so bitten as to draw blood, and Sylvia had a sprained thumb.

That Summer, in an effort to go and socialise, they went to New York on an excursion. They went to listen to Marianne Moore, though they had retained a grudge against her, for returning the poems that Sylvia had sent her, with a stinging remark, a little piqued, no doubt, at having been sent only carbon copies. Ted found the old lady charming, but her reading awful, for she kept bringing in impromptu commentaries in the same steady monotone which meant you could not tell whether they were part of the poem or not. They took advantage of their being in New York to go out sometimes in the evening. At a mixed party on Fifth Avenue they met some of the people who were most in the public eye: the black novelist Ralph Ellison, some pundits from Columbia, the old Farrar, from Farrar, Strauss and Cuhady. But, on the whole, social life in New York seemed to Ted to take place in a vast tube station, and the bohemian life of Greenwich Village seemed direly pathetic to him with all its drunkards asleep on the pavements. So they went back to Boston, where they moved into a two-roomed flat at 5 Willow Street in the district of Beacon Hill, nearer the centre of the town, where it would be easier for them to lead the life of serious artists. Reverting to the precarious sort of life that he had led in London and Cambridge when he had no permanent job, Ted thought he had saved enough money by now to do nothing but write for a certain time. They had both decided to give up teaching. Their near relations and friends did not disguise their disapproval because they could not understand why they would turn their backs on the paths which lay open to take them to the places waiting for them in American society. Sylvia herself, in the wake of her family, was none too sure that Ted was right to have taken such a radical step. What was so terrible, she thought, in the security of a regular income? Ted was a fanatic. For a start, there were those warm-up exercises before starting to write, during which he went to such extremes that he would sometimes crick his neck and be too stiff to move for days, aching all over. Moreover, he was dictatorial, a would-be Pygmalion, bossy and domineering, whose orders were sometimes contradictory. It eventually reached a point when she began to feel that their marvellous complementariness was turning them into Siamese twins, as if they were inside the same skin at two ends of the same continuum. That summer, they resumed the Ouija séances that they had dropped since their arrival in the States, and Pan, their familiar spirit, began suggesting new subjects for their poems and first names for their future children. One day, he even recited a poem of his own invention. He claimed to draw his information from a household deity called Kolossus. Meanwhile, they went on steadily with their routine and their training. They got up early to go through their regular set of tasks at fixed hours. Sylvia was still trying hard to learn German, but with no great success. During one of their periods devoted to rest and relaxation, they had made the ascent of Mount Holyoke, but, most of the time, they went for walks in the neighbouring parks where they sometimes played with grey squirrels. One day they found a young bird fallen from its nest, that they took home and tried to feed with bits of mashed meat made to resemble worms, but the bird did not do well, scratching and screeching in his cardboard box all night, until they took it back where they had found it to see if there was a nest in the tree from which it had fallen. A head furtively appeared at the opening of a hole in the trunk, then the bird turned round and defecated in their direction. As a result, they took their protégé back home and Ted decided in favour of mercy-killing. The bird was placed in a shoe-box, a hole was made to insert the pipe from the gas cooker, held in place by sellotape. Sylvia never stopped crying. Ted opened the box too soon, and found the bird, its bill wide open, fluttering piteously. After a second stay in the box, it at last died peacefully, and they went to bury it in the park under a stone of druidical appearance on which they laid a few fern fronds and a glow-worm.

Since the month of August, the quality of Sylvia's writings in her diary tended to deteriorate. It had become so disjointed that she no longer formed sentences, which seemed to betray some psychological suffering. Either because she herself had noticed that her mind was again slipping away from her, or because she was in fear of becoming over-dependent on Ted and wanted to counter his influence, she secretly resumed her psychotherapy sessions with Dr. Beuscher, the psychiatrist who had attended her after her attempted suicide in 1953. Maybe on the advice of the analyst, but also perhaps to avoid having to find herself face to face with a blank sheet everyday, she took up a part-time job as secretary in the same hospital where she had once been given medical attention, and where she had now resumed treatment. Among its most famous patients the institution numbered Anne Sexton, and Robert Lowell whose lectures on poetry Sylvia was attending as an unregistered student. Her work at MacLean Hospital consisted in noting down in shorthand the dreams of patients. This furnished her with raw material for small texts which she found good enough to preserve and which she collected under the title *Johnny Panic and The Bible of Dreams*. These were not exactly the funny, tender stories for women that she had dreamt of writing. But one had to start somewhere and things would eventually find their proper course. In her diary, she wrote long accounts aiming at self-justification. Dr Beuscher permitted her to hate her mother, whom she then held fully responsible for all her miseries since the death of her father.

During the winter of 1958, the desire to have a child took hold of her and, whereas a year before at Cape Cod she had been in a panic at the thought of being pregnant without wanting it, she was now consumed with dread at the thought that she might be sterile. Could it be that she was as incapable of bear-

ing children as of writing poems? She would sometimes think with regret of her own desire, of the all
too common way she had of sliding into the most ordinary form of the American dream: a house and children. Ted Hughes had already written twenty-five
poems which he deemed worthy of being published. It
was to be called "The Feast of Lupercal", after an
ancient Roman fertility rite during which the Luperci,
the priests of Lupercus, ran naked through the streets
of the city, striking women suffering from sterility or
wanting to become pregnant with strips of goat skin
soaked in a mixture of goat milk and bitch blood.
While putting the final touches to his volume prior to
publication, Hughes was still reading extensively, in
particular Aldous Huxley, the author of *Brave New
World* who had, a few years back, published *The
Doors of Perception* in which he described his experiments with psychotropic drugs, with a view to
enriching the field of literature by opening it to non-
verbal perceptions. It was also at that time that
Hughes was rediscovering Nietzsche, whose intellectual flamboyance was not much to his taste and whose
continual imprecations against the barbarism of the
Germans seemed to him ridiculous. At that time, his
preference went to Goethe, who confirmed and comforted him in his religion of great men. For he would
be himself the greatest English poet of his time, Sylvia the greatest American poetess, she thought, with
the possible exception of Marianne Moore. Ted had
applied for a Saxton or a Guggenheim scholarship for
next year. Meanwhile, they fought more and more
often, so that Sylvia's thumbs were tender to the touch
and Ted's ears were in bad shape.

But there were also good times. Lucas Meyers
came to visit them. They were invited to dinner at
Robert Lowell's house where they met Robert Frost.
On New Year's Eve, they went together to a fancy
dress party. Sylvia got herself up as Little Red Riding

Hood and Ted wore a big bad wolf-mask which he made for himself with an old sealskin belonging to Aunt Agatha. But they also made disconcerting Freudian slips. Ted drew Sylvia's attention to the fact that she had unmistakably written *woe* instead of *love* on a New Year's greeting card to his parents. Sylvia could not believe her own eyes; visibly, her left hand did not know what her right hand was about. This fell right in line with Hughes's dualist theories. But it was not exactly the sort of life he wished to live. The American way of life was decidedly not to his taste. He found Bostonians pedantic and artificial and he dreamt of quite a different existence for himself. He thought that one ought to strive to retrieve the real sense of one's life. Indeed, the adoption by the masses of this industrial and standardised lifestyle seemed to him to be due to some regrettable collective error of the people. He refused, for his part, to fall into line with the bleating sheep of consumer society, and he did not believe in the need to make money at all cost. Most people's lives, he said, resembled the behaviour of lemmings, those small rodents which are said to jump off the edge of a cliff in large numbers and die without knowing what they are doing. He was convinced that fortune only smiled on those who stuck strongly by their own desires. The thing to do was therefore to listen to the needs of what he called one's true self.

More and more, he would speak of his wish to have a farm. No doubt, a farmer's life was hard, but it was the price to be paid to preserve one's human dignity, of which a city worker was so cruelly deprived. A farm: that was his ideal of a life, but somewhere in Europe, not too far from a great cultural capital such as Rome, Paris or Madrid, and also with English private schools at hand, the prime requirement if his future children were to have a decent education. Besides, insofar as he thought that he should turn his back upon the times, it seemed to him all the more obvious that, as a poet, his task was to wage a sort of ideological war aimed at drawing his adult readers out of their chronic stupor, and at fostering in the young the capacity to develop their true nature freely. On the reverse side of prevailing American culture, he had discovered the Native American tales and legends in which the trickster, a character much given to tricks and pranks, plays a central part. This trickster could be a raven or a coyote or some such animal fond of practical jokes whose tricks had the cathartic power of getting rid of the sadistic impulses and evil urges of the human mind, which thus lost their harmful power by being openly expressed in small myths and funny tales. Whereas Christian American society invented the devil in its desire to repress evil at all costs, the Natives knew how to exorcise it by giving full play to maleficent instincts, which lost some of their force when given free utterance. Instead of which, resentments accumulated, building up to a bursting point behind the façade of proscriptions. Because it was rich in what he called psychic symbols, the primitive form of literature, seemed to hold the promise of a genuine, sincere literature for children. Its commercial exploitation by the American film industry, however, with its cartoons and rustproof star tricksters pointed to ways of developing a mode of writing from it beyond the scope of children's books. His intuition indeed told him that this form retained the power to arouse genuine spirituality in the human mind. Ted was rediscovering for his own part, in Native American folk tales, the rich potential that the German Romantics had found in the Märchen and old Germanic legends: the promise of a new style of literature capable of restoring a spirituality ill-used by the mechanical philosophy of the Enlightenment, itself deriving from the empiricism of the Renaissance and the humanism of the Reformation. The spirit of Protestant

dissent was still very attractive in the USA in the cari-
catural form of the religious revivalist movement, an
exacerbated vision of Methodism which had influenced the way his mother Edith brought up her children. This seemed to him the worst example of the
way religion had been misappropriated by the mer-
chants of the temple for their own purpose. In his
opinion, the style of the sermons of Billy Graham had
less to do with religion than with the sales talks of a
mountebank serving his own interests. In his letters to
his brother Gerald, who had joined the Catholic
Church under the influence of his wife, Ted wrote that
the Roman Catholic and the Anglican Churches alone
afforded an organised system of belief necessary to a
genuinely religious life rooted in prayers and a daily
adherence to one's task. True, he was grateful to their
mother for having drummed the respect for the Gos-
pels and the principles of Christian morality into
them. But he had come to think that the Catholic
Church was perhaps the only organisation capable of
barring the way to materialism and communism, as
well as offering resistance to this consumer society.

However, despite his personal reflections on the
subject in his letters to Gerald, Ted Hughes refused to
attend religious services in any of the numerous
churches that flourished in the States as well as in the
United Kingdom. Sylvia, for her part, spoke of her
desire to join a church, if only to be part of a community. She felt the need to be with other people.
Why couldn't she go to church alone? She tried not to
let Ted into all her thoughts. Sometimes she would
cry, when she was by herself, for no definite cause;
she noticed that it brought her a certain pleasure, and
she welcomed it because she would feel perfectly
cleansed afterwards, as if her tears had done wonders
washing her. If Ted did not go to church, he remained
faithful to the Methodist education he had received as
a child in the discipline he continued to impose upon

himself, apparently with great delectation. Early to bed and early to rise: this simple practice considerably raised the level of his creative energy. Perhaps this was just due, he said, to the force of habit or because that was what he had been told all his life, so that obedience to this rule gave him the salutary feeling of being at peace with himself. He had also decided to lose weight and he imagined that he could do so on a strict confectionery diet. Every night, the two would read in bed before going to sleep. Ted was then discovering the novels of Georges Simenon, which he recommended to his father. While he got up early to go and work in the library, Sylvia liked to stay in bed late. At that time she was working part-time for the head of the Sanskrit department at Harvard. Meanwhile, Ted was to received a grant of $1,000 from the Guggenheim foundation to help him complete his *Feast of Lupercal*. Each of them worked in the recess of a bow window on makeshift tables that Ted had made for them, but these joint efforts did not produce the same effect. Sylvia complained continually of her lack of inspiration; she would succumb to panic at the thought that she might never succeed in being pregnant. Sterile! She was sterile. How could she continue to force Ted to be married to a sterile woman? Since the beginning of the year they had decided by common consent to go back to England because they wanted to have a child and Ted desired that the child be born on English soil. However, they had enlarged the circle of their literary relations. Robert Lowell, whom they both held to be mad, but who was charming with it, had put Sylvia in touch with Anne Sexton and a mutual sympathy had grown between them, in spite of the fact that Sexton was certainly more well-known and better-looking than Plath. They began to talk about their attempted suicides as spontaneously as more ordinary women would have talked about clothes. Sexton's lover at the time was a certain

George Starbuck whose job consisted in casting about for new talents for Houghton Mifflin, and by degrees they made the acquaintance of other poets and some of the literary figures of Boston. At Harvard, there was Richard Wilbur and Archibald MacLeish, and also Robert Frost who had rooms in Brewster Street in Cambridge, Mass. Through Anne Sexton, they also made the acquaintance of Maxine Kumin, of Kenneth Koch and John Ashbury, both of them poets in residence at Boston. There were also Philip Booth, M. S. Merwin and Peter Davison, poetry editor of the *Atlantic Monthly*. All these people considered Ted Hughes as a writer of real merit, while Sylvia Plath, who helped him in his work, was regarded as a poet's wife who occasionally dabbled in literature.

Both of them had a sneaking feeling of unease and tended to think that they would feel better if they moved elsewhere. They thought of Rome, or perhaps Ireland. Sylvia asked herself if she ought not to do research for a PhD thesis in comparative literature; after all, the discipline required by academic work might do her a lot of good. Ted Hughes was attempting to read the great poets of American modernism but his preference went to Petronius. He did not like William Carlos Williams; he found *Paterson* both pretentious and trite. He also disliked Hart Crane; to his mind his poetry lacked humanity, and it made him think of some electronic sound. E. E. Cummings, he thought, might well be a genius, but he was most certainly a fool and a self-server at that. He had met John Crowe Ransom, and he admired his poems and much enjoyed his company. On the other hand, they had both recently become Tolkien enthusiasts — so very British — while reading *The Hobbit* and *The Lord of the Rings*. However, if Ted was soon to address himself to the task of developing original ways of using myths in literature, Sylvia, on the contrary, did not follow Tolkien's example and set about exploring her innermost feelings and thoughts under the influence of Robert Lowell and Anne Sexton. Her name would later be joined with theirs as examples of confessionalist poets, so called because they were revisiting a certain romantic lyricism in their own name and right by making the exploration of the secret recesses of their minds into their favourite theme. But for the moment, she met with a refusal every time she tried to publish something, plunging her ever deeper into a gloomy frame of mind, which was further darkened, if that was possible, by her reading of Virginia Woolf. Anne Sexton, who had been wise enough to take a lover in the publishing house, had submitted her book that Houghton Mifflin preferred to that of Sylvia Plath. It was hardly a surprise, but Sylvia could not get over the disappointment. The emotional damage was further aggravated because, in March, she insisted that they should visit the tomb of her father, Otto Plath. Once there, she was seized by the mad desire to dig him out to make sure that he had really existed and that he was really dead. In such a climate, Ted now came to fear for his own inner balance, and he was more and more worried that his poetic inspiration might be in danger of running dry. He was aware that he was developing a growing tendency to check on every word he wrote, at the risk of freezing his own writing power. His emotional life, he said, had become sluggish, even non-existent since his arrival in the States. His familiar spirits seemed to be kept away from him, as if in quarantine. Nevertheless, he admitted that America was not the problem. It all came from him. He had also noticed that this state of affairs had rendered him indifferent to people around him. If the whole truth must be known, one should also mention that at the time, in addition to Provençal poets in translation, he was also reading Alfred Jarry's *Ubu the King*, which could not but colour his daily experience and increase his depressive tendency. Last of all, he had been aware for some time now that his writing was best when he did not have too preconceived an idea of what he wanted to do; his best poems tended to come to him when his mind was turned elsewhere. Life in America, however, was very unfavourable to that sort of intellectual experience, because of the way the massive objectivity of the present is constantly pressing upon your mind. Many American poets, William Carlos Williams among them, had remarked on that American conundrum before: there seemed to be an incompatibility of sorts between poetic reverie and American civilisation. Such a cleavage between outer and inner experience was what T.S. Eliot had called "dissociation of sensibility"; according to him, it had taken place at about the time of the Reformation and had begun to reach its limits with the Romantic reaction against the too narrowly rational spirit of the Enlightenment. Ted Hughes, for his own part, linked this movement to the social conflict in England itself, intimately connected with the question of language and the repression of its dialectal element. The language that he called dialect had been, he thought, the native idiom of Shakespeare, but it had been reduced to silence since the time of the Glorious Revolution in 1688 that had opened the very objectively standardised era of the Enlightenment; it had had to wait until the advent of the Romantic movement, particularly with Blake, Wordsworth and Keats, to be accepted again. In other words, this American period in the life of Ted Hughes was not without its influence on the shaping of some of his most strongly established opinions concerning the history of ideas.

In June, to celebrate their third marriage anniversary, they gave one another a book on Paul Klee. And, by way of marking the end of the American chapter of their life in common, they embarked upon the grand traditional sightseeing trip in North-America: the crossing of the continent from East to West and back, going through Canada on their way west. For this transcontinental drive they bought — at knock off price — a tent that was the size of a small house. Thus equipped, they set off on July 1st in Aurelia's car towards distant California where they had arranged to visit Frieda Plath Heinrichs, Otto Plath's sister, who lived in Pasadena. After driving around the Great Lakes through Canada, they crossed North Dakota and arrived in the Bad Lands where erosion has left tall columns rising above the grass of the Prairie, then went right through the state of Montana. The rolling landscapes offered them many occasions for literary descriptions. In Yellowstone National Park the tourists were being disconcerted by grizzly bears. A woman had been killed at West Thumb and, every evening, people making camp for the night tried not to give way to fear. In the course of their trip, the Hugheses would count 67 bears, which they referred to by their numbers. In the end they had to take tranquillisers in order to snatch some sleep without being disturbed by the noise that the animals made stumbling into the guy-ropes of their tent and stealing their food supplies. One of these nocturnal visitors had broken the rear window of their car to gobble up the oranges and cookies that they had left inside. As they had been told that only red pepper and gasoline could keep away the plundering beasts, they ended their trip in a car whose rear window was broken and reeking of petrol. The episode with the bears would later inspire several texts, among which "The Brother's Dream", a poem that remained for a long time unpublished, in which Ted Hughes abandons himself to the masochistic phantasy of being devoured by a she-bear, associated in this particular case with the theme of the double that had haunted the hunting parties of his childhood. Two years later, Sylvia Plath was also to publish a short story called "The 59th Bear" in the

London Magazine, in which the heroine owes her widowhood entirely to an obliging bear. For the time being, however, conjugal happiness seemed to have been restored. Just when they were about to set off on their trip, Faber & Faber wrote telling Ted that they agreed to publish his second collection of poems, albeit on condition that he change the title just a little. He thought of replacing "The Feast of Lupercal" by something like "Lupercalia", the name of the grotto at the foot of the Palatine Hill. Be that as it may, in some obscure way, the magic of this ancient rite seemed well to have worked, for Sylvia felt practically sure that she was pregnant. Her new-found confidence in her creative powers found expression in the long conversations she had with Ted on the necessity to go in search of her real self, which had supposedly been repressed by the puritan education she had received in New England. They crossed the Golden Bridge at San Francisco in a glorious Summer mood, buoyed up by the stereotype of California as a land of plenty, a dreamland of perpetual holiday.

Once back on the East Coast in September, Ted and Sylvia settled for two months in Yaddo, an artists' community founded at the beginning of the century by the New York financier Spencer Trask and his wife Katrina to enable creative people to express their talents in a favourable environment. As there were but few people in residence at the time, Sylvia had the first floor all to herself. The large grey stone ivy-covered house stood in the middle of a large verdant park shaded by trees. Ted had a bungalow at his disposal, standing among pine trees; equipped with a wood stove, it was very light inside. Ted was at leisure to put the final touches to his *Lupercal*. Both of them spent several hours a day reading and writing. Sylvia, who was now certain she was pregnant, was working on the poems of her *Colossus*, trying to plumb the buried world of her worst nightmares. She was reading the experimental poems of Theodor Roethke in which the poet tries to render in words the fantasies and images observed in cases of severe depression. She attempted to do the same by writing in her turn what she called "mad poems". She considered her sudden changes of mood as a host of creative incentives that deserved to be exploited in writing. Never for a minute was she visited by the thought that such an extreme case of manic depression would one day ensure her the honour of having her name immortalised in certain books on psychiatry as a classic case of bi-polar affective neurosis with a strong depressive syndrome. For her own part, she simply considered that, as had been the case for a great number of poets before her, her life seemed to be placed under the magic spell of two contradictory experiences, one of them being positive, the other negative.

During their periods of relaxation, Sylvia and Ted would hypnotise each other, trying to put their subconscious in what they thought were the best possible conditions for producing great literature. In October, Ted was correcting the proofs of his short-story "The Rain Horse" that was soon to appear in *Harper's Magazine*, and under hypnosis Sylvia suggested he might complete some others in the same vein. One month before, Ted had earned $1,000 through selling his poems to various magazines and winning first prize in the Guinness Poetry Competition. He was also working for a Chinese Composer, Chou Wen Chung, on the libretto of an opera based on the *Bardo Thödol* or *Tibetan Book of the Dead*. The opera would never come off, but Hughes's reading of this book in the translation of Evans-Wenz was a strong influence on his future poems. These sacred texts of the ancient religion of Tibet before the country was converted to Buddhism, describe the trials encountered by the soul after death. They reminded him in part of what he had read a few years before about the shamanic practices of the peoples of Siberia and of most Native Americans in whose folk tales he had recently discovered the importance of the trickster. From all these stimulating readings done at Yaddo, he drew the plan of a play based on Euripides' *Maenads*, which he entitled *The House of Taurus*.

Finally, the young couple returned to Wellesley, Massachusetts, a few days before Thanksgiving, traditionally set on the fourth Thursday in November, to celebrate the religious festival with Aurelia Plath, before taking leave of her. Sylvia's waist was now noticeably filling out. Ted had just learnt that he had been appointed Guggenheim fellow for the coming university year 1959-1960. Aurelia accompanied them to the railway station where they took the train for New York, and her son-in-law had leaned out of the train to shout that they would be back in two years' time. They embarked on the *USS United States*, which set sail for Europe on 9 September 1959, due to arrive at Southampton on September 14th after an uneventful crossing.

IV

THE WRECK OF AN IDYLL

On their return, they went to visit Ted's parents at the Beacon and spend Christmas in Yorkshire. They had no sooner set foot in the old world than Sylvia felt that all Europe resembled a vast poorhouse and she experienced a sudden spasm of homesickness. While sipping a Guinness in a pub in Heptonstall Slack, Ted decided that what was needed to cure Sylvia of her sadness was a house in the country. This was in keeping with the dream he had long had of leading the life of a farmer. But Sylvia was a little dubious. She was convinced in fact that living in a large town was indispensable to a poet's career and, moreover, if the truth had to be said, she had no desire to live too close to Ted's family. On the contrary, Ted firmly intended to keep his distance from the so-called intellectual world. In his eyes, it was just a bunch of often the least interesting and most insolent people to be found in London. And so he began to keep an eye out for houses that were still to be picked up at a reasonable price at the time in Yorkshire. A few days after their arrival, a letter from Aurelia arrived at the Beacon addressed to Miss Sylvia Plath in a typed envelope bearing inside brackets the handwritten mention "(Mrs Hughes)". To pass the time, Sylvia taught the Hugheses tarok, a Viennese version of Italian tarot. There were also Vicky, a cousin of Ted, aged 21, Aunt Hilda and Uncle Walt, and also Olwyn, Ted's sister who still felt very jealous of "Miss Sylvia Plath's" possessiveness towards her brother. Worse still, Ma had done irreparable harm by transforming an old mauve dressing-gown of Sylvia's to fit Olwyn's measurements so that the two women were soon looking askance at each other. While Ted was working upstairs, Sylvia stayed downstairs listening to the rain beating ceaselessly against the window panes of the small living-room beside the humming stove, nursing her feeling of boredom laced with a twinge of disgust, for she found that her mother-in-law's kitchen was really not too clean.

On 31 December, they were already back in the flat at 18 Rugby Street that Ted had sub-rented from Dan Huws in the past. Dan and his wife Helga occupied the third floor with their new-born child, Ted and Sylvia the second floor, sleeping in a bed with a sagging mattress and sharing the only bathroom on the ground-floor. Sylvia, who was now six months pregnant, found such conditions sordid to say the least, and the young couple tried to find a place with hot water, a central heating system, and large enough for the child to come. For his wife's amusement, Ted built a birds' restaurant, which consisted of pieces of fat strung on a cloth-wire suspended outside the window. But the poet's mood was as sombre as it could be. He reflected that the question was no longer to diagnose the diseases of Western society with the possible risk of having to sign its death certificate, but rather to look for signs of life that might still linger here and there. To his mind, modern man seemed to be characterised by a sort of intellectual dilettantism coupled with an immoral voracity, while his inner life had been willingly suppressed altogether. He compared Western civilisation in general to that of the Polynesian islanders who, when brought into contact with American civilisation, had given up all their beliefs and ancestral values, had scattered and dispersed, and eventually died of despair. The poem "Strawberry Hill" in *Lupercal* is a metaphor of the way in which the West is being emptied of its soul like a rabbit drained of its blood by a weasel that has crept upon it unawares. But, for all that, the situation was not as desperate as it looked, and rescue was at hand. It was to come from friends they had met in Boston, the poet Bill Merwin and his wife Dido, who were a little richer than they were. The couple owned a flat in London and a house in the South of France. It was thanks to their help that, in February, the Hugheses were able to find a small flat within their financial means at number 3 Chalcot Square, not far from Primrose Hill and Regent's Park. Sylvia, moreover, was enchanted to hear that they would reside within a hundred yards of Fitzroy Street, where a plaque was affixed on the house where Yeats had lived. They hurried to buy a bed from a second-hand shop, Ted painted the walls of the living-room white and hung up a poster of the goddess Isis, Magna Deorum Matris, taken from one of his books on alchemy. But Dido found Sylvia's insistent demand for a fridge somewhat strange, for this sort of modern appliance was not yet in current use on this side of the Atlantic. Besides, the studio apartment of Chalcot Square was so very small that there was room for only one table, that they had to share when they both wanted to write, unless one of them went to work on the bed; in the end Ted arranged a little corner in the hall for himself, where he wrote on a small folding table. Such conditions of life, as one may imagine, were not conducive to serenity and they did nothing to placate Sylvia's chronic state of anxiety. She would repeatedly interrupt Ted when he was trying to work. This became so excessive that one day he yielded to the curiosity of keeping count of how many times she called him, and found that she had done so 104 times in a single morning. Soon, he made an arrangement with the woman living on the floor above who allowed him to go and work in her flat when she was out working; similarly when the Merwins went to spend the Summer in their house in Dordogne it was agreed they would be allowed the use of their flat with garden in Saint George Terrace. In the hope that better days would come, Sylvia now slept more than ten hours a day, and they resumed their old habit of one spending a whole day in bed once a week in turn, while the other attended. Though Sylvia was now seven months pregnant, she made a point of going alone to a pub in Soho to sign a contract with Heinemann for her collection *Colossus and Other Poems*, while Ted waited for her in another pub nearby with a three-volume edition of the poems of D.H. Lawrence he meant to present her with for the occasion. Since their return, a meeting of the ex-members of the *Saint Botolph's Review* had been arranged, but Sylvia preferred to receive them in a pub, as they were too heavy smokers for their small flat. They would go out at night, sometimes, with Bill and Dido. On such occasions they saw Eisenstein's *Ivan the Terrible*, and some plays by Ibsen and also Ionesco which they found rather ridiculous. The Theatre of the Absurd was capturing the London stage at the time, and Ted sensed that it would certainly not be too difficult to do at least as well, which might prove an easy way of making money.

In March, he read his poems to the members of the Poetry Society of Oxford. Then he was awarded the Somerset Maugham Prize for *The Hawk in the Rain*, consisting of the tidy sum of £400 which was designed to finance travelling costs meant to broaden the poet's general outlook on the world. *Lupercal* was due out on March 18th. Would the baby be born on that date, so that this second book could be dedicated to it? No. Once more it would be "For Sylvia". There were some laudatory reviews. The second book fortunately confirmed the great talent already noticeable in the first. Moreover, it was published in England instead of the USA, which undoubtedly added to the merits of the book. The return to nature-centred poetry was greeted with great applause. Mr. Hughes was praised for resolutely turning his back on a certain superficiality of contemporary society, and was admired for his remarkable technical skill which enabled him to change tones and modulate his voice at will. The *Yorkshire Post* expressed its satisfaction with the fact that the lad from the North had forgotten neither his old friends nor the land of his birth. But, more than anything else, what retained the critics' attention was the strength and Nietzschean vitality of this new style of poetry, which did not wince at violent subjects and metaphors, and was remarkable for the alliterative clout of the language, even if flexing its muscles in such ways sometimes gave a painfully strained twist to his expression. But it was the literary journalist Alfred Alvarez, self-appointed star-maker — whose poetry was considered by Hughes mediocre and his critiques inept — who was nevertheless to contribute greatly to his fame, thanks to his review of *Lupercal* in *The Observer*, where he greeted the book as heralding the advent of a new style of poetry. The episode of the Movement had had its day, with its poems written by pusillanimous gentlemen, too polite to be able to face raw truth. For his part, Ted Hughes merely observed that *Lupercal* set him free from the demons that had been clogging his imagination throughout his American period. He felt that writing had again become easy for him, as if living in England, in some mysterious way, was indispensable to the free expression of his talent. But he also found that England was changing rapidly, as if the prosperity he was sure he had seen predicted in the stars a few years before was now starting to materialise in the country. His personal success seemed to be part of this general renewal, but he was already conscious of the unfortunate consequence attending the restored vitality. Rural England, it seemed, had definitely ceased to exist, other than as a specifically preserved décor.

Blessings, so the saying goes, never come alone; the creative spirit, it seemed, cannot be parted from the vital power of the body. Sylvia gave birth to a girl, who was to be called Frieda, after her maternal aunt and after the wife of D.H. Lawrence. She was also given the name of Rebecca because, Ted Hughes said, it meant man-trap, but above all because it was a powerful name. If the newborn had been a boy, his second name would have been Major, after a Scotsman who had fought in the past against absolute monarchy. Frieda was born in her parents' home like most babies at the time because of the difficulty of getting a bed in the maternity ward of a hospital. The doctor had no drugs to relieve the pain, and nor did the midwife, so that the lucky father had to soothe the anguish of the panicked mother by hypnotising her several times in succession. Moreover, Sylvia so energetically refused the idea that her first child should be born on 1st April, that after two nights without sleep she had taken two sleeping pills but without succeeding in befuddling a mischievous fate that had decided that the birth would occur at 1 o'clock on the morning of April 1st, 1960. As soon as she had recovered some strength, Sylvia had called her mother to let her know the first name they had chosen for the child, exclaiming in the tongue of her ancestors: "*Ein Wunderkind, Mummy! Ein Wunderkind!*"

"For Frieda Rebecca" — The little girl had been born just in time for Ted to dedicate his collection of tales for children soon to be published by Faber & Faber to her. A few days only after the birth of the child, her parents had been invited to a restaurant to discuss the choice of illustrations for *Meet My Folks*, a book composed of a series of portraits of the members of an imaginary family. Seeing that he was not doing too badly, Ted Hughes entertained the hope that he would earn enough money this coming year to enable him to dispense with the necessity of getting a job to support his family. As for Sylvia, motherhood had opened up a new creative period for her, which began with the laying out of a plan for her novel *The Bell Jar*. The Hugheses indeed seemed well engaged on the way to success, and while they were rejoicing at the news that their cat Sappho, which they had had to leave behind them in Massachusetts, would soon have kittens, the favourable reception that *Lupercal* got was bringing them many invitations. They were even invited for dinner at Mr. and Mrs. Eliot's. This meant the child had to be weaned early so that her parents could leave her in the care of a baby-sitter to be free to do due honour to the invitation from the great man. After a romantic taxi run in the streets of Little Venice, whose wealthy residences were mirrored in the dark waters of Regent's Canal, the Hugheses were surprised to find that the Eliots lived in a very ordinary-looking brick house. They were a little taken aback at first, but they were soon overcome by the feeling that they were in front of some living god, rendered more human, however, by the presence of Mrs. Valerie Eliot, who was also from Yorkshire. Fortunately, other guests soon joined the party: Stephen Spender and his wife, the pianist Natasha Litvin whose lively conversation was much welcome. It soon emerged that Eliot and Spender had played a non-negligible part in Hughes's Guggenheim scholarship, as well as in the resounding reception of his second book. Of course, Hughes would have found it more elegant not to talk shop. However, Eliot assured him that he was looking forward to reading all that he would go on to write.

The passion that the Pope of Modernism had been nourishing for a renaissance of poetic drama since before the 1940s encouraged Hughes in his attempt to revive the genre within the more recent context of the Theatre of the Absurd, and soon he was submitting to the BBC a dramatic poem entitled *The House of*

Aries, which was produced with great actors in the leading parts. In it he tried to expose the fragmented psyche of the modern subject, but he had got carried away by his widespread use of symbolism, to such an extent that, on November 1960, when he went to listen to the performance in the flat of his upstairs neighbour — not having a radio set himself — he was utterly horrified to hear what he had allowed to be produced under his name. Still, he managed to sell a few other plays to the BBC, such as *The Wound*, for example, a text based on a dream, that he would later describe as his own version of the *Tibetan Book of the Dead*. But these were never given a public airing, for a producing director judged that it all lacked dramatic interest, the characters were hollow, the scenes were static, and the language was too flatly rhetorical. Hughes had no doubt overestimated the capacity of the market for the Theatre of the Absurd, which was just a passing fad. He would laugh over it in secret, asking himself if one day he would see the genre pushed to its limit, as for instance in the story of a wolf's entry on stage: first showing the tip of one ear, then a quarter of an hour later one lip, then, after another quarter of an hour, the other ear, so that when he appears entire upon the stage, one or two hours later, all the spectators have died of boredom or of fear. But these failures were to put an end to his theatrical ambitions. He would not, however, abandon all interest in drama, but it would take the form of adaptations of famous classical plays. The fact remains, however, that the month of April 1960 established the reputation of Ted Hughes among the poets of his generation as indisputably the successor, in a manner of speaking, of the poets of the first half of the century. On April 21st, Faber & Faber gave a reception in their commercial premises at 3 Queen Square, in honour of W.H. Auden, and on this occasion the photographer Mark Gerson immortalised the new poet among his peers: Ted Hughes can be seen standing in a large doorway, with T.S. Eliot and Louis MacNeice on his left and, on his right, W.H. Auden and Stephen Spender.

Already the first edition of *Lupercal* was out of print; a second edition was in preparation and due to come out in June. Ted Hughes was learning to get used to receiving abundant mail from readers and to having perfect strangers coming up to him in the street to offer their congratulations. At the same time, he was trying to brighten up their lodging at 3 Chalcot Street by painting the hall and one kitchen wall bright red, because this colour had a soothing effect upon Sylvia's anguish. He was also hunting mice, but he had to catch them alive and go to Primrose Hill to set them free, for they would not run the risk, if he had poisoned them, of their rotting under the floor. Sylvia dreamed of a house in Fitzroy Road where Yeats had lived as a child, but the owner wanted nearly £3,000 for it, which was quite beyond their means. They were taking it in turns to look after Frieda; Ted was prompt to notice that a young child is like an antenna catching the slightest change of mood of the people around it. It seemed more and more obvious that they should remain in the vicinity of the literary circles of the capital, but Ted held strongly to his idea that they should buy an old farm, in Devon perhaps, or in Cornwall. Ideally, he thought, they would also have a pied-à-terre in London, so as to be able to share his time like the traditional squire, between the life of a hermit in the country and the necessity to spend some time in town to meet people socially for the benefit of his career. He had also taken up astrology again and his friends came to consult him on his future. He was, for instance, able to provide astrological advice to Lucas Meyer and Bill Merwin. But concerning himself, he once made the disquieting remark that, had he been a serious astrologer, he would have lost no time in going to bury himself in the country for the coming two years. And so, he went out to visit farms that were for sale, and the rest of the time he spent reading Heraclitus and Mayakovsky, when he was not writing dozens and dozens of pages to explain his poems to Mrs Prouty. He had also begun to do the rounds of a few dealers in rare books to try and make a few extra pounds with the sale of the manuscripts of his poems. He was even on the point of selling the manuscripts of his first two collections to the University of Indiana for a few hundred pounds. The life of an artist is sometimes not very different from that of a student, and on occasions when he met Peter Redgrove they would test their respective beer-drinking capacity, and Ted was pleased to find that he could still hold his nine pints without being unduly elated. They also went one day to Trafalgar Square with some friends, wheeling Frieda in a pushchair that they had borrowed for the occasion, to join the Aldermaston March against nuclear weapons. But their relationship was becoming stormy again. Sylvia could not help being envious of Ted's celebrity. A photographer who had had the bad luck of coming to take a photograph of him for his publisher one day after they had been squabbling, was forced to retreat nearly empty-handed after having had to face the bad temper of his subject. There was no doubt that a break was needed. They decided therefore to buy a car. It was their first car and Ted wanted to buy it new with the money from the literary prizes prudently laid by on a bank account in Boston. They chose a Morris 1000, with the wooden frame apparent in some van versions. Then they set off for the continent to visit the Merwins in their farm in Dordogne, at Lacan de Loubressac near Bretenoux. But Sylvia suspected Ted of being attracted to Dido and she spied on him intently. They were soon back in England to spend some time in Yorkshire. However, it was not long before they grew fed up with the visits to the bathing station in Whitby with cousin Vicky — the place was too working-class and dirty for Sylvia's taste — or with playing darts with Uncle Walt who insisted on slipping pound notes into the pockets of poor Ted, whom he persisted in regarding as a good-for-nothing. Besides, Sylvia was now definitely on bad terms with her in-laws. Her sister-in-law Olwyn never called her by any other name than "Miss Plath" and she reproached her with behaving as if she were the mistress of the Beacon, whilst each would blame the other for her possessiveness towards Ted.

On their return to their small flat on Chalcot Square, Ted got back to working five days in the week in the neighbour's flat on the floor above theirs, whilst Sylvia got it into her head to learn Italian at a Berlitz school, making ready for the journey they vaguely planned to make in the land of Dante and Leopardi using the money from the Somerset Maugham Prize that they had saved for the purpose. In October, *The Colossus* came out just before Sylvia's birthday. Ted's reputation was by now so well established that he could afford to decline several invitations to read his poems in public and he even went so far as to refuse to appear on television as "poet of the year". He would only, on occasions, accept an invitation to dinner at Stephen Spender's with Louis MacNeice and his mistress of the moment, Rosamond Lehmann. The rest of the time the poetic couple preferred to remain quietly at home over a bottle of rosé champagne, going to bed to read Proust's *In Remembrance of Things Past*, the poems of Yves Bonnefoy or *The Lord of the Rings* once more. Ted could well be satisfied; this year he had derived a comfortable income from the BBC and he already had a tidy sum in the bank for the day he found the farm of his dreams. Occasionally, they would exchange small gifts and various tit-bits. In keeping with the trend of the time, they contemplated buying a hand loom or a potter's oven, and meanwhile, Sylvia proudly sewed garments for Frieda. They even bought a small radio set to listen to a reading of *The Rain Horse* that was due to be broadcast soon. One day, perhaps missing the close contact with nature he had enjoyed as a child, Ted very nearly bought a young fox from a man who was walking in the street with the animal ensconced in the folds of his coat, selling it for one pound. But wild animals are not easy to domesticate.

In the year 1961, the by now famous couple was to sign an engagement with the BBC to participate in a series of programs entitled *Two of a Kind* in which they were featured as an exemplary couple of writers. This was an image of them which was more mythical than real. It was the impression they would have liked to give but it did not correspond to the reality of their lives. In February, Sylvia had a miscarriage due perhaps to an attack of appendicitis for which she had been hospitalised in Saint Pancras. The aseptic whiteness of the hospital had a soothing effect upon her, and her husband at her bedside, for her alone, did much to restore the image of the chivalrous colossus she liked to have of him. Ted looked after the "Pooker" (for such was the name they had given Frieda) and came to the hospital regularly, bringing her big sandwiches of red meat to speed up her recovery. Also, seriously boosting her morale, a check for £100 arrived accompanying a first reading contract for one year with *The New Yorker*. Above all, Sylvia was much impressed by the atavistic pluck shown by the English patients in all circumstances, as if it were the most natural thing in the world: innocent practitioners of autosuggestion, who never complained, bravely smiling and joking all the time from hospital beds as a matter of course. However, she had not been long out of this clean, white paradise before her recurrent jealousy was revived when she heard on the telephone the suave tones and torrid Irish lilt of a BBC woman producer. As a precautionary measure, Sylvia vented her frustration on Ted in advance by tearing up the manuscripts of the texts upon which he was working at the time — plays and poems — as well as his precious red book of the complete works of Shakespeare which had saved him from mortal boredom a few years back, in the Pinewood studios. These fits of temper had become so frequent and were so manifestly excessive that certain of his friends were beginning to be alarmed and they let him know their surprise at his accepting these outrageous outbursts of bad humour without a word. He put them down to his wife's unrecognised genius, which some day would inevitably find more artistic expression. But he himself began to be seriously disturbed when he saw how she would exploit the incidents of their daily life in her poems. Yet, in May, he wrote to Aurelia saying how highly he thought of the poems that Sylvia had managed to produce. She had, he said, begun to write "permanent" poetry, that would surely stay.

As he saw it, genuine poetry demanded from the poet total devotion to the art, so he continued obstinately to refuse to be tied down to a regular job as long as the success of his books could enable him to survive without it. Sylvia, however, would have preferred him to have a regular income which would have given them more comfort and a standard of living closer to the level of wealth they might have hoped for if they had followed an academic career in the States. She was now learning to drive and imagined herself at the wheel of a big family sedan. The debate was relaunched when they met the American poet Theodor Roethke in London, whose "mad poems" Sylvia had admired in Boston. This tall and broad-shouldered Viking had said that he could get a university job for Ted in Washington if he so desired.

But that was exactly what Hughes did not want. Had he not just won the Hawthornden prize? If course it was only £100 but a tradition has it that the prize was handed over to the laureate by the winner of the previous year, and it had been the occasion for them to meet the novelist Alan Sillitoe, the famous author of *The Loneliness of the Long-distance Runner* and figurehead of the "Angry Young Men", and his companion the poet Ruth Fainlight. Moreover, Ted had just given a fifteen-minute interview on television to talk about his book for children, so that Pa and Ma were rather reassured and indeed very proud to have seen him and heard him talk on screen. Was all this not more interesting than buying fridges and washing machines? Besides, all would be well when they could settle in a large house in the country and have a home of their own. And so, in June, Aurelia once more crossed the Atlantic to look after Frieda in the Merwins's apartment while the two poets, after a brief holiday in France, went in search of a large house in the South-West of England.

By the end of August, soon after Ted's thirty-first birthday, they literally fell in love with Court Green, a very old house in the village of North Tawton in Devon, not far from Exeter, a four-hour train journey from Waterloo Station. Their substantial savings made it possible for them to buy it outright, thanks too to a complementary sum of £500 advanced by Edith and a further loan of the same amount given by Aurelia. When they moved in on 31 August 1961, Sylvia was already five months pregnant. Court Green was a large thatch-roofed house. It had been in the possession of the Arundel family, whose ancient name is immortalised in a poem by Philip Larkin. It was a large house of great character, the oldest part of which dated back to the 15th century. It was within the village but looked withdrawn, surrounded by a piece of land of three acres containing a large orchard where

Ted numbered seventy-two apple trees of different varieties, among which he had recognised the Devonshire Quarrendon, red as tomatoes then, in August, the Early Victoria and the Bramley, as yellow as quinces, and the hardy Pig's Noses, green at heart and orange on the edge like Irish flags. The rose shrubs had grown long shoots, pale purple and green. The corollas of gladioli on the spikes with their long sword-shaped leaves, and also the zinnias with their coarse heads of flowers around a yellow core, resembling many-coloured feather-dusters, were just visible above the wild growth that had invaded the flower-beds, surmounted by the cone-shaped clusters of the lilacs and the drooping long stems of yellow laburnum flowers. There were also cherry trees, red and black currant bushes and a huge honeysuckle hanging ramshackle over the entrance of the house. Two large box trees stood on either side of the front door, glazed with eight small panes and protected by a slate-covered porch-roof supported by a latticework structure, on the right side of which grew a Virginia creeper. The different buildings were arranged around a square yard paved with pebbles coming right up to the two steps of the threshold whose stone had been so much worn over the years that it seemed to be subsiding in the middle. The house comprised about ten rooms, a great number of bedrooms, many bathrooms, two kitchens, a storeroom, a wine cellar and various other outbuildings, a cottage, a stable that could be converted later on, and a tennis court in a state of abandon. As this property, shadowed with great elms, was an old presbytery, it was close to the church and bordered the churchyard, whose tombstones could be seen from the windows of the large upstairs room that Sylvia immediately reserved for her own personal use. Just beyond, a swelling in the ground announced the presence of one of the barrows containing the graves of prehistoric people which so much abound in some parts of the English countryside.

Delighted with this opportunity, the two poets hastened to isolate themselves in different quarters of the house: Sylvia in a large room on the first floor, Ted in a vast attic under the thatched roof. But he had no sooner carried his books and his manuscripts up than he came down again and, remembering that he was a joiner's son, he set about knocking up a makeshift barrier so that the little lass who was following him everywhere should not fall down the stairs. He made a large writing table for Sylvia with long, heavy elm boards, then a small sewing table, shelves and a toy trunk for Frieda. His brother-in-law sent him a toolbox with a characteristically American aerodynamic outline. Soon he became a member of a purchase club and could buy furniture at very low prices. He also bought seeds from a mail-order firm and with a set of garden tools picked up at an auction, he set about digging a large patch of ground for strawberry plants. Frieda followed him like his shadow in her diminutive Red Riding Hood dress, imitating every one of his gestures with her small spade. Meanwhile, to brighten up the rooms, Sylvia painted the woodwork and the floors white and the mouldings grey. Later, she would spread carpets on the floors: a bright red Wilton for her study since the colour was almost a fetish with her. It would be a room of her own, such as Virginia Woolf had so much dreamed of having for herself. It would be her private place of meditation where nobody else would come. She bought a sewing machine second-hand, and a Bendix washing machine for which Aurelia had sent her the money, and a lot of red velvet material for the walls and the curtains, the pillows, and the bedspread. Ted put animal skins on the floors and seats and carefully chose shamanistic objects such as eagles' talons and tigers' teeth, badgers' and foxes' skulls that he had boiled a long time to bleach, which he then displayed in different parts of the house. It was a pleasant surprise for him to discover that the old house, so full of charms, responded well to the slightest gesture he made to take possession of it, as if it were endowed with a soul; Ted saw it as a large bird cage or a vast glass house bathed in sunlight all day long. From inside the house, nothing but treetops could be seen, through which a few roofs could be glimpsed.

In London, the Hugheses gave several dinner parties to take leave of their friends: Alan Sillitoe and Ruth Fainlight, the Portuguese poet Halder Macedo and his wife Suzette, and a few of the rare persons who had remained in the capital in the heat of August. Ted and Sylvia remained in town just long enough to sublet their flat at 3 Chalcot Square for the rest of their three-year lease. They did not have to wait long. They had made friends with a Canadian poet called David Wevill and his wife Assia, who made such good first impression that Ted and Sylvia instantly tore up the check left by another candidate for the flat who had been prompter to make up his mind. They then called back the young couple of such distinguished appearance who resembled them so much. Then they returned to their pastoral idyll and their various settling-in tasks. There were plenty of red and black currants waiting to be picked. Ted resumed his old habit of getting up before dawn to go and fish for trout for breakfast in the Taw nearby. Sylvia baked apple tarts all the time, making stews with the rabbits poached by her husband, and dishes with potatoes that had grown at random in the abandoned garden. Then, as soon as he finished sowing the winter lettuces, Ted set about cultivating what he called his "mental cabbage", enjoying the privacy of his refuge under the thatched roof of the attic, to read and write at ease for weeks on end, free at last to follow the drift of his thoughts without being disturbed. For over the past year London had been weighing on him as much as Boston before, and he had written nothing, all things considered, of real merit; it was as if all the time spent in London had been like a bad nausea spell about which he could do nothing but wait till it passed away. In the spring, he came across a very fine book on the Loch Ness monster which, he thought, convincingly established its existence, if not perhaps under the form of a single animal but of a resident colony of plesiosauri, a sort of marine reptile whose genus was not totally extinct. As this was a subject which particularly excited his imagination, Ted plunged into writing again, beginning with a long poem for children that was due to appear in *Vogue* under the title *Nessie the Mannerless Monster*.

And thus, they spent days of quiet happiness, punctuated by the sound of the church bells nearby. On Sundays, skilled bell-ringers would give virtuoso performances. The peals of bells had revived Sylvia's deep-seated attraction to religious rituals, and with renewed intensity she felt the urge to join a community of some sort, be it only to take part in the monthly reunions of the young mothers of the village. Going to a maternity home to attend regular pre-natal sessions encouraged her to meet people. Of course, her new house filled her with the benign feeling that time and space was hers to enjoy and thrive in, but she was not naturally inclined to live a hermit's life. So she went to pay a visit to the Anglican vicar of the parish. He was an Irish clergyman who had travelled the world, and he had assured her she was welcome in his church in spite of her heretical Unitarian opinions, for she belonged to the denomination that denies the doctrine of the Holy Trinity. She therefore taught little Frieda her prayers and would soon send her to Sunday school. Meanwhile, as she had only the churchyard to cross when the bells called the faithful to prayer, she attended Vespers to enjoy the beauty of the songs and the stained-glass windows, and the solemnity of the liturgy, but she stopped her ears to the sermon. Was it because of her pregnancy? She was surprised to feel flabby all over, and she said she could no longer take an interest in anything but cooking, sewing and women's magazines. Indeed they wondered sometimes whether it was very reasonable to bring children into the world in such a cold-war atmosphere, with Kruchtchev and Kennedy engaged in a nuclear stalemate and America in a headlong rush to build antinuclear shelters in the imminence of a nuclear war. "The future is no calamitous change", Ted had written in a poem of *Lupercal*, called "A Woman Unconscious", "but a malingering of now". Was the world about to burn? Just then, Ted spent much time looking after Frieda, doing the washing, going shopping at Exeter. Then, one day, as he was digging a patch of ground to plant potatoes, he suddenly did not feel well: hypochondria had taken hold of him. He was convinced that he would not live much longer for he could feel all the symptoms of a fatal heart disease, he had no doubt of it. Immediately he began treatment, dosing himself on Beethoven at top volume for he maintained that there was nothing better to flush out your aorta.

With her second pregnancy Sylvia's anxieties seemed to vanish as mysteriously as her blank page syndrome. She finished the first draft of her novel *The Bell Jar* even before they moved in. Ted would read to her of an evening, mostly from Conrad's novels, while she did sewing or got on with some manual work; he was so much engrossed in their domestic happiness that he seriously thought of declining the Somerset Maugham prize that was intended to finance travel expenses. Husband and wife indulged their natural inclination to remain quietly at home. Ted Hughes wanted to convince himself that they shared a form of common unconscious to which they could have permanent access through a sort of telephone line made of intuitions and telepathic vibrations. From time to time they would play games to develop their inspiration. Sylvia would ask him to think as quickly as he could of a topic for a short-story, giving no time for second thoughts, and Ted would say, for instance, that he saw himself alone, sitting on a chair in a world entirely covered with snow, and he went on to make up a story on the theme, while at the same time furnishing Green Court with Windsor chairs that answered to those he had spontaneously imagined. And yet if such great mutual understanding existed between them, with its pleasant and even its creative aspects, Ted Hughes would later look back on this time when they were as inseparable as twins as a suffocating period of their life together. The short story "Snow" is a metaphor of the truth that Ted Hughes had somehow perceived concerning Sylvia's type of inspiration. Ted realised that the possibility of gaining access to the inner life that for him could be reached by unrolling the thread of some half-conscious image, did not exist for Sylvia. He would later picture Sylvia's inner life as a vast blank, and he saw that when she tried to apply the methods that he recommended to her it was as if she found herself in the middle of the Sahara, as if the forests of her unconscious had been shrivelled up by a sudden flash of amnesia. Her method of composition was rather that of a gleaner picking out minute details of ordinary life in the hope of arranging them later into a beautiful bunch of literary flowers. Ted was beginning to think that Sylvia was entirely given over to what he called the "world of things", as if the severity of her Protestant education and the scientific turn of mind, part of her German-American inheritance, had in fact shut her out from the world of spirits. Ted was somehow extremely wary of anything that might, at this time, jeopardise the privileged relationship he entertained with the spiritual world of unconscious energies, for it was there that lay the source of his special poetic gift, of his vocation. It was of vitally important for him to feel constantly related to the spiritual dimension of myths, invisible though it might be to the brains of too narrowly rational people. His life with Sylvia, precisely because of the ever increasing domestic pressure she exerted on him, however unconsciously, was, he felt, strangling his creativity and thwarting the growth of his mental cabbage for no legitimate reason whatsoever. More alarming still was Sylvia's peculiar sort of negativity, a kind of death ray, he said, which threatened to irradiate and in the long run destroy people around her, like the mythical *upas* tree whose shadow was reputed to blight any living thing that came beneath it.

Sylvia was quite aware that her second pregnancy plunged her into a sort of bovine apathy which extended out into the rest of the family, creating an atmosphere of female animality which was markedly different from the knife-edge wakefulness inspiring Ted Hughes's poems. Their settling in had been like the feverish preparation of a nest and the generative process culminated in one more delivery at home with its sequel of raw concomitants disturbing the comfort of the young domestic atmosphere. On January 17th, 1962 Nicholas Farrar was born, so named in memory of a maternal ancestor of Ted's. The delivery was long. Sylvia was given ether in a mask while Ted stood by her side making conversation with the midwife. It was winter, and with festivities still fresh in their minds, the event took on the atmosphere of the Nativity which extended its grace over the family. To his own surprise, Ted did not experience the sort of joy he had felt at the birth of his first child. Sylvia who, not so long ago, had been impatient to wean her daughter, now took pleasure in nursing her plump newborn boy. Ted reserved most of his attention for

Frieda, who was avid for affection with the arrival of her little brother. Ted even seemed to take no interest in his son, as if the coming of this other male between his wife and him disturbed him more than would have seemed reasonable, however unconsciously. He would have much preferred to have ten daughters, he thought, for a son was somehow like a hypodermic syringe, a banderilla thrust into the father's neck. However, these negative feelings were most certainly due to a temporarily confused state of mind and would soon disappear. The astrologer's son was a Capricorn, born under rather auspicious stars, and other preoccupations soon came to take the poet's mind off his fatigue and to dispel his black mood. True, sitting on the jury of the Poetry Book Society, of which Ted Hughes was now a member, had been mortally boring and they had ended up awarding the prize to some insignificant poet whose sole merit was that he was less well-known than the old suspects like George Barker or John Heath-Stubbs for instance. The PBS jury did not have the prescience to award the prize to an amusing young West Indian called Derek Walcott, but this future Nobel Prize winner would lose nothing by waiting. A small anthology of American poems chosen by Sylvia Plath for the *Critical Quarterly* had just been published, and another one, edited jointly by Ted Hughes and Tom Gunn, the homosexual teddy boy and a Cambridge man like Hughes, who had gone to live in the States, was to be published by Faber & Faber. At the time, their names were being artificially linked, because they both made use of the theme of violent energy. But Ted found other occasions to go to London for a change of air. He had agreed to read his poems aloud for the Jupiter record company and for the British Council. His friends at the *New Statesman* also sent him interesting books to review. These welcome diversions had attenuated Sylvia's postpartum depression to a certain extent. Their future, Sylvia thought, looked promising: during the last five years, hadn't they seen their wildest dreams come true? Ted, whose inspiration was again going full throttle, seemed to look forward hopefully to a future as the responsible head of a family and he was planting walnuts, plums, peaches and pears to give companions to his old apple trees.

In March, they prepared to baptise the children. Frieda had not been brought to the baptismal font immediately after her birth, but the good old custom would be revived with Nicholas's birth. With the sound of the neighbouring church bells the call of the Gospel had surreptitiously worked its way into the placid indifference of the family. However, Sylvia now regarded the vicar with abhorrence ever since one Sunday, when he had unsuitably attempted to appease the fear of a nuclear apocalypse among his flock by explaining to them that it would be nothing more than an anticipation of the second coming of Christ. Good Christians had no grounds for fear. After that, Mrs. Hughes stopped going to church for a long time; she preferred to sit at home with tears in her eyes reading the Unitarian sermons, in all their freshness, that her friend Marcia Plumer kept sending from Massachusetts as soon as they were delivered. How she missed her Unitarian Church of Wellesley! However, she would send Frieda to Sunday school and it was very important for her that the children should be baptised. Ted was rather indifferent in this respect and concerned himself with digging the garden. The prayers he uttered were entirely practical, of the sort that helped plants to grow. A quite simple experiment had shown him that if he prepared two seed boxes in the same way, the seeds on which he repeatedly concentrated his prayers would grow much more vigorously than those on which he did not. He had likewise noticed that, when he went out angling, if he concentrated his energy on imagining a dip of his float he did not have to wait long to see it happen. The same with playing cards: he had observed more than once that he could force luck to be on his side if only he concentrated his mind hard enough. He was convinced that there existed telepathic powers in the human mind that modern man was no longer able to use because of his hare-brained cocksureness. He thought that he had developed similar skills in himself, a sort of keen sixth sense he felt he had acquired in the course of his long practice of hunting and fishing in his early years. The peculiar cast of Ted Hughes's spiritual life inclined him towards immemorial pagan practices and beliefs but, after all, if Sylvia wanted to baptise the children, he had no serious reason to object to it.

Although Ted's manners could sometimes be rough, his innate good nature easily made him the providential man, around the house of course, but also in the neighbourhood. In April, it was he that Mrs. Key called to help when her husband had a series of strokes. Their large house also welcomed visitors who might stay a while. In May, for instance, the Sillitoes came to spend some time with them. Then it was Edith and William Hughes's turn; they had come for a week with Uncle Walt to spend time with the children. All this was not very favourable to intellectual work, and the result was that family life tended to crowd out literary creation. Ted also helped a neighbour's daughter, Nicola Tyrer, with her school work, explaining Shakespeare and Hopkins to her. Sylvia, however, was aware that her charms, temporarily dampened by her recent pregnancy, were no match for the bloom of a sixteen-year old adolescent; she soon found the girl was coming a little too often and gave in once more to one of her furious outbursts of jealousy. All that was transitory and short-lived turned in her mind to stone-like permanency, and she was certain that the state of mind in which she was trapped for the moment would never let up. And so she wrote the poem called "Event" in which she depicts herself one night, glazed hard and shiny by the light of the moon and the flowers on the apple-trees, being woken up by a child crying to be fed. His face is that of a wooden statue painted red. She is submerged by a sense of guilt mixed with resentment. Her soul resembles an insect larva. She notes that the love in which she trusted is gone forever. To his dismay, Ted could not but see that she was once more overtly turning a jot of their private life into the subject of a poem, and though he objected to her doing so, she insisted on publishing the poem in *The Observer*.

In May, the Hugheses were visited by the couple to whom they had sublet their flat at 3 Chalcot Square, the Canadian poet David Wevill and his wife Assia who came down to the Devon House. David had met Assia Gutman, then Mrs. Lipsey, on a boat crossing the Atlantic from Canada to the United Kingdom. When three years later she divorced, it had been to join him in Burma. Assia was a Jewish woman whose family had fled from central Europe to the United States under threat of Nazism. She was a short, dark woman of sombre charm. She liked men, and she enjoyed sporting an artistic bent, painting water-colour miniatures and writing charming little poems. The Wevills both worked in advertising. They lived now in a house in Belsize Square which had been once that of Sigmund Freud, and they moved in circles where the reputations of Ted Hughes and Sylvia Plath were well established. Hughes and Plath of course attracted the sort of jealous fascination that celebrities will inevitably excite. Many of Ted's friends who had known him during his glorious period at Cambridge found it rather amusing that the great seducer he had been was now tamed down and henpecked by Sylvia Plath, who had had her fling, too, when she was a student there. It was rumoured that Mrs. Hughes now went to church, while Mr. Hughes went digging in his garden, and that the great man, whose booming voice was regularly heard on radio, had now become a tame home-bird. It seemed incredible. But perhaps one should not entirely judge by appearances, for some had heard it said that the world of Philemon and Baucis was not quite as rosy as it looked, and that the two lovebirds did often fight. You don't say! This roused Assia the Babylonian into action. She liked to make herself up, to dress in a vaporous style, to douse herself with perfume: the woman loved to seduce. She playfully promised herself that she would test her charming powers upon the man who had so ironically sketched himself in his poem "A Famous Poet". So she went for the week-end to North Tawton in her war paint after betting — of course just for fun — that she would get Ted. It is just possible that it was a rather safe bet. Her charms were indeed so powerful that, after dinner, the conversation freewheeled long into the evening. When Sylvia went to bed, Ted stayed on to compose a poem — which was to remain unpublished — on the light of the sun. The final blow was struck, no doubt, the following morning at breakfast, when Assia came down and told Ted her dream of the night: a big pike was rising to the surface in a pond; in the pupil of its golden eye there was a foetus. It was a dream she could easily have had with her eyes wide open, simply by reading the first poems written by her host. But Ted was taken aback: "You know," he said, "what has happened to us?" The rest of the week-end passed without incident, the Wevills went back to London and, a few days later, Assia sent the lady of the house a warm letter of thanks with a delightful tapestry outfit, a wide-meshed canvas printed with roses and ribbons. Sylvia set to work on it on the spot and kept at it for the following five weeks while listening to French and German lessons on the radio.

The rhubarb was making spectacular progress, so much so that it looked as if it would soon make an assault upon the house, while swifts were wheeling back and forth around the roof discharging their excrement and screeching like Stukas. Ted had the impression that he could no longer hear his own thoughts. He dreamt that Hitler was breaking into his house, wild with rage, requiring that he execute his orders on the spot. He was not well. He tried to pull himself free of this nervous bind by writing a play for the theatre which ought to have been called *The Difficulties of a Bridegroom*, inspired by the Third Rosicrucian Manifesto, *The Chymical Wedding of Christian Rosencreutz*. The moral of the play was that by a sort of tragic irony we are, in the end, always overtaken by the very things that we fear most. His depression would not give up. It was even fuelled anew by the situation next-door. Mrs Key was now calling on him in a panic nearly every day to help her pick up old Percy, now an emaciated moribund, and bring him back into his bed. Meanwhile the BBC was broadcasting his radio play *The Wound* for the third time, in which two wounded soldiers are dreaming that they meet enticing furies who tear one of them to pieces while the other manages to repulse them, only to discover on coming back to his senses that his companion is dead. Ted Hughes did another broadcast in the memory of Keith Douglas, an English poet who died, aged 24, during the Normandy landing in 1944. Sometimes, Ted was feeling he was leading a double life, and he was at some distance from either: if, on certain days, he was in London playing the man of letters, most of the time he was playing the factotum at Court Green, a sort of stronghold from which he issued forth now and again like a medieval knight of old for brief sorties into civilised territory.

For some years, now, Sylvia had wanted to have a bee-hive and a few hens to follow. So Ted joined the

Devon beekeepers' club. They both attended meetings of the club in villages where they met gentlemen-farmers in tweeds and other aficionados among whom they were less overjoyed to see the midwife and the moralising vicar. To start them off, they were given an old bee-house as a gift. They painted it green and white and set it at some distance from the house, in a quiet corner of the orchard, and they ordered a swarm of Italian bees reputed not to be too aggressive. Ted had a special outfit except for the head covering that he replaced by a handkerchief under which the docile Italians lost no time finding their way, forcing him to leave the ground with their cruel stings. His angina attacks had immediately reappeared, and the pain in his chest that had worried him so much the Autumn before had returned, with a deep need to rest, so pressing that he wondered if it would ever give up. Meanwhile, his neighbour Percy Key died of a last stroke after many days spent on morphine to relieve the pain. Ted had fortunately not had to take care of him then, having at last been replaced by a nurse.

During this time, Sylvia was preparing the house in anticipation of her mother Aurelia's arrival who was expected in June. As was the fashion in the sixties, she painted hearts and flowers here and there in the house, upon door-jambs, window frames, the baby's cradle, and even the bee-house. She also began to write a novel based on her life with Ted Hughes, a long-time project of hers. Her first thought had been to call it *Falcon Yard*, but she changed her mind and called it *Venus in the Seventh*. It was dedicated to Ponter, her pet name for Ted, in remembrance of the time when they had tried to earn a few dollars by taking part in competitions for coining advertising slogans under the pen-name of Ponter Hughes. She trimmed down her first draft and came out with a watered-down version, a sort of sugary novelette that she planned to offer him for his birthday. Around that time, she also composed sinister poems like, for instance, "The Rabbit Catcher" in which Ted in caricatured as a poacher setting traps, while his innocent victims, caught in the immobility of death, wait for him in the silent undergrowth. In this poem, her relationship with Ted is explicitly described as being that of the rabbit. Was not Ted's spirit like a wire loop tightening around her neck to kill her?

Towards the end of June, when Aurelia Plath arrived for a several weeks' stay, she found herself in a strained family atmosphere. Ted was still suffering from the bee stings, but you could also sense that a grave misunderstanding had arisen between husband and wife, both of whom were doing their best to cover things up by trying to put a brave face on it. Ted was thinking of divorce. He wanted to persuade himself that it was basically unhealthy not to make a fresh start every ten years. After all, had Robert Graves not constantly maintained in *The White Goddess* that the Muse was not at her best in a domestic atmosphere, and that no woman could hold that role for more than a few years? In his personal view of the world, considering as he did that civilisation was a prison exerting a pernicious influence, he came to look upon adultery as a necessary escapade to ease the pressure — at least for a time — that society brings to bear upon individual man. They journeyed to London, travelling together but hardly speaking to each other, to make separate recordings of their program at the BBC. Once back at Court Green, Ted could see that Sylvia and her mother were spontaneously drawing closer to each other, entering into a female complicity with a strong American accent, from which he felt excluded. Since they seemed to manage so well without him, he decided to go to town for a change of air. Seizing the opportunity of his being away from home, Sylvia read passages of her autobiographical novel aloud to her mother, while Ted was in London seeking to get in touch with Assia. He went to her office, but had been unable to talk to her, so he had left her a word saying that he had come to see her in spite of all marriages. As an answer, she sent him a blank sheet and a rose enclosed in an envelope. Then, after doing the round of some pubs and a few other special places where he knew he could find good company, he returned to the delights of family life at Court Green. A few days later, Sylvia had just come back from shopping with her mother when she heard the telephone and hurried to answer it. The voice at the other end of the line, low-pitched and a little cracked, was Assia's; to Sylvia it sounded like that of a woman trying to cover up her voice to make it sound like a man's. Once more, she abandoned herself to one of her spectacular jealous fits, bursting into tears and ripping out the telephone wire. Then she rushed into her room upstairs where Ted followed her. Forced into a corner, Ted confessed, that strange smile of his playing on his face, twisting one side of his mouth. Ordered to leave the house on the spot, the poet packed his bag, humming to himself, seemingly unconcerned. Then without a word his wife and his mother-in-law drove him to the station in his own car. With a queer sarcastic laugh, he cast them a good-bye that stayed unanswered.

In London, Ted Hughes roomed for a while with Al Alvarez, the critic who had done much to build his reputation as a poet when *Lupercal* had appeared, and who was himself divorcing. At the time, Alvarez was living in Swiss Cottage, not far from Primrose Hill where the Hugheses had been living some time before, and also a few streets away from the Wevills. Ted started to court Assia assiduously, and she felt so proud of it that she began to brag about it to all who cared to listen. Then, on July 13th, Ted rented a hotel room near King's Cross station and he made love to her with his customary animal-like conviction, tearing through the delicate underwear that she had bought for this special occasion. Somewhat bruised, she swore never to see him again, but after a few days, she yielded once more to the fascination. From then onwards, they were to be seen together everywhere, starting with the evening parties given by the poet Nathaniel Tarn in his sumptuous house in Hampstead Gardens. During that time, Sylvia Plath was writing letter upon letter to all their friends and acquaintances to let them know that Ted, disreputable and disloyal individual that he was, had abandoned her. At the end of July, when Ted went back to Court Green, he saw that Sylvia had made a huge bonfire of all the manuscripts of his on which she had been able to lay her hands. They drove Sylvia's mother to the station in the car that Sylvia had dented and scratched by driving it off the road, no doubt voluntarily. Then they began taking steps to legalise the breakdown of their marriage. Towards the end of August, Ted Hughes received the visit of John Malcolm Brinnin, American biographer and poetaster, who was known to have accompanied Dylan Thomas during his lecture tours in America. He had come to offer him a post at the University of Connecticut for the next year. In September, having abandoned the somewhat unrealistic project of fixing up Sylvia in Spain for the winter, they went to Ireland to look for a house that would suit her. They went through Dublin for the sake of its oysters and its Guinness, then they made brief stays in B&B milk farms on their way to Connemara, on the West coast, where they met the poet Richard Murphy who survived on the money he made by renting out two fishing boats to tourists. After a night spent playing Ouija with Murphy and the Irish poet Thomas Kinsella, Ted went to pay a visit to the painter Beryl Cook in County Clare and did not come back. From London, he sent a telegram to Sylvia saying he would not be back till October and he left for Spain with Assia. Husband and wife had agreed on a one month separation at the end of which Sylvia did not want Ted to come back for fear that it should jeopardise her divorce plans. She had been encouraged meanwhile to do so by her psychiatrist Ruth Beuscher and her patron Olive Prouty who had convinced her to start legal proceedings for a divorce action against Ted. It was at this time, in this gloomy house in which the telephone that she had ripped out no longer rang that, depressed by the ceaseless crying of Frieda who grieved the incomprehensible absence of her father and could not be comforted — a grief that reminded her with a pang of her own feeling of unjust abandonment at the death of her own father — that she composed her famous "Daddy" in which the character of her husband and that of her father Otto Plath, whom she calls a bastard, combine into the phantasmagoric figure of a sadistic nazi dressed in black from head to foot. In her heart of hearts, she wrote, every woman adores a fascist and, unabashedly going over the top, she compares her lot to that of the Jews in extermination camps during the Second World War.

In London, Ted Hughes first relied on the hospitality of some friends before moving to 110 Cleveland Street, in Soho, not far from Regent's Park, in a small bed-sitter which appealed to him because it was within walking distance of at least three bookmakers. In November the telephone was in working order again at Court Green, where Aunt Hilda arrived to give a hand. However, Sylvia would soon move to the capital with her two children, for she had by now made up her mind not to return to live in America. She adopted a new hair style, for she thought it appropriate to fit her change of life with a change in her looks, and Ted indeed hardly recognised her when he came to meet her at the station. He helped her to find an apartment, accompanying her on her visits while she explained to everyone they met that she was the one wishing for a divorce, for fear that she might be mistaken for a semi-literate housewife shrugged off by her genius of a husband. She eventually chose to move into a street that ran parallel to Cleveland; by a surprising piece of luck, she obtained a duplex at 23 Fitzroy Road, in the house where Yeats had lived as a child and which had been the object of her most ardent desires two years before, when they lived in Chalcot Square. She started to sue for a divorce and, following the competent advice of her Massachusetts Egerias, she hired the services of a private detective to obtain evidence of adultery as grounds for a divorce, in spite of the fact that Ted Hughes was quite willing to grant it to her. She received the financial support of her American friends with whom her aunt Dotty, as if by magic, had come to join forces. She also hired the advice of a solicitor and an accountant who assured her that, as she was the forsaken spouse, she was perfectly justified in withdrawing all the money from their joint bank account. Ted Hughes, whom she regularly met in restaurants, was quite resigned to it, as much out of genuine indifference as because it could not be helped. As a last resort, he was obliged to borrow money from his own family to help him survive until they reached a final arrangement. He would then consent to pay an alimony of £1,000 per annum. He would also leave her the interest of a life insurance he had contracted for her benefit and which would now ensure her a guaranteed income. He also gave her the car, since she needed it for the children, and he himself had the use of an old round-eyed Ford van of the 1950s that Bill Merwin lent him. He used it to go and fetch a few potatoes and various pieces of furniture from Court Green, and indeed it pleased him to be thus obliged to burgle his own house. There was always a spinning rod in the back of his van to better his daily fare by poaching the big cannibal trout that feed on fish alone, in the blue dawn, when detectives are still asleep and slumbering herons reluctantly take their flight at your approach.

All things considered, he felt rather happy in his new bachelor's life. Alone, deep in his private thoughts, he would think back to all the episodes of his intellectual life, and he was saddened to realise the wide gap there was between what he might have been and what had become of him. When he looked back upon his youth, his reflections bore upon the way he had tried to shape himself by imposing rules on his life derived from his reading of Jung. He had thought that, if he strove methodically to hold back the conscious activity of his mind and keep clear of it as much as possible, his unconscious would necessarily compensate and resurface hale and strong; as a result, his poetic inspiration could not fail to develop: the logic of this deduction he deemed undeniable. There were seven rules of life that had enabled him to build a screen in favour of the visionary turn of his deeper self, to which he had enjoyed such free access as a child. But he now felt that his fear, no doubt a little foolish, of losing touch with his inner self, as well as the defence he had so painstakingly erected against it at great cost to himself, had been a hindrance of sorts, neutralising in part the force and agility of his mind that would have stood him in good stead to keep control of the vicissitudes of his life. It was a little as if he had perpetually been a stranger to himself. The idea which had been his, during his student's years, of inventing, as Pessoa had done before him, literary personae with whom he could play at will, had never really left his mind. And yet it seemed to him that he had never had more than two of them. The internal dialogue that he had with an alter ego who shared all his secrets when he roamed the Yorkshire countryside had found its application in literature. When he now considered his experience as an author, he could see clearly that there were two poets in him. One of them exerted an iron discipline upon himself, attempting to make a detailed, objective description of the world, while the other indulged his whims freely, allowing him all sorts of experiences, taking all sorts of liberties. At home in these split residences, he resembled many an English poet, and, in more ways than one, the Bard himself, but also all the anonymous poets since Caedmon had spoken the dialect of the tribe. Moreover, he saw it as a consequence of his Puritan education. The dourness of Protestantism had left him alone to cope with a moral law dictated by his deep-down convictions. He was quite aware that his poems were produced by either of the two poets that he harboured in himself, or by both of them felicitously entwining their voices. Whatever the case, such considerations had to be kept jealously private, for they touched on the secret of his poetic mint.

At about Christmas 1962, with her heart still wavering between her two loves, Assia went back to live with her husband. Ted and Sylvia were seeing each other more and more often. Sylvia had thinned a lot. She was now wearing her hair long, plaited in braids rolled on top of her head above a fringe because she thought it gave her a German look. They were no longer sure of what they were to think of each other. Ted Hughes found Sylvia Plath sometimes coldly aggressive and firmly determined to get a divorce, and at other times extremely desirous of a reconciliation. Ted sometimes seemed charming to her and sometimes unbearable. As she was in great need of money, he gave her as much as he possibly could, but some inexplicable reflex of prudence made him set down all these sums in a notebook. Then, after January 14th 1963, there came a great change. On this day, he had been invited to a cocktail party held for the launching of *The Bell Jar*, a novel that Sylvia Plath was publishing with Heinemann under the pen-name Victoria Lucas. Around that time, they were seeing each other several times a week though it was not easy for them to communicate. For Sylvia was still without a tele- phone, and she had to queue up in the cold to make a call from a public booth. The winter was one of the coldest in recent memory. They both went on expedi- tions for food in Devon that took up the whole day, on roads that were often icy and sometimes covered with snow, until the Morris refused to start; Ted fortunately had the knack for coaxing his borrowed Ford into action. One day he had ran over a hare, which pro- vided him with food for several days and a pair of slippers that he made with its fur. The streets of Lon- don had to be cleared of snow nearly every day; the whole city was paralysed by power failures and gas cuts; water-pipes burst because of the frost. People died of cold in a strange silence, all sounds muffled by the cruel wadding of winter. In February, Sylvia and the children had to go and shelter from the cold at a friends' house which was better heated than her own. She also came to visit Ted Hughes at 110 Cleve- land Road. She found lying on his desk a sort of ghost, but a strangely real one: the very same Shakes- peare, bound in red leather, that she thought she had destroyed two years before. When she opened it, she found in the front an inscription from Assia who, she realised, had replaced the book she had wasted for Ted. She shut it down without a word. Then there was a sunny winter morning when she burst into tears, saying that the divorce business was merely a bluff. But what about him? Did he believe in her? Did he promise to meet her in the summer in their home, under the yellow laburnums? Yes, three times yes had been his answer. Deep down he felt it would be even sooner. Ted was ready to go back to Court Green with Sylvia and to take up their family life. It would only be a matter of weeks, he was sure, of days perhaps. Then, three days later, in the morning of February 11th the telephone rang. Sylvia was dead. She had turned on the gas, then she had gone to sleep, her head inside the oven, having blocked up the door of the children's bedroom in which she had prudently placed some food. On her working table he found a typed collection of her last poems and her hand-written journal. There was also a poem by Ted Hughes: "Full Moon and Little Frieda", in which the child discovers the moon at the same time as the name for it: *Moon! Moon!* Was it not what the wolves of the zoo at Regent's Park were howling now in the cold night?

V

THE CROW YEARS

Sylvia's death was reported to the coroner as is the legal practice in such cases. Ted had to go to the Camden Town mortuary to identify the corpse of his wife and he asked Al Alvarez to accompany him for this last farewell to Sylvia Plath. The burial was deferred for a few days to allow Aurelia and Warren Plath the necessary time to arrive from the States. It took place at Heptonstall churchyard where most members of the Hughes family were buried. Ted's sorrow was shot through with surprise, because her death seemed so much in contradiction with the impression he retained from her last visit a few days before. Later he would think that he had discovered evidence that she was allergic to Parnate, a tranquilliser prescribed by Dr Horder who had treated her depression without having been fully informed of all her medical antecedents. Hughes was also trying to fight off a feeling of guilt which seemed to him particularly unjustified as he thought he had very nearly been reconciled with Sylvia just before. Obstinately, the same thought recurred telling him he could have saved her; that, had he been present by her side, the tragedy would have been avoided. Perhaps she had not really wanted to die. Perhaps she'd thought they would once more find her in time, since she had taken the precaution of leaving her doctor's phone number plainly visible by her side. But perhaps, too, she'd had only her children in mind. He was firmly convinced she'd been asking for help, and he reproached himself for having been unable to hear her call. He moved to 23 Fitzroy Road, into the flat that Sylvia had painted blue all over, only because she knew he disliked the colour. Her aunt Hilda came over to help him take care of Frieda, then aged three, and of Nicholas who was but three months old at the time. Then Assia joined him; to the indignation of Aunt Hilda who thought it scandalous that such things should be possible; as a result he had to find a nurse to replace her.

Ted Hughes was thirty-three years old, the age at which, it was supposed, Christ went to Calvary, and he felt as though he had been crucified. Sleep seemed to have deserted him for good, as he lay on his back at night, nailed to his bed by a stabbing pain in his left shoulder, the same, he felt, that a hanged man must endure. He saw this as the sign that in the invisible world of spirits which was for him the reverse side of conscious life, never seen but always present, he occupied the position of Prometheus, chained to his rock by divine punishment; more exactly, he was like one half of a pig's carcass hanging from a butcher's hook, with absolutely no hope whatsoever of being rescued or redeemed. During these days of intense suffering, when pain made him blind to the possible consequences of his words, he was to write to Aurelia Plath, somewhat imprudently, saying that if there was such a thing as an afterlife, he would certainly be among the damned. The wolves howling in the night in the zoo nearby, in the town stunned with cold, seemed in the icy air to have broken into a chant to console him and his two motherless children, as if by some strange animal empathy they had somehow sensed their grief. But he would write in "The Howling of Wolves" that it is a senseless song, a haunting primordial cry disconnected from the world, expressing nothing but absurd desire and the painful meaninglessness of being a survivor. Hadn't Sylvia died two days before the Ides of March which marked the opening of the Lupercalia in ancient Rome, the adopted daughter of the she-wolf which had suckled the founders of the city, the twins Remus and Romulus whose mother was Rhea Silvia?

The poems in the typescript entitled *Ariel,* that Sylvia left as her only testament, contained the same number of poems as *Lupercal*, which placed it under the supposedly favourable auspices of the collection of poems that had made Ted famous. As he read on, so his conviction grew that these poems were such as to ensure their author's immortality, that this poetry was, so to speak, the permanent soul of Sylvia Plath. Since their author had died without making a will and since Ted Hughes happened to be her sole heir, free to deal with them as he liked, he would soon publish them, though at first in a slightly different order. He was also discovering her journal and her correspondence; he spent many a long sleepless night poring over them attentively. Admittedly, certain of the poems described him in very hostile terms. He was in a constant state of anger when he realised the extent to which the women who had written to her from the States had been poking their noses into their marital problems. Ruth Beuscher and Olive Prouty, as well as to a lesser extent Aurelia Plath, had been insistently pressing her to divorce, all the while giving her plenty of advice on how to better her financial interests. Here was a sufficient explanation of the surprising shifts in Sylvia's feelings towards him, swinging pendulum-like from a desire for reconciliation which he believed had been sincere, to an inexplicably grim determination to divorce him. And yet, when he read her journal, he was stirred to the very depths of his being by the viciousness of the resentment that she had nurtured against him. The hatred that spilled over from some of the last pages she had written left him stunned, in a daze, unable to react, like a boxer caught off his guard. Assia shared his state of mind, as she read the same pages, sitting silent by his side, as if hypnotised by the spell that this dead woman was casting upon her from beyond the grave. The damage was such that Ted soon decided to keep this last copybook concealed, even letting it be known, that he had destroyed it to put an end to any further questions.

In the days that followed, the shock was so brutal that, in order to draw him out of the nervous prostration in which the discovery had plunged him and to try at all costs to surmount this impossible mourning, Assia invited a few friends to 23 Fitzroy Road. Many years later, *The Independent* published an article about a funerary gathering of a special sort, of a questionable taste; though it has never been firmly established, the article was to contribute to the blackening of Ted Hughes's reputation. Be that as it may, he continued to be seen everywhere in the company of Assia, until many of his friends from before distanced themselves from him. The fact that some people were openly turning their backs upon them hurt Assia more than Ted, who tried to retreat into indifference. They were both visibly perished with shame, and they could be seen for a while going out in London, in a gesture of defiance, perhaps. They formed a shadowy couple with wan faces, blaming each other for the tragedy. Then David Wevill returned at last from Canada, where he had gone to look after his dying mother, and once more Assia went back to live with him. Ted Hughes put Court Green up for sale, letting it meanwhile to Sylvia's friends Elizabeth and David Compton. He left his children in the care of his aunt Hilda and made arrangements in anticipation of his mother-in-law's visit due to take place in June. He wrote asking her to try, as far as possible, to spare the children the weight of her own grief. However, he would soon realise that Aurelia had come with the purpose of persuading him to consent to her taking her grandchildren back with her to the States, where they could be brought up properly in a decent American school. He was to learn later that she had secretly contacted Dr Holder, who had been Sylvia's and her children's doctor, to ask him to help her realise her project. To this end, she had explained that what she had seen in Yorkshire had given her some fears as to her son-in-law's ability to assume the role of a responsible father. Dr Holder had been wise enough to ignore her demand, and Ted Hughes, for his part, had confined himself to holding his ground. But there were few things that he could have wished for less than this project of hers, for he had always been of opinion that Aurelia's anxious possessiveness had played no small part in Sylvia's neurosis. In the future, he would do all he could to protect his children from it, and the first step that he took to this purpose was to prudently maintain good diplomatic relationships with their American grand-mother.

Ted Hughes was now thinking of going to live in Yorkshire. Quite early in his search, he located the estate of Lumb Bank, a gentleman's residence dating from the 18th century, halfway between Heptonstall and Hebden Bridge, standing in 17 acres of wood and open grassland. He could fell the trees in order to set up a plantation of firs that he would sell as Christmas trees and use the grazing land to raise cattle. He hesitated, however, to take the plunge because the house was not very far from that of his parents who, he was sure, would never accept his coming to live so close to them with another man's wife. There were even risks that it would mean his mother's death, for any additional worry would certainly aggravate her already very bad state of health that was all the more preoccupying for not being related to any well identified cause. He thought of founding a community there as Coleridge and Southey had once wanted to do in Pennsylvania. The notion was much in fashion then but, for various reasons, it never got done. Then, when a sale agreement for Court Green fell through at the last moment, he decided to go back and live there. His sister Olwyn convinced him to do so when she decided to resign her job in Paris and come back on purpose to keep house for her brother and look after the children; that is what she did for the two following years.

That Summer, between a brief trip to Germany and the First Arts Council International Poetry Festival at the Queen Elizabeth Hall, Ted Hughes received a review copy of the English version of Mircea Eliade's book *Shamanism and the Archaic Techniques of Ecstasy*. He learned in it how, in this form of religion peculiar to certain tribes of Siberia and North America the shamans, as these wizards or medicine-men are called, go through psycho-somatic crises in which they undergo a disintegration and recomposition of body and soul. They have no choice but to repeat these harrowing experiences as otherwise they would fall gravely ill, sometimes even mortally so. But they thus become acutely responsive to the world of spirits; they acquire a further knowledge of this world through a methodical training under the guidance of older shamans. They are afterwards obliged to shamanise very often to guard against the return of fatal illness. Ted Hughes was deeply interested in the famous Romanian anthropologist's, having read his *Treatise of Religions* during his third year in Cambridge. He indeed perceived a profound analogy between the flight of the shaman, in the particular crisis during which his personality is shattered and reassembled, and the sort of death in life into which he had been plunged by Sylvia's suicide and from which he now glimpsed the way out. Besides, it seemed to him that there was only a difference of degree, not of nature, between this dreadful ordeal and the recurrent bouts of chronic depression that had regularly plagued him for many years. Was it not the same thing as the descent into the infernal regions that Orpheus had made to rescue his Eurydice, or that of Dante guided by his Beatrice, and of so many other poets besides? It was quite possible that those shamanic practices described by Mircea Eliade were, in essentials, basically the same as the secret of poetic genius, if not the very secret itself. Hughes shared the view that there was a close relationship between bouts of depression and poetic inspiration with his friend Lucas. At the time, they were reading and discussing the poetry of Frederico Garcia Lorca and his essay on *duende*. A profoundly Spanish notion, the word designates the irrational earthly spirit, a peculiar way of playing with death which manifests itself best in music, dancing and also bull-fighting. True poetry, it seemed, poetry that takes the poet on the uphill climb to the top of Parnassus, had first to be brought up from the underworld. It could only be conquered by repeated passages through the cavernous jaws of madness and death.

Hughes's notebooks during these years were covered with hysterically gaping animals' heads, full of sharp-pointed teeth, of birds whose bills were drawn open to tearing point. The obsession with the female sex that these drawings betrayed showed how, for Hughes, the doors of the underworld were connected in his imagination to the doors of birth. In one of the most powerful poems of *Lupercal*, "Mayday on Holderness", he had described poetic inspiration as something that could only be found beyond death or in some antenatal limbo by a return journey into the regions where the souls of the dead meet with those of the children yet to be born. Hades, from which Persephone came back every year in the spring, was for him no more than the place outside time and space, the *illud tempus* of which Mircea Eliade spoke so eloquently, that the so-called primitive people knew so well, but that western civilisation had purely and simply occluded, amputating thereby one half of its own consciousness. He had found the same notion in Huxley, whom he had read again and again in Boston, in an America that wanted so much to forget the existence of the world of spirits. In *The Doors of Perception,* a title that Huxley borrowed from William Blake, he writes about his own experiments with mescaline and LSD. But as Hughes said to the Hungarian poet Janos Csokits, one does not enter into poetry through the back door. To his mind, drugs were no more than a sort of psychedelic tourism. They ensured an illiterate ignoramus outside the poetic fold could enjoy a free ticket for a trip into very secret regions, whose keys and maps were only known to a very ancient form of wisdom that was now partly obliterated or lost. Poetry that deserved its name was compelled to stake its claim to this heritage, which had been submerged beneath the deluge set loose by the need to perceive the world objectively. Yet there were still obscure forces, malignant energies that he liked to call simply spirits working with a viciousness that was boosted by our denying their existence.

He was now back at Court Green, surrounded by his children and assisted by his sister, and he returned to his old quarters in the vast attic room, beneath the thatched roof. The table on which he worked was a thick board of elm wood over two yards long, salvaged from a disused mill and laid on two barrels. Sylvia's manuscripts lay on another table, but he had already noticed that certain pages were missing. Before he moved his belongings and those of Sylvia from the flat in Fitzroy Road, things had begun to disappear: her books, but also her personal linen, things bearing her signature and her initials. The lesson he learnt from this was double: first, that Sylvia's manuscripts were already worth money, that they would soon be worth a fortune, and that he could not indefinitely postpone their publication. Her death had irresistibly set on the course to her posthumous fame. It was as if her spirit was impatient to obtain justice. But, meanwhile, life must go on. He had his children to attend to. He compared himself to Pushkin, for he was now obliged to write above all to support his family. In January, he received an invoice for the rent of the flat in Fitzroy Road. In February, he refused an offer from Syracuse University in New York for Sylvia Plath's manuscripts. His poem for children on the Loch Ness monster, *Nessie the Mannerless Monster,* was due to appear in April. As he was particularly eager to learn as much as possible on folk tales, he wrote to magazines asking if he could be sent review copies, as far as possible, of everything being published in the field. Among other things, this critical activity afforded him the opportunity of defending astrology against general opinion and more specifically, against Puritan Christianity, but also of discovering the English translations of the novels by Isaac Bashevis Singer, a New York author writing in Yiddish, about Jewish life in his native Poland before the war, and Hassidic beliefs derived from the Cabbala; these greatly interested Hughes, because they privileged prayer over study. This extensive reading was nourishing an intellectual transformation, slowly nurturing the second phase of his poetic career.

He was very deliberately turning to earlier periods in English history. He was also curious about literatures that were not directly linked to English civilisation, with which he felt, more and more clearly, that he was at variance if not in downright conflict. In 1963, at a New Year's Eve party, he advanced the idea that it would be a salutary shock to publish English translations of the works of foreign poets in one way or another, to hustle this too provincial nation out of its insularity. His friend Daniel Weissbort took him at his word and founded a literary magazine called *Modern Poetry in Translation* with the object of making poems written in other languages, primarily by poets of eastern Europe who were considered as dissidents in their own countries, available in English. The magazine was thus to publish and bring into public notice the works of the Polish writers Tadeusz Roszievich and Zbigniew Herbert, but also of the Czech poet Miroslav Holub, the Yugoslav Vaska Popa, then of Nadeshda Mandelstam, Akmatova, Bulgakov, and many others besides. Behind the enterprise, there was of course the avowed ideological intention of opposing those totalitarian regimes that they regarded as the most regrettable apotheoses of the narrow-minded rationalist spirit. It was this, they believed, that had swamped humanity, causing it to err out of its proper evolution path; an error that, they hoped, might still be remedied. For there was in Hughes a deep-seated desire to change things through literature, prompting him to act via his poems upon the ideas, both conscious and unconscious, of his contemporaries and of generations to come. But if his determination was strong, he knew very well that his chances of success depended much upon discretion. Moreover, there was nothing naive or irresponsible about the influence he wished to have in shaping the intellectual climate in England, and he was quite aware of the undesirable right-wing dangers that might lurk behind a certain romantic celebration of brute force. At this period of his life, when he set his mind on exerting an action through his writings on the ideological climate of the times, he met Henry Williamson, the author of *Tarka the Otter*, a best-selling novel for children in the pre-war years. Ted had once received a copy of the book as a school prize at Mexborough. In the novel, Williamson described the life of a young otter in terms extolling the innocent violence of predatory animals. It was an idea with which Hughes had some sympathy, but he would never make the same mistake as Williamson and indeed he condemned his going astray in the direction of right-wing politics, that so regrettably caused him to throw in his lot with the handful of people who would have liked to do in England what Hitler had done in Germany. Hughes had a fundamental horror of dictators and instinctively abhorred all the different constraints that society tends to impose on individuals. He was a typical member of the rural middle class — enduringly attached to the land and individualist to the core — which had long been the power base of the conservative party.

The same year, no doubt because it felt it had a natural affinity with the underlying theme of his poetry, the University of Vienna brought him a ready-made answer to his financial difficulties by granting him a £1,500 annuity for a period of five years to pursue his poetic activities as he thought best. He was again free to tend his garden. When he was not studying folk tales he found relaxation in mowing grass with a scythe as in the old days. He was also taking time to play with his children, and he felt legitimately proud of the great strength of character of his son Nicholas, a hefty boy who did not shirk a fight, who would not allow anyone to tread on his toes any more than the stubborn Yorkshire lad that Ted had never ceased to be. As canny with his money as a Scotsman or, for that matter, any good Englishman worthy of the name, Ted Hughes availed himself of every opportunity to make his pile. He would, for instance, make fair copies of his own poems on purpose to put them on sale. He was doing business with a certain Winifred Myers, a London dealer in articles for bibliophiles and autographic documents. In February, she had sold some manuscripts of his poems for him at prices varying from ten to twenty-five pounds each. The "Pike" manuscript, for instance, was among those fetching the highest prices because the poem was then considered as probably the best that Ted Hughes had yet written. Alas, one of Mrs Meyers's assistants had forgotten to add the ten per cent profit margin for the dealer on the customer's invoice, and the sum was charged to Ted Hughes who, as a result of this mishap, lost twenty pounds. Upon receipt of the amputated sum the poet lost no time taking up his pen to write personally to the buyer, asking him to pay him back the twenty pounds. The collector, who very appropriately answered to the name of Gold, was much surprised to see his idol suddenly knocked off his pedestal, descending to the vulgarity of such "a sordid incident"; he declared himself shocked by the proposal and proposed in return to send back the "Pike" manuscript, which the poet accepted, convinced that its price was sure to rise in the future.

In May, a couple of ravens took up residence in one of the elms standing on the opposite side of the courtyard. They had surprisingly built two nests but were using only one of them. Ted was fascinated by the strange splendour of their deep harsh call, so sad and so desolate. Assia, always irresolute, had once again gone to live with her legitimate and tolerant husband, forever wondering if it was really possible to love two men at the same time. But she soon found herself pregnant and there was no doubt that Ted was the father. It indeed seemed to the poet that he would never be done with getting tied up with the female tribe; and he found it strange that although his sister had placed herself at his service to take care of his children and promote his poetry he did not proceed more briskly with his work. The anxiety born of such a situation seemed to him to be best summed up in the Portuguese proverb which held that the wolf will eat the donkey that has many masters. However, he found a certain relief in the tusks and pelts of animals and other talismans that he asked his brother Gerald to send him, and whose presence in his house could but have some effect on his creative energies. To escape the boredom of living permanently in the country and to renew the dual life he liked so much, he took lodgings at Chalk Farm in April, always in the same district of London, though this time, a little further north of Primrose Hill. In July, he seized the opportunity of a change of air and went to the poetry festival of Spoleto in Italy where he met a whole array of contemporary poets. The Chilean poet Pablo Neruda was there, but also the Austrian Ingeborg Bachmann, the Russian Yevgueni Yevtushenko, the Hungarian Gyula Juhasz, the Czech Miroslav Holub, and a large number of those whose works were being published, in translation, in Daniel Weissbort's magazine. He even caught sight of Ezra Pound, but the old fascist, always the showman, just put in an appearance, draped in marble silence.

Once back in Devon, he was soon to learn that the Washington University Library, which was desirous of acquiring all his manuscripts, was asking him to name his price. If things had already gone that far, what heights would the bidding reach if only he had the patience to wait a few years more. In the immediate future he had to face the much less promising prospect of a daily life fraught with difficulties. Edith had had a heart attack, and from then onwards her health had gone from bad to worse until his parents had come to live with him. They were both at a loose end since Billy Hughes had retired and put his business up for sale. Gerald, sensing that Ma was seriously ill, made an unplanned visit from Australia, and his return seemed for a time to restore Ma's health. Soon after, Assia also came to live at Court Green, much to the dismay of the other guests, not to mention the fact that the overcrowding in the North Tawton house did not allow Ted much leisure to write. The number of letters he received from his readers had increased so much that he had stopped answering them. A woman admirer from Nottingham had written saying that she did not know if it was considered acceptable to importune living poets to ask them what they had wanted to say but she did absolutely want to know how to pronounce one particular word in such particular poem. At Glasgow University a disagreement had arisen among teachers marking papers over the interpretation to be given to one of his verses. Could he please settle the dispute? Some journalists wanted to interview him, less to have him speak about himself than to weed out some details of his life with Sylvia Plath, which he would always make out as an ideal of complementariness. There were also poetry readings to be made for a national children's poetry competition organised by the *Daily Mirror*. All in all, he had no time left to concentrate his energies on the poetry he would have liked to write.

In March 1965, on a day when a vexing snowstorm further deferred the laggard spring, Assia bore him a daughter whom they officially named Alexandra Tatiana Elise but whom they would call Shura. Ted Hughes, much moved but also made happy by the birth, was surprised to see his handwriting suddenly change without his knowing why. The same month saw the publication of *Ariel*, a collection of Sylvia Plath's poems that he himself had set in order. He set off with Assia and the children for a long stay in Ireland, then they went abroad for a boat trip on the Rhine. His poetry notebooks were never far from hand. On some pages, on which Frieda had once written down questions from Sunday School, Ted jotted down free verse considerations on the proper way to create poetry. One had, he wrote, to forget words, forget oneself, forget the world. The world of spirits could not be raided. A stable and lasting relation had to be established with the inner world, and for that one had to turn away from the world of things, the worthless outside world. In the interviews he gave to journalists he would explain that his poems did not speak of violence but of vitality. If he had chosen to write about animals, he said, it was because in human beings vital animal energy had no occasion to manifest itself, particularly in the too well-groomed English civilisation in which all expression of feelings was being kept in check, and the satisfaction of certain desires, no less genuine for running counter to all those artificially contrived properties, were always strongly refrained. His attachment to his Yorkshire accent had the same origin. His dream was to write a type of poetry that would be an equivalent of dialect English, a language closer to essential truth than the standard English, with its refined vocabulary and county pronunciation, that was rife in schools and at the BBC.

In September, he was planning to take up residence in Ireland, preferably in the West, because of its still intact nature; his idea was, in part, to find conditions of life more favourable to his writing but also to preserve his children from what he referred to as "this rotten English civilisation." In English schools they would necessarily be exposed to the materialist ideology that had so much hurt his feelings at Cambridge. Ireland would be just ideal for them because they would continue to be brought up in the English language, but out of England and away from the English people, whom he viewed as having become besotted with the enervating blandishments of the consumer society. It was above all necessary that his children should grow up in an English-speaking environment that would be closer to nature. But he was adamant that they should not end up speaking that devitalised English, that "paralysed English" which was such a pain for his ears when he heard it pronounced by so many young men and women of the new generation. So, at the beginning of the following year, he settled in Connemara, on the West coast of the Republic of Ireland, in the county of Galway, where for two Irish pounds per week he rented a house contiguous to a farm. Looking out of his window, he could see, beyond the moor, the bay of Cleggan and the Atlantic ocean. Assia and the children were perfectly happy.

Shura was very beautiful and very mature for her age; her horoscope was surprisingly concentrated, so much so that, had it been a male horoscope, something extraordinary might have been predicted. He would deny, however, that he attached too much importance to these astrological remarks, and he said more than once that the interest he took in them was merely pseudo-scientific, since exceptional people did sometimes have quite an ordinary personal horoscope. Therefore, he did not waste much time studying the stars, and set to work for many long unbroken weeks to the silent sound of the wind and the retreating roar of the sea a little further off. Everything here was much less expensive than in England. He had resumed his dear habit of getting up before dawn to go and catch fish for his family. In England his parents, having at last succeeded in selling their shop, were a little more serene, and his sister had taken up another job in London.

But, once again, money was scarce. Barclay's Bank wrote, warning him that he had a one hundred and fifteen pounds overdraft that would have to be set right as soon as possible. Perhaps the sale of a few manuscripts would be enough to cover it. In any case, the Cleggan house was only at their disposal until March. So, after a week in London and a detour via Edinburgh for a poetry festival, he took his whole tribe, as he said, of five people including himself, directly to Germany, where a university had invited him to come and spend a few months as poet in residence. Then he came back home to deal with his inescapable mail, and also to have his photograph taken for Faber & Faber, who would no longer tolerate the odd quirk of his of refusing to have his picture taken. Then, Nicholas and Frieda went to spend their holidays with their grandmother in America. In the autumn, Ma was again hospitalised with pneumonia. Ted was preparing himself to the idea that, from now on, his parents would be living in his house. It really looked as if his own existence was fated to slip out of his control, all the more so because the posthumous success that had come to Sylvia Plath gave him the impression of living in a mausoleum. A second edition of *The Bell Jar* had just come out, no longer under the pen-name of Victoria Lucas but under the author's real name. At the same time, in what one might have been tempted to see as a sign of sorts, he could no longer lay his hands on a single copy of *Lupercal*, and he was naturally led to the conclusion that they must have been pinched, one after the other, down to the last copy. By friends, no doubt, since none but his friends ever came into his attic. It was as if, at Court Green, the literary objects of some value were growing legs or wings, since they so unaccountably disappeared. The feeling of guilt mixed with resentment that the memory of Sylvia Plath inevitably brought in its wake found for a time a strange echo in the deleterious misogyny of Tolstoy, at a time when he was reading *The Kreutzer Sonata* and experiencing a renewal of his passion for Beethoven. This reading inspired him to write a poem that he judged good enough to be included in his next collection. He had spent long hours drawing the portrait of the Russian author, copying a photograph, and then dedicated it to Assia. The rest of the time, despite Olwyn's return in London to act as his literary agent, he still had to deal with far too abundant a correspondence, especially since he had set about contacting a whole galaxy of poetic luminaries with a view to inviting them to a poetry festival organised by the Poetry Book Society.

However, his finances were soon to be in better shape, owing to Olwyn's expert management. For instance, she had insisted that the £1,000 fixed salary he was to receive to translate Seneca's *Oedipus* for the stage manager Peter Brook be raised to nearly £400 a week. Meanwhile, on the domestic front, the situation continued to deteriorate, for hostilities were being reopened between Assia and his parents. Billy Hughes was decidedly allergic to her international English accent, which he found unbearably affected. It reached a point when, on certain days, Assia and Shura would have their meals separately while Ted would take his with his parents. The house was full of wailing and gnashing of teeth against which the attic itself did nor afford enough protection. His writing suffered much from this state of affairs and his poetic responses seemed to run dry. The crisis was at its worst when the overcrowding in the house reached its peak with the arrival of aunt Hilda and cousin Vicky. Ma was distraught even before they arrived, and Ted and Assia had to go and rent a room in a hotel for a few days to get away from the tension that was becoming truly unbearable. He was beginning to understand, he said, how Buddha had reached the stage of giving up on everything and had gone to find refuge in the jungle. At last, despairing of any other issue, and in the hope of recovering some peace, he let Assia go back to London. He then retired to work in a garden shed that his father had built with clapboards painted green. For some time now he had been thinking of writing what he called crow poems, which would be a sort of literary analogue of the voice of the large black birds that had made their nests in his elm trees. The vague project took more precise shape when Leonard Baskin, an artist with whom he had felt a bond of sympathy when they had met in Boston, sent him drawings of birds in black ink, asking him if he could not write a sequence of poems to go with them. Hughes had developed such a passionate interest in the distinctive myths of the North American Natives, in which the crow plays the role of a trickster, he perceived at once how he could make use of his documentation and of the reflections he had accumulated on folk tales.

While this new work was in hand, he corrected the proofs of a third collection just about to be published. He had assembled a sufficient number of poems for a volume that he proposed to Faber & Faber to be published under the title *Wodwo*. The word was an allusion to one of the best known poems of English medieval literature, *Sir Gawain and the Green Knight*, in which is briefly evoked, among the savage adversaries that the Christian knight has to fight, a man of the woods, a vague reminder of a satyr or a faun, halfway between man and beast, called *wodwo* in the North-Western dialect of the 14th century. The wodwo that Ted Hughes endows in his poem with the faculty of speech is a being whose consciousness of the world is not the sort of rational objectivity that, in the Western world, seems to define a human being. It is, one might say, an entity that cannot quite separate its own self, its body even, from the things that surround him. The *wodwo* is in fact a proto-shamanistic state of mind: that of a shaman whose return from the world of spirit was imperfect and who would remain on the threshold of the sort of consciousness that characterises ordinary human beings. It is also the very structure of the collection named after the character that gives an extra resonance to the journey into hell, comparable to the catabasis that Eliade speaks of in his book on shamanism. The first part of the book comprises poems in the vein of *Lupercal* or of *The Hawk in the Rain*. The second part is a succession of short stories to which has been adjoined the radio play *The Wound*, whose two main characters have been sent into the world of the dead, from which one will come back and the other not. The third part, whose tailpiece is "Wodwo", also contains such poems as "The Full Moon and Little Frieda" and "Wolf Howl", but a quite different voice can be heard in it, which might be that of another poet. A note is sounded that already announces the voice of Crow, sarcastic and full of black humour, which does not bother either to please or to displease, but exerts on the reader a strong fascination, only equalled by its radical originality in English poetry. A fine example is the short poem "Theology" which asserts in three small unornamented quatrains in free verse that it was not Eve who yielded to the snake's charms; she was simply eaten by him after having herself eaten Adam who had eaten the apple. Our world today is but the bowel of the snake, indifferent to the vain protest of God. Then, in a chilling triptych, the Beast of the Apocalypse addresses the reader as the new Messiah: it is Gog, so called in memory of Gog and Magog who stand in the Bible for the archetypal enemy of Israel. In the centre, Death reigns over a world of dust that has returned to dust. On the third panel, Saint George the dragon-slayer, the Christian knight, the perfect type of Western man, is represented as an iron warrior riding full gallop on a horse shod with iron vaginas, desperately and endlessly striving to escape the gaping mouth of hell

The critics did not fail to point out that a split was clearly to be observed in *Wodwo*, a fact most of them regretted. It was as if Ted Hughes could no longer conceal the secret of a break in his poetic voice, and perhaps in his personality as well. His readers could not but notice what, on the face of it, looked like the stages of an evolution in his writing towards something more in accordance with the tone of modernist poetry. It had visibly no longer anything to do with the anti-modern, even reactionary tone of the nature poetry and animal descriptions that had until now been Ted Hughes's trademark. Rare indeed were those who would have thought of using the adjective Parnassian when speaking of *Wodwo*. One such exception was Donald Davie, one of the main figures of the Movement that, in the years immediately following the end of the war, had wanted to acclimatise the notion of neo-classicism. Risking a comparison of Ted Hughes with Leconte de Lisle, he said that what he meant by such an epithet was that the collection contained anthology pieces. But, if he had wanted to say that it was a purely formalist exercise of art for art's sake he could not have been more wrong. For behind these poems there was manifestly a revolt and a radical questioning of the time-honoured values of English society that, in some of its pages, might well send a chill down the spine of its readers. A few months later, Ted Hughes would explain to Janos Csokits that *Wodwo* marked a turning point in his poetic career. He considered that after a first period privileging the relationship with the outside world, the world of nature, he had felt something like a demand, or rather an order or an injunction coming from another world. He thought that he had refused to obey this command at first or, perhaps, that he had not understood it soon enough, so that he had tarried too long before doing what poetry demanded that he should do. He had paid, he thought, a high price for his refusal and his negligence. The price had been a psychological collapse and a nearly total destruction of his energy, that had left him in a sort of animal lethargy. Perhaps he was himself the wodwo, after all, living below the human condition, returning painfully from hell to bear witness to its existence. He then went on to explain that, in the second part of the book, the short story "The Rain Horse", in which the protagonist is fleeing in the pouring rain, chased by a horse right into a wood, was a metaphor of this request and of his refusal. But now that *Wodwo* was at last published, he suddenly felt exempt from all the difficulties that he had experienced in his writing during the last seven years. The poems that he wrote now came to him much more easily than they had done for years. The wodwo had been the larva from which crow developed. It was a slow metamorphosis. The bird at last spread its wings: he felt an excitement that he did not quite dare taste to the full, for fear that it might bring ill luck.

Whether he worked in his attic or in his garden shed, whose door he always carefully left padlocked so that his manuscripts should not make a bolt for it, Ted Hughes covered page after page of his exercise books, glad to find that poetry was coming to him of itself, as if dictated by the funny bird, which seemed to want to take him to unknown regions whose existence he would never have imagined without it. But Assia still could not come back without Ma manifesting her visceral disapprobation by mysteriously falling ill one way or another. Then, by an annoying coincidence, Ted put out one of his vertebrae. As the prejudices he entertained against modern science included traditional medicine, he preferred to call for help upon a bonesetter. The quack played havoc with his spine, leaving him worse than ever, unable to move and half stoned with useless drugs. Stiff with pain, he at last agreed to be dragged to an osteopath's. There it transpired, that nine of his vertebrae were supposedly disjointed, and it was an excruciating job to set them right. After a week's rest he had still to endure physiotherapy exercises so that the crow was of necessity reduced to silence. Ted Hughes took advantage of this imposed break to finalise things with his correspondents concerning the international poetry festival he had agreed to organise for the PBS at the Queen Elizabeth Hall and at the Purcell auditorium on the South Bank. Among the participants there would be the French poet Yves Bonnefoy, who would have an English version of his choice of poems published in the autumn by Jonathan Cape. The American Allen Ginsberg did not have enough money to cross the Atlantic; Ted must absolutely advance him fifty pounds for his plane ticket, then Arnold Wesker would pay for his return journey. "Oh oh oh did you think of Pound?" wrote the exuberant beatnik, excited to the point of forgetting his exclamation marks. For no very clear reason, Ginsberg feared he might be refused entry in the United Kingdom. It was therefore necessary to check with the Home Office to ensure that there was no reason to refuse him entrance into the country. A few poets of the older generation, over-favoured by glory, like Basil Bunting, Robert Graves or Hugh MacDiarmid, found various reasons to decline what they may well have considered as a polite proposal to come and grace a festival in honour of the poets of the new generation. But Yehuda Amichai would be there and also Pablo Neruda, Giuseppe Ungaretti, Anne Sexton, John Berryman, Austin Clarke, and a long list of the stars of contemporary poetry who did not hesitate to regroup around the name and person of Ted Hughes.

In July, *The Scotsman* published a poem from *Crow* called "A Disaster" that metaphorically represented language as a calamity. A word, that is a sort of allegorical figure of language that crow perceives in the form of a giant lamprey or of a huge mushroom comes to empty nature of its substance, poison what is left of it and consume the human race, leaving a desert behind it. While Ted was thus gently preparing his readers for a change of style of which he had already given some signs, Assia, who was now settled in London in the working-class district of Clapham Common on the South Bank towards Brixton, was beginning to publish poems of her own in *The Observer, The London Magazine* and *The Atlantic Monthly*. She also worked with Ted at translating the Israeli poet Yehuda Amichaï from Hebrew for Cape Goliard. Their relationship could no longer be described in marital terms; it was very much now in the tone of the liberated life-style of the sixties. Hughes was also working with Peter Brook on the staging of his translation of Seneca's *Oedipus* and the production promised to be in the obscene vein characteristic of the period, with phallic totem, thirty-yard-long penis snake and final happening in the form of a gigantic orgy to the beat of tom-toms. Hughes was once more caught in the whirlwind of literary and artistic events, uncertain whether he preferred to go into a solitary retreat and produce immortal poetry or allow himself to be snatched into the hectic turmoil of the public scene. In any case, he understood that he did not really have the choice. The royalties from *Ariel* seemed likely to make his fortune but they obliged him, on the other hand, to adopt a certain attitude, if only to try and alter and if possible counter the image of himself that the posthumous glory of Sylvia Plath was inexorably building among the public. He was beginning to understand, though as yet in a confused way, that, born in the mental universe of Sylvia Plath, there now lived in her poetic work a dark and malevolent character who also bore the name of Ted Hughes and who, for the general public, was in no way distinct from himself. It would take him long before he fully realised that he was being haunted by his own ghost much more than by that of the memory of Sylvia Plath. He must continue to publish and to appear in public if he wanted to hold his ground on the literary stage, but he had to face the extra challenge of bracing himself in order to survive this death, while staying at the helm to maintain the course of his career and continue to exist by himself. At the same time he was publishing *Poetry in the Making,* a collection of theoretical texts written originally for a radio series, aiming at expounding in detail his own method of poetic creation. In it he developed the idea that poetry bore a resemblance to angling and hunting. But he insisted on the fact that poetry begins, above all, with a photographic observation of the outside world. All this, no doubt, did correspond to the Ted Hughes of the first period, for it was not difficult to see how the poems that he had published so far, and above all the first to have been published, might have been written along those lines. But these explanations did not at all fit the poetry he was practicing himself at the time for Crow, whose dark ironic eye that looked unresponsively through appearances, did not care a fig about objective delineation or the outside surface of the world

Just as the crows whose tricks he admired in his elms had more than one nest, Ted Hughes, it became increasingly clear, had more than one life. The independence that Assia had been more or less forced to take had made him free to come and go as he liked so that he could, as he felt inclined, now be a bachelor in his London flat in Chalk Farm and now a widower apparently living the life of a recluse in his retreat at Court Green. A combination of circumstances led him to establish friendly relations with Brenda, the wife of Trevor Hebden, a mature student in English literature at Exeter University, to whom he entrusted the care of his house whenever he went away for a long time. For instance, Trevor and Brenda came to live at Court Green with their children when Ted and Assia went to Ireland with theirs for a while. In due course, familiarity bred intimacy between Ted and Brenda. Trevor, like Ted, was a fervent supporter of liberated sex. All the same, quarrels between the jealous women at times raised the decibels in the house, and were not unconnected with Assia's departure. But this was only the beginning of the sentimental imbroglio, and the vaudeville plot thickened when Ted also started going out with a young girl from the village called Carol Orchard, the daughter of a neighbouring farmer. Rumour had it that he met her in an antique shop where he used to go now and again in search of old swords that he was sending to his brother Gerald in exchange for animal pelts. Ted Hughes liked to say that when he read D.H. Lawrence's novels it seemed to him that he was reading his own autobiography. But he shared far less in his mystique of monogamous union than in his articulate protest against the disastrous consequences of repressed sexuality. For Ted Hughes, this was part of a radical criticism of the staid and stuffy habits in which English society was hopelessly grounded, though, in his opinion, it would have everything to gain by being set afloat as soon as possible. In those years, Ted made no secret of his polygamous tendencies and he announced far and wide that he was determined never to fall into the power of a single woman again. One day when he had taken his children to the airport, he heard Nicholas and Frieda talking together while waiting for the plane that was to take them for a holiday to their grandmother's place at Wellesley; they agreed that the best solution would have been that he married the three women, so the three children would then have one mother each.

But being separated from his children, even for a little while, always severely depressed him. Their departure for the United-States in the summer of 1968 left him in a state of great distress. He indeed had no immediate scruples about leaving his children in Aurelia's care for a while, but he saw nonetheless that his anguish had serious ideological grounds. American civilisation seemed to him the apotheosis of Puritanism which he considered as responsible for all the misfortunes attending Western civilisation. Reformed Christianity, which had plainly climaxed in North America with its extravagantly urbanised mode of life, stood in his eyes as the institutionalised divorce of man from nature. The Reformation had paved the way for scientific empiricism which held that nothing existed but an outside world, a world of natural objects. He therefore considered Christianity responsible for the condemnation and the destruction of all that belonged to the realm of the spiritual, vital forces of nature. The natural energy active in sexual desire was precisely what the religion of Christ called the Devil. Since in Jung's theory objective rational thought is considered as the masculine part of the human psyche, just one more step was needed to convince oneself that the open war that was being waged between the world of things and the world of spirits was a clear case of the *animus* attempting to destroy the *anima*, of the feminine part of the psyche being oppressed by the masculine one, and it was, without any doubt, a Christian crusade. Had not the Puritans always persecuted witches and burned them at the stake? Had not Christ gone so far as to disown his mother, saying "woman, what have I to do with thee?" Was it not, again, in Christ's name that the misogynist Tolstoy had defended the idea of capital punishment for the woman suspected of adultery in *The Kreutzer Sonata*. However, it seemed to him that contemporary society was characterised by the dissolution of this Christian ideology and its baleful consequences, since the age was unmistakably in favour of a return to nature. Somewhat contradictorily, nuclear physics itself showed that science ended up invalidating empiricism, since the theory of relativity had proved that our realistic vision of the world erred wide of the mark. In the end, science confirmed the intuitions of the visionary poets of the past, chief among whom was William Blake. Besides, did not the radical incomprehension between man and woman, that had developed in western society, spring from the same root? The war that had been waged for thousands of years in the unconscious world of spirits was finally emerging into consciousness. It appeared more and more evident that the tragic incomprehension between Sylvia Plath and himself had its final explanation in this symbolic equation. The feeling of guilt and the responsibility in the death of Sylvia Plath were his. But it was also the reflection of a much deeper reality, the final outcome of the activity of spiritual forces far greater than them, for which they had been mere toys. Had Shakespeare not said that we are to the gods as flies to wanton boys? Be that as it may, during those days of anguish in the summer of 1968, Sylvia very often appeared in his dreams. On one of these occasions she had come back to see her children and spend a day and a night with them. They had gone together to dig a hole in the park of Smith College to bury her manuscripts. The traces that death had left on her were only visible on the photographs that were taken of her. She was the same as she had always been except for a sort of theatrical style informing her gestures. Just as he had been aware throughout his dream, when she had gone to sleep, at the end of that day spent among the living, it had been to return to the realm of the dead and never to come back. Another time, he thought he had seen her in an empty train in the underground, he had briefly looked aside and, when he wanted to look at her again, she was no longer there. Assia too thought she had seen Sylvia enter a tea room one day and make a move in her direction. Indeed, more and more often, she thought that she suddenly recognised her in the crowd.

The two lovers appeared on television to talk about the translation of Yehuda Amichai's poems, but Ted, in the course of time, had come to feel a little resentful towards Assia, tempted as he was to make her responsible for Sylvia's suicide. He became distant, affected even to lose interest in her, contacting her as little as possible. Assia was manifestly unable to bear the solitude to which she was confined. David had finally left her and taken a post at Austin University in Texas. Shura cried in her sleep and her cries depressed her mother. Then, wretched with grief, she would call Ted on the phone, but most of the time on the other end of the line she would hear the impassive voice of a man just as depressed as she was. Then she undertook a treatment to try to overcome her depression. At the beginning of 1969 it seemed that they were their normal selves again, and they even began to look for a house in the north of England. They often travelled by train with Shura. Ted composed certain *Crow* poems on the train, Assia and Shura sitting drowsily by his side, the three of them rocked by the obsessing sound of the wheels on the rails while the rain was being driven against the window panes and the desolate landscapes of England in winter endlessly glided past. Then one evening in March, Assia, feeling depressed, had called Ted, and he had not found the words to comfort her. Alone with her daughter in her flat in Clapham, she gave sleeping tablets to Shura, downed several whiskies herself, opened the gas, and the two of them went to sleep, their heads in the oven. She died like Sylvia, but she had taken her child with her into death.

As Ted Hughes learnt later, the idea of suicide had long been in Assia Gutman's mind, for she had made several wills. The presence of Shura had probably kept her long undecided, for she had stolen some of Sylvia's manuscripts and taken the precaution to send them to her sister Celia, instructing her to sell them at the best possible price as a provision for Shura's future. Since the child had died with her mother, Ted Hughes soon had the surprise of finding these documents in his mail. At the time, however, he had been stunned since he heard the dramatic news, like a man thinking he would soon wake up and find it was only a nightmare. He attended the double burial in his everyday clothes, too troubled in mind even to think of changing. Mentally exhausted, unable to cry, he got into his car and drove he did not know where. He landed up in a ferry for Ireland. Speechless still, he let black ink flow from his pen forming haphazard words signifying nothing. On the other side of the Irish Channel he drove towards the setting sun as far as the Atlantic. He arrived, as if by pure chance, in the county of Tipperary, at Cashel, whose fairy-tale castle stands at the top of a rock. Two children were playing at the edge of the cliff. Grief was like a torturing poison running through his veins. He wrote in his notebook as a man who clings to the face of a cliff, by the sole force of his fingers so as not to fall into the gaping void at his feet. He was engulfed by the desire to let go; to stop these useless efforts, routinely repeated every day, to lead what could pass for a normal life. Nothing was important any more. His temples hurt, as if caught in a vice. The pain seemed to spread to his whole body. It increased slowly but continually. Brandy and coffee at the hotel did not help. The two boys, out there, were still playing at chasing each other at the edge of the cliff. Sleep had abandoned him. When he shut his eyes he saw the face of Assia, the face of Shura. It could not be true. All this, surely, could still be stopped. It was all a horrible mistake. Grief seemed literally to be tearing him to pieces slowly as if with an iron hook.

He returned to England just as he had left it. Edith had died in her turn. He thought that she may have been unable to stand the horror of the events. She was buried not far from Sylvia's tomb in Heptonstall churchyard. Right after the burial, he went to buy Lumb Bank with the prize money from the city of Florence. Life had felled him. Then life had chewed him slowly. Now life was digesting him interminably. But what would be left of him under the sun, he wondered, when this infernal intestinal process had ceased to run its course? What supernatural force imposed such punishment on him? It was from him, from him alone that those death rays emanated, destroying those who came to close to him. Perhaps, his depression was catching and those coming too close to him could not but be affected by the melancholy oozing from his person like some deadly venom. Then the death of his mother transformed his suffering, turning it into a sort of torpor, leaving him numb, deprived of sensation, like an automaton, as if he'd been lobotomised, he thought. Soon, he would ask Brenda Hebden if she'd agree to come and live with him at Lumb Bank. But Brenda was still a married woman and Heptonstall a small village where they might have caused a scandal. Olwyn and aunt Hilda strongly disapproved of the plan. As Lumb Bank was situated in a damp hollow where the light of the sun rarely penetrated, he soon found the solitude too heavy to bear and he went to live with Brenda for a time in a farm that they rented in Devon, where he could also more conveniently continue to see Carol. The following year, all things considered, Brenda preferred to step out of Ted's life and go find a more favourable climate to bring up her children at Welcombe in Cornwall. Ted, for his part, arranged that Nicholas and Frieda should go to a boarding school run by Quakers at Waterford in Ireland, because he had heard that they formed some of the best students of Trinity College, in Dublin. They would begin to learn Irish, as was the rule in the schools of the Republic of Ireland at the time.

By October, Ted Hughes had decided to fight back. Fortune had been so persistently cruel to him that he felt he had no choice but to meet the challenge of such brutal events. He had always thought that poetry held the answers to all the questions that he encountered, and so he chose more than ever to place his trust in it. Beneath his very eyes the examples of poets from Eastern Europe like Popa, Herbert, Holub, but also the Jewish poet Amichai, whose works he had translated with Assia: they all shared the belief that poetry was a form of resistance and a means to survive. Some of them had had to survive totalitarianism, others a holocaust. For all of them, art was poles apart from the easy complacency in the supposed loss of sense that in the West characterized the modernist and post-modernist materialistic climate that hope had deserted. These poets were not the sarcastic celebrants of despair. They were men who had turned to poetry to find in it the resources necessary to survive the absurdity and cruelty that life had decided to inflict upon them. Here was the proof that poetry had in it something that could help a human being not to collapse, body and soul, into madness and death. Ted Hughes was firmly bent on steeling himself for the task. He would take up his pen and write in order to survive, and he would live for the sake of poetry. So he buried himself in literature like a partisan going underground; from now on poetry would be for him a permanent spiritual struggle.

While the thatcher was finishing the new covering for the roof at Court Green, Ted Hughes, who had bought a new car exactly the same as his old one, had also knocked down the stone sides of his fireplaces in order to have larger hearths on which to light big fires all winter. He resumed his Crow chronicle with renewed faith and the conviction that he was breaking new ground in poetry. It was also just possible of course that he had given birth to a monster. But it seemed much more likely that he was inventing a kind of poetry surpassing all that was being done in English, be it in England or in the United States. It might well be that those fashionable ignoramuses about town that he lumped together under the generic term of "*literateurs*" would fail to notice its radical novelty at first. But he was sure he had hit upon something important, for he had managed to tap, in the evocative voice of Crow, the primal source of ancestral literature, the immutable poetic tradition whose existence was for him as undeniable as the productions of nature. Sylvia Plath, too, when writing the poems that she collected under the title *Ariel*, after the name of the horse on which she was learning to ride, had been certain she was riding Pegasus, the winged horse of the Muses that would take her to Parnassus among the immortal poets. Likewise, when writing the poems of *Crow, from the Life and Songs of the Crow*, Ted Hughes was certain that he was writing a poetry that would live long after him. In one of his poems entitled "Examination at the Womb Door" one reads that death is stronger than hope, stronger than life, stronger than love. But who is stronger than death? Me, evidently, answers Crow. Apart from the fact that he had a model that was quite real in the world of things, Crow was an allegorical figure of the spiritual force of the absurd that Hughes called God's nightmare. Crow was in fact the voice of God's mother buried alive and forgotten by her unworthy son. The God of which he spoke here was very much like the God Blake called Urizen, a totalitarian God so bent on being unique that he would deny his own origins. Crow keeps coming back like a facetious ghost to sow tragic discord in the allegedly well-ordered creation of the Almighty. Like the tricksters in Native American folk tales from which he is derived, Crow is as indestructible as a character in an American cartoon. He is thoroughly stupid, so perfectly idiotic that it is impossible to thwart him. He will always have the last word. Of course, as in cartoons and folk tales, there is a story, of which Crow is both the main protagonist and the anti-hero. At the end, in a parody of the Eucharist in which Christians claim to symbolically eat the body of Christ, Crow ends up swallowing God. By so doing he liberates the mother of God, who is the one true divinity since she is the mother of all the gods. Crow will eventually marry her. But in order to achieve such a titanic task it was necessary that Crow should not be totally human or, more exactly, not only human. In many respects he resembles Wodwo, for he is like a being that is not completely endowed with the faculty of speech. Crow is not the prisoner of human language, and he wants to free humanity from language. The verbal God that Crow destroys is none other than the Word that in "A Disaster" consumes the universe and presumes to take its place. Here Ted Hughes hit upon a tradition of English poetry going back to Milton at least and running through the works of some of the great romantics. It is the tradition of mythopoeia, mixing the mimetic with the mythical by staging allegorical characters. They are not the personifications of virtues and vices as in ordinary allegories or in medieval mysteries, but forces at work in the minds of men at particular moments in the history of ideas. His anthropological studies had orientated Hughes towards the elaboration of a myth for our times, which in modern England could serve the same function that myths and traditional shaman tales played in so-called primitive societies.

Laying aside their complicated metaphysical substratum, the *Crow* poems are instantly striking for their disconcerting simplicity. They are written in very ordinary, unornamented language, and in an economical style. They have the straightforwardness and transparency of tales for children. The world of Crow, as one would expect, is extremely black, but the very extremity of its blackness makes it comical. Black humour pervades the whole sequence and asserts itself as its natural colour: laughter irrepressibly bursting out in the face of despair. But they have yet another striking characteristic: one feels it is not a collection of independent poems carefully arranged to form a beautiful anthology. While reading them one has the vague feeling that these poems are the separate episodes of one single adventure, not disposed, perhaps, in a natural order but asking to be included in a meaningful sequence pointing, one feels, towards the story of a transformation. Crow is defined as a being undergoing a metamorphosis. But in what terms? Ted Hughes dealt with the subject on various occasions, in his letters and in interviews, but he always carefully avoided translating his poetic enterprise into rationalistic terms. To his mind, poetry belongs to quite another dimension of language. And language indeed is a central issue here, for Crow serves as an intermediary between the God of the Word, the God of the Bible, and another divinity whose domain is precisely all the rest, all that is not Logos. The tale relating the adventures of Crow is the tale of a war of the gods, between the masculine god of Logos and the feminine deity of anti-Logos. But all this metaphysics is far too complicated. So the poet chose to reformulate his myth in a much less forbidding and far more amusing manner, in the style of the North-American Native tales that he liked so much. He would say that it was also a tale about Crow, who wanted to cross a river but found it could not do so without the help of a big fat female that he had to carry on his back. When they were halfway across the river the female started asking him a string of riddles in succession. Every time he gave a wrong answer her weight increased and Crow sank a little deeper into the river at the risk of being drowned. If he gave the right answer, she became lighter. After many adventures he would finally make it, and he ended up marrying the female whose beauty had eventually been revealed by all the various incidents of the story. It was an amusing way of saying that the metamorphosis of Crow was the search for a common ground for the male and female principles, as they are evoked in Jung's theory as well as in Far-Eastern cultures of the Yin and the Yang, and in many other visions of the world which could not fail to excite the interest of a poet well versed in anthropological literature. In short, Crow had evolved from the spiritual state of mind of the Christian knight of which Saint George, the patron saint of England, was the archetype and Tolstoy a borderline case. In certain poems like "Crow's Account of St George" he slaughters his wife and children by mistake, thinking that he is killing the dragon.

It is inevitable that this good Christian should in the end be punished for such a tragic mistake. Crow is also the charred remains of the saint, so to speak, once he has finished burning in hell. The indefinitely multiplied destruction of this indestructible cartoon hero who keeps reappearing to explode into a thousand pieces, is meant to represent, in a simple and humorous way, the shaman's flight to hell and back again. Another way of expressing the same thing would be to say that Crow himself, owing to his perfect blackness, impersonates the pupil of the eye, the door through which he comes and goes between the outside world and the inner world of spirits. Nothing can resist Crow's sarcasm except his blackness itself which comes in handy as an efficient antidote to death-dealing melancholy. In many respects, Crow's laughter has the old familiar satanic ring when he sets about making fun of Christian beliefs and values. But this merely, if somewhat crudely, adds a faint odour of scandal to the poems, which is very much in the mood of the time.

If Ted Hughes embarked with such energy on the composition of the *Crow* poems it was because, by so doing, he had the impression that he was turning over a new leaf. Edith's death, at first, had left him dazed, then he had felt strangely liberated. It was as if his mother's death had brought about the annihilation of the past. Uncle Walt, the old folk, his family in Yorkshire: it seemed to him that they belonged to a world that was irretrievably gone. A slate had been wiped clean. In particular the slate of the Methodist education his mother had given him, the self-imposed discipline, the incessant nit-picking in your life leaving you, in the end, as if caught in a vice between remorse for the past and cares for the future. To hell with all that! It seemed to him that since the age of seventeen or eighteen his life had been a fake. Assia's death, then his mother's death, had destroyed this false construct, making it possible for him to start a new life. From Edith he would retain her power of clairvoyance and the memory of a loving mother, but he had taken the plunge and resolutely turned his back upon Christian values. He was sure of it: Christianity had been nothing but a long mistake. The religion was now at the point of death. Something else had to be found, and it seemed to him that poetry was perhaps capable of providing an answer to such an enormous problem. A profound change was taking place in him. His handwriting had become so bad that he was no longer capable of reading what he had written. The situation was so self-evident and he was so clearly unable to do anything about it that he was obliged to use a typewriter in spite of his theories recommending that as direct a link as possible should be maintained between the text and the brain that produced it.

For his letters, in any case, he used a typewriter and checked his text with a pen, for he received an ever more abundant mail. His children's poems brought him letters from readers which were sometimes touching and often comical. For instance, a girl writing to wish him a speedy recovery attached to her letter a drawing representing a bird of prey carrying away a bleeding fish in its claws, to illustrate the notion of animal instinct. In quite another vein, he also received letters from puzzled readers like the one from a French teacher in a secondary school in Marseille, concerning the poems in *How the Whale Became* published in 1963, who wondered what could have made him write about animals as he did, pointing out with typically French logic that it was incomprehensible that animals should have thought of existing before existing as they precisely did not exist yet. But Ted Hughes took pleasure in this sometimes naive but always sincere correspondence which this part of his work for children was bringing him. It was a facet of his poetry much less exposed to criticism and, for that reason, he placed great hopes in it. In the ideological battle in which he was engaged, he did not doubt that he would achieve results in the long run. His teaching vocation, which did not develop to the full in the classroom, found a mode of expression that suited him better in writing for children. Ted Hughes indeed had less the soul of a teacher than of a preacher. He sought less to awaken the capacities and enrich the minds of those that he addressed than to fascinate and convince his readers. The year before, a tale entitled *The Iron Man* had met with some success, in which a robot from outer space, a modern version of Saint George's dragon, barely escapes destruction at the hands of an English society far too prompt to hunt down foreign objects. The monster soon comes in very useful to the village that has befriended him, and in the end he saves the whole country from utter destruction. Soon Hughes was also to publish *The Coming of the King*, for he was always determined to have more than one string to his bow, advancing on a variety of fronts to press his ideas into the heads of his countrymen.

By March 1970 he had ceased to write *Crow* poems, like a miner who has worked out his seam. He was still convinced that this was the highest level of excellence he had ever reached. In Northampton, Massachusetts, Leonard Baskin began composing a sumptuous edition of some *Crow* poems, illustrated with his own engravings, in his small art book publishing house, the Gehenna Press, while in London Faber & Faber made ready to publish *Crow, From the Life and Songs of the Crow* in October. Ted Hughes then entered one of his unproductive periods that regularly followed his bouts of intense creativity. He went fishing more and more, and started thinking very seriously again of buying a farm. He made arrangements for Gerald to send him pelts of blue kangaroos with which he covered the seats and the floors at

Court Green. It had occurred to him, as Gerald could obtain pelts for him at prices defying all competition, that he could profitably trade in pelts while indulging his interest for commerce. Prices in England, he observed, were on the rise. He was continually receiving offers for his land and his house, but also for his manuscripts and for those of Sylvia Plath, each bid higher than the one before. Had he not been offered twenty thousand pounds for the manuscript of *Ariel*? Patience and poetry, it seemed, would suffice to make a prosperous man of him.

That summer, he received the visit of Seamus Heaney and of his wife Marie who gave him a talisman to protect Court Green from bad luck. He went out sometimes with the two poets, Peter Redgrove and his wife Penelope Shuttle. One evening they went out to dinner in a haunted restaurant and Peter saw the ghost. In September 1970, two days after his fortieth birthday, Ted married Carol Orchard, a young country woman, the daughter of a neighbouring farmer, little attracted by London life, a perceptive reader but with no literary ambitions of her own, and whose surname — Hughes liked to say — was that of a gipsy family from Wales. They went to Jerusalem for their honeymoon. Ted Hughes, having thunderously celebrated the awakening of Gog, and whose favourite deity was not far different from the goddess Astaroth that Jehovah had supplanted, felt suddenly deeply moved when he found himself in Israel. At the Rock of Sacrifices he felt the power of the spirit of the place and he was deeply touched by the welcome that he received. The visit, he said, had opened his eyes and, like many visitors from the West on their first visit to an oriental country, he said that he would have liked to live there. This was only a few months before Crow, the arch contemner of the God of the Word made its resounding entrance on the English literary scene. In October, the poet and critic Peter Porter hailed the publication of these new poems by Ted Hughes, saying that English poetry had found its new heroic figure and that, from now on, no one could read or write verse without feeling the shadow of the black bird pass over the page.

VI

MOORTOWN PASTORAL

For Ted Hughes the publication of a collection of poems was always followed by a more or less total incapacity to continue writing in the same vein. After the publication of *Crow* he found that he was unable to go on writing in the same mood, and he saw clearly that he would have to move on once more to something different. Crow had marked an important departure from his first manner but if he was to continue writing he would have to operate another radical change. While it slowly dawned on him that he would not make any progress until he found a way out of this impasse, finding himself at a loose end for the moment, he could only slide back into his old depression. So he kept moving with his new wife, often accompanied by his sister Olwyn, between Lumb Bank, where it was increasingly obvious that he could not bear to live, and Court Green where, much to his surprise, he realised that he was getting bored. Always keen to provide the best possible schooling for his children, he brought them home from Ireland and sent them to a school in London. At the beginning of 1971 Olwyn started the Rainbow Press. They had long intended to carry out the project of setting out a small publishing house like that of Leonard Baskin to produce limited editions of certain *Crow* poems that had not found their place in the Faber & Faber edition. It would also be a means of drawing a profit from Sylvia Plath's poems as well as from Ted Hughes's unpublished manuscripts, but also from those of Ruth Fainlight, Alan Sillitoe and Seamus Heaney, among very close friends, by offering to the public deluxe editions on fancy paper at fancy prices. The logo chosen by Olwyn for the books was a colophon, probably drawn by

Blake, showing a rainbow arched over a seascape at night, with the crescent of the moon, seeming to ride the waves, surmounted by a dove with its wings outspread bearing an olive twig in its bill. The engraving is framed by a garland of twigs in which one recognises the berries of the hawthorn. For some years, the Rainbow Press produced nice slim booklets on thick brown vellum which would later gratify the senses of book lovers who were fond of spending. This was a venture much in the spirit of the Hughes family, and of Ted especially, who had always nourished the dream of a poetry that would be produced like good confectionery, genuine English tweed, or quality Swiss watches, within the restricted circles of a family enterprise reputed for its craftsmanship.

But soon the winds of change were blowing on him again. Peter Brook, the innovative stage manager of the Royal Shakespeare Company, was then beginning to work in Paris for the International Centre of Theatrical Creations and would soon establish himself in the Théâtre des Bouffes du Nord. At his request Ted Hughes had worked on the translation of Seneca's *Oedipus*, produced at The Old Vic in London in 1969 with John Gielgud and Irene Worth in the leading roles, but without much success. But much more was needed to dampen the enthusiasm of Peter Brook, whose ambition was nothing less than to revolutionise Western theatre, starting with the mentality of the audience. His experiments were quite in accordance with the mood of the times; the decade was rediscovering Antonin Artaud and his Theatre of Cruelty, the inspiration for which he had drawn from Bali; it had replaced the Theatre of the Absurd as practised by Beckett, Ionesco and Anouilh among others, who had so masterfully dominated the stage in the years following the end of the war. Brook had evidently understood the message of Crow perfectly, as well as the significance of its sarcastic imprecations against the language of men and the Word incarnate, for he came to Ted Hughes with a new project along the same lines. It consisted in a stage production aiming to impart emotions and feelings to the spectators without having recourse to articulate language. It was thus hoped to clear the ground for a more direct expression of truth by disentangling it from the adulterating mediation of words. This sort of fantasy was very much the fashion in the early seventies, as the then flourishing linguistic studies and sciences of language were busy flogging a horse that had been killed thousands of years before by countless poets and metaphysicians. What Brook proposed to Ted Hughes was to go one step further, if that were possible, in exploring the croaking of meaning at its birth, which still retained for him, it seemed, secrets of fascinating novelty. The play was to be called *Orghast*, a term invented to designate the ectoplasmic spirit through which meaning supposedly emerged direct from the flesh. Everything was to be done in Teheran. The first performance would take place in the ruins of Persepolis, the capital of ancient Persia, with a troop of actors of different tongues and nationalities.

Ted Hughes thus spent the summer of 1970 in Teheran where he was received in the Shah's palace and accommodated in luxury hotels with abundant financial resources at his disposal to write the text of a play without words. His job was to produce a maximum number of scenes, drawing inspiration from Avesta, the sacerdotal language of Zoroastrianism, the ancient religion of Iran, but also from Manichaeism, a dualist system which derived from it in the 3rd century, when it came to rival the Christian religion. Ted Hughes took a particular interest in Manichaeism because of its belief in the demoniac nature of the flesh and the earth, both considered as a prison from which the soul must liberate itself. It seemed to Hughes that this was at the root of the error committed by the Puritan variant of the Christian religion. According to Mani, the soul of man sprang from Light whereas the earth-bound body was held prisoner in Darkness. Hughes was soon to consider that this light was the same thing as language, tending through its conceptual clarity to throw the factual world into the shade. In Greek mythology, the myth of Prometheus bore a striking resemblance, he thought, to this doctrine. Prometheus had stolen fire from heaven and brought it down to men. For Ted Hughes, fire was light, and it stood for language and its power of abstraction at the origin of science and technology. Ted Hughes would therefore organise the story of *Orghast* around the myth of Prometheus. It was also the story of a conflict between two opposite forces. On the one side, fire and light, standing for the Logos, that is to say language and the rational conceptual thought of science; on the other side, darkness engulfing all that does not pertain to the reign of Logos, all the irrational sphere of matter and primal instincts. This opposition between darkness and light recalled the ancestral conflict between the male and female principles. The fire, stolen by the Titan, is the lightning wielded by Zeus, the father of gods and men, and Prometheus' punishment for this act consists in being chained to a rock, that is to say the body of his mother the earth. In certain versions of the myth Prometheus is delivered by Heracles, and Hughes had the pleasant surprise to find equivalents of this outside the sphere of Greek culture in Armenian mythology with Artashes and Artavazd, but also in the *Vedas* where very similar heroic figures can be found under the names of Pramanath and Agoluz.

Hughes was leaving no stone unturned, collating different sources in support of his project. His starting point, of course, was the play by Aeschylus, *Prometheus Bound* but he also drew on *Life is a Dream* by Calderon de la Barca who, at the beginning of the

17th century, had meditated on the possible reversibility of dream and reality. At the same time, he was also reading various books on the Gnostics who had imagined other dualistic theologies very similar to the doctrine of Mani. He was naturally fully aware that with *Orghast* he was following in the steps of Shelley, who, in the years of the romantic revival, taking Aeschylus as a model and modifying the legend, had written *Prometheus Unbound.* Ted Hughes in his youth, like T.S. Eliot before him and countless other English-speaking adolescents, had for a time been a Shelley enthusiast. He was quite familiar with the totality of his work and knew his *Adonais* by heart, but his interest had somehow taken another course in Cambridge, when he had abandoned the idea of writing an essay on his translation of Goethe's *Faust,* though deep down in his heart the yearning remained, and he would have liked to write like him. Besides, if Hughes, unlike Shelley, was not a proclaimed atheist, like him he pursued the dream of liberating Western man from the tyranny imposed on him over thousands of years by the great monotheist religions. As is the case with Shelley's lyrical drama, Hughes's play takes place within the soul of man, inside the body of Prometheus. While he wrote to his brother Gerald to send him more pelts, especially fox pelts if he could find them, Hughes feverishly jotted down the myriad of thoughts that all the reading he was doing was stirring up in his mind. He was ceaselessly writing and drawing on exercise books that he kept close at hand. There was one in particular, of French format, in Angouleme vellum with large squares and a spiral binding called reversible, on the pale green cover of which he had drawn, seen from three-quarter back, a lean-flanked cow grazing. Inside the notebook there were, repeated on several pages, pictures of a man pinned down to the ground like a butterfly on a cork slab by an amateur entomologist. In another of these notebooks, of British make, with pale blue lines printed across their pages and a margin ruled off by a pink line, he drew a much more elaborate picture of his Prometheus tormented by his internal drama. It is the figure of a man, arms and legs spread-eagle, a little like Leonardo da Vinci's Vitruvian Man, bearing the word Man written on his right arm and the word Woman on the left. His face is nearly completely masked by a bird of prey with its wings outspread, driving its claws and beak into his skull. The bird's name is Krogon. It is an allegory of the Logos God taking brutal possession of the mind and body of Prometheus in the name of rational thought. Just as Blake's Urizen prevented access to truth, Krogon blocks out the light of the real and usurps its place in the world of man. This true light is represented in Hughes's drawing by the sun shining behind Krogon, whose name, Hoan, evokes original unity. The same image of the god Krogon was already present in a *Lupercal* poem called "Hawk Roosting" in which Hughes tried, as he said, to make nature, that is to say the divinity of this world of things that we are mistaking for reality, speak. The hawk, he said, spoke like a fascist, and his speech had a totalitarian ring, for he behaved as if he were the master of the world, since he thought that he could mete out death as he wished. He said: "the sun is behind me". The torture that Krogon inflicts upon Prometheus literally cleaves him in half from head to foot. But Krogon on the head of Prometheus reveals the presence of another force whose seat is in his belly and that Hughes calls Moa. Moa stands for feminine energy, an organic, earthly force that Krogon had repressed into an inferior region. The entire being of Prometheus is the seat of an interminable warfare between Krogon and Moa, reason and passion, the conceptual and the organic, the masculine and the feminine principles.

In Milton's *Paradise Lost,* Death, begotten by Satan on the body of his darling daughter Sin, having sprung fully armed from his head, incestuously rapes his mother Sin at the gates of hell, who hourly conceives and gives birth to monsters. Similarly in Hughes's *Orghast,* a generic Krogon indefatigably rapes Moa, and every son thus conceived rises up against his father, kills him and automatically takes his place, faithfully reproducing the Oedipus complex, which seems to guarantee the perpetuation of the maleficent demiurge. Such is the fate of Agoluz, the rebellious son, who only succeeds in becoming a tyrant himself in place of a tyrant. But in Hughes's drama the deliverance of Prometheus is accomplished by the coming of a son of quite another stamp, whose name is Sogis. Sogis manages to put an end to the drama by abolishing the baneful opposition between reason and feeling, male and female principles, science and poetry. But this metamorphosis of the human race is only made possible by the evolution of the species towards a new type of man, not unlike Nietzsche's superman, but who is also silhouetted on the horizon of several 20th century philosophies, like Jung's psychoanalysis, which exerted such a strong influence on Hughes. Indeed his *Prometheus Unbound* bears a curious resemblance to the ideal subject as defined by Jung, who would perfect what he called the process of individuation by reconciling in his own being the masculine and the feminine parts of his personality, the *animus* and the *anima*, never harmonised until then.

The whole action of the play could also have been set in a cave sheltering prehistoric people about nine or ten thousand years ago, at a time when the language of men had begun to take the regrettable turn in its evolution which was to culminate in its deification on Mount Sinai, when the God of Israel would give His Decalogue to Moses, saying "I am that I am". The poet was filling his notebooks with fragments of dialogue between characters standing allegorically for the forces astir, at this fateful moment, in the human soul. He strove above all to avoid the temptation of starting from English words and to concentrate on purely sensuous states of mind, to make them produce their own equivalents in sound, eschewing the trap of any known language. It was not an easy thing to do. Very soon, the stress incurred began to take its toll on his health. He felt very tired and developed eczema. However, an important breakthrough had been achieved when he had suddenly realised that the right approach to the difficulty was to abandon the path of the playwright for that of the musician. The thought came to him when he remembered the twofold advice that he had given the year before to his niece Ashley, Gerald's daughter, who was beginning to learn music. Uncle Ted's first rule for the piano, he had said, was: if it isn't the devil it isn't music. The second rule was to take possession of the musical phrase like a tiger pouncing on a pig. Just so with *Orghast*. The staging had to come last. The first thing to do was to find a purely musical expression for the state of mind that you wanted to convey. It was just a matter of tone and tempo and of volume of sound. It all boiled down to the idea of music as a universal language, as a purely formal form of art, hardly figurative at all, with no coded correspondences between the forms it uses, and no permanently fixed meaning.

In July, Carol came for two weeks with the children. It was the occasion for a much welcome break. Ted played with Nicholas, chasing the magnificent lizards living in the ruins of Persepolis. They were extraordinarily difficult to catch and, much to his disappointment, they always returned from the chase empty-handed. With the snakes, they were more successful and they caught some specimens that Ted killed and flayed for their skins, such beautiful papery skins. At Persepolis Ted felt that he had definitely shed his old life. He could not imagine returning to live at Court Green, which Carol was doing up to suit her own tastes during his absence. He conceived the vague project of letting the house to rich American academics, as he was resolved to start a new life elsewhere.

His exercise books had now been replaced by large-sized jacket-files in which he accumulated plans and maps that he constantly reshaped for his play on the stocks. There were also long dialogues made up of cries and confused jumbles of words, the extreme length of some vowels being noted by a long string of the same letter. Whole pages of the play also contained an interlinear translation of these pure sound words. More and more often, Ted was led to draw lists of these sounds with their English translation facing them. It was the sign that Orghast, imaginary as it was, tended to become a language like any other, since it was necessary, it seemed, that sounds should be linked to sense, in one way or another, by some sort of convention. Even if Ted Hughes would be long to admit it in so many words, his annotations bore witness to the logical contradiction inherent in his initial presumption, which quite invalidated the project of *Orghast: Talking without Words.* It indeed seems quite clear that there can exist no expression of meaning outside the articulation of certain sounds with something else, by a rule or a law of some sort, rudimentary though it be. Plato had met the same problem in his *Cratylus* without being able to decide one way or another. Ted Hughes was no more successful in a similar enterprise, and it would have been easy to guess from the start that it was inevitably bound to fail. There was little more than a single performance of the play at the Fifth Festival of Arts of Persepolis, and there is every reason to believe that it proved a disappointment. The actors could just be made out gesticulating in the dark, dimly lit by rare torches, belching forth enigmatic imprecations. One part, at least, of the play was filmed. Some extracts were published in specialised reviews which reported on an experimental enterprise that would soon be confined to oblivion. Some time later, Peter Brook admitted in an interview that with *Orghast* they had attempted to tackle an impossible task. But Ted Hughes was to keep all his notes, as he was in the habit of keeping all the first drafts of his works, meticulously stored in cardboard files. He would later draw on them for the raw material of a series of metaphysical poems called *Prometheus On His Crag.* In the last poem of the series, there appears one of the beautiful Persian lizards that father and son had never succeeded in catching; it perches on the shoulder of Prometheus who hears its mysterious whispered voice in his ear telling him how lucky he is to be human.

Once back in Court Green, at the end of summer, he found his past still dogging him. The year before, he had authorised the publication of *The Bell Jar*, a little against his will, but because American law allowed the copyright of the works of American citizens published outside the United States only for a term of seven years. Even if he had refused, there was the risk of the book being published one day without his agreement. As soon as it appeared, Sylvia Plath's novel remained among the best-sellers for many months in succession. As a result, and much to his regret, the attention of the public remained fixed on that controversial period of his life. However, what he considered as most unfortunate for his reputation brought him fifty thousand pounds in royalties straight off that he immediately laid by, declaring that it would be "the kids' money". At about that time, Aurelia Plath expressed the desire that he should allow her to publish the letters her daughter had addressed her. The motivation behind her demand was

perhaps less financial interest than the desire to redress the wrong that her daughter's novel was doing,
she thought, to her own character. Ted Hughes had no
objection whatsoever, too much preoccupied himself
by the growing embarrassment that the posthumous
celebrity of Sylvia Plath was causing him. Two years
before, he had been vilified in a first biography of
Sylvia Plath written in the United States. In England,
the literary critic Alvarez, who had already written a
tactless article in *The Observer,* was now taking advantage of his having met Sylvia Plath in the days
preceding her death to place himself in the light of her
sudden celebrity. In a book he devoted to the subject
of suicide, he did not hesitate to spread scandal about
Sylvia Plath as well as about Ted Hughes himself and
the supposedly magnetic attraction that he exerted
upon women. He justified himself by saying that her
death, in a way, had put her in the public domain. Ted
Hughes's reputation was such, he said, that even Sylvia Plath must necessarily have known what sort of
man he was. Hughes wrote him a letter in which he
declared himself deeply wounded by the unforgivable
things he had said about him. This was the beginning
of a long series of attacks from American readers, as
enforcers of outdated morals, upon the womaniser
who could no more bear to have his conduct exposed
than Oscar Wilde, in his time, had been able to accept
the epithet, publicly applied to him, that was certainly
just as justified.

When he saw the inheritors of the Salem witch-
hunters blowing on the dying embers of his shame,
Hughes was quick to exaggerate the risks that this
could represent for his children's future happiness. As
he was above all afraid that they might learn of their
mother's suicide through the jibes of their school-
mates, he imagined that it would be preferable for
them not to go to school rather than be exposed to
public shame. So he fetched them back home, remov-

ing them from their London school, unsure which way was best to let them know the truth about their mother's death. He was then to find out that Frieda had discovered it long ago. But it was a great shock for Nicholas when he heard the truth, and from that day onwards he refused to speak of his mother and to hear people talk of her until he was in his twenties. Acting on the spur of the moment and partly as a bitter reaction against American public opinion, whose verdict he considered unjust, Ted Hughes made his son sign official documents formally renouncing his American nationality. It might appear illogical that he did not do the same with Frieda but, when staying with her grandmother, Frieda had always seemed to be more at ease than her brother with the American way of life. It may also be that in his world the symbolic significance attached to nationality was, between father and son, of special importance. Then, having kept his children with him a long time to counter the impression, that cut him to the quick, of having been attacked in his family life, and very anxious that his children should pursue their education, but in a pleasing environment, he chose the very special school of Bedales for them, standing in the green and peaceful countryside of Hampshire. All this while, Carol was imperturbably pursuing her painting at Court Green, quietly taking her place at the head of the household. Ted eventually managed to regain some calm by once more seeking protection in angling. He would later say that, of all his follies, angling was the one that had succeeded in absorbing all the others. He dreamt again of fabulous catches and he supposed that it was a good omen. His passion for tanning animal skins had taken hold of him again. He skinned a few badgers that he found dead on roadsides here and there, and he tried to find the best way of scraping and curing the skins so as to render them as smooth as possible. This activity must have seemed

particularly odd or, on the contrary, most characteristic of him, because there exist two photographs of
him that had, with time, merged into one in his memory, but to which he attached enough importance to
express the regret of having mislaid them. On these
photographs, he is not seen actually skinning the
badger but preparing its skin. He wears a plaid over-
shirt with the sleeves rolled up and black trousers
tucked inside rubber-boots. Under his over-shirt, the
collar of his shirt is held round his neck by a black tie.
On one of the photographs, he stands near the trunk of
a big apple-tree working on a skin hanging upon a
line stretched between two trees of the orchard. Behind him, Nicholas, in shorts, is staring at the scene,
one of his cheeks bulging from the big chunk of apple
he has just bitten off. On the other one, Ted is standing, his legs spread astride, showing a badger's skin to
the camera between his uplifted arms, his knife still in
his right hand. In front of him, Frieda, in white socks
and pleated skirt, her hair kept in place by a hair slide,
and with a roguish expression on her face, is symbolically bound, her arms held close to her sides with a
thong whose end is left free to hang around her neck.
It is just possible that Ted had thus wanted to exorcise, for himself and for his family, the Bluebeard
character that his detractors sought to impose on him.
The unfair hostility that he felt was being released
against him encouraged his natural tendency to isolate
himself. These were the years in which he began to
acquire the reputation of a recluse avoiding as much
as he could all worldly obligations that were not
strictly necessary. He was still entertaining his old
dream of reuniting his family around him, but he had
abandoned the hope of seeing his brother Gerald
come back from Australia, either to become a gentleman farmer in England or, at least, for a few days'
hunting with him. Gerald continued to evade giving
an answer. Ted was also delighted that his son should,

in his turn, develop a passion for fishing, for with him he was rediscovering something of the joy he had known, when he was his age, of getting up early to go on an expedition with his elder brother, a role that had now devolved upon him.

His dream of buying a farm to breed cattle was still very much with him. It increased, rather, as he intensified his research with a view to acquiring an estate. He discovered, as he did so, that it was not as easy to find a more or less run-down old house in the country as it had been some ten years before when he had bought Court Green. In the space of hardly ten years, the fashion for a cottage in the country and the back-to-the-land craze had doubled the price of land and increased fourfold the price of houses. He came to believe that real estate would prove the best investment in the long run if he wanted to preserve his capital to ensure the future of his children. Even if he had to borrow money to do so, his only thought, was then to acquire landed property. Lumb Bank was definitely not a place where he wanted to live. Moreover, someone had attempted to set fire to the house by piling up old papers in the upstairs room with typewriters on top, as if to hold them in place, before setting them alight. But the house was so damp it had simply refused to burn; just one hole had been burnt in the boarded floor, and the fire had died out when the embers had dispersed as they fell on the ground floor. Not wanting to spend too much time looking after it, but anxious to prevent it getting too derelict through not being lived in, he decided to let it.

In 1972, Ted Hughes bought Moortown, a nearly one hundred-acre farm near Winkleigh in Devon, five miles from Court Green and not far from Dartmoor National Park. He went immediately to live there with his father-in-law who was bringing to the enterprise his rough-and-ready knowledge and his experience as a farmer. Ted's idea was to breed bulls and compete for prizes in agricultural shows; if possible they would have to be Charolais because he admired their white coats and firm muscular build. Besides, as he was sure that the Common Market was going to cause a profitable rush for English beef, he decided to fatten livestock. He therefore bought a herd of thirty cows with their calves and a flock of one hundred and forty sheep. Ted Hughes made his debut as a farmer learning how to start an old refractory tractor on a raw frosty morning. Ted and Carol, on arrival, found the Moortown farm already occupied by a female badger that had burrowed her way under a wall and dug a labyrinth of tunnels under the floor of the cowshed. At once Ted had started to feed her nearly every night, hoping that she would stay. As a farm hand, Ted Hughes had a lot of learning to do. He was not always a great help and sometimes proved awkward, but he was always full of admiration for the work being done on the farm. However, the pastoral adventure required infinitely more energy than might have been expected judging from Virgil's eclogues. Ted did not spare himself, for he was naturally hardworking. Very soon, this farmer's life administered the proof that it could renew his sources of inspiration as well as his methods of composition. In truth, he found the affected and pretentious ways of the professionals of literature utterly unbearable. It seemed to him, therefore, that poetry had everything to gain if it were raised to the noble state of an amateur's pursuit. He was now writing in the evening, after his day's work on the farm, with the more or less conscious hope that these new conditions must necessarily lead him towards new horizons. The incidents of his everyday work brought him new sensations and unexpected occasions of wonder that had to be snatched from the succession of works and days. These fragile spurts of emotion were in danger of being lost as soon as the accumulated experience of the days that followed blunted their memory. His poetry had therefore to cultivate the freshness of what his life in the fields brought him everyday and preserve in its verse, as soon as it appeared. And so, he came to write the poetic diary of his everyday life. This practice recalled the journalistic approach to poetry of the poets of the thirties. But for poets like Auden, MacNeice or Spender, a preference for urban subjects was the signature of their poetry, whereas Hughes was revisiting the ancestral genre of pastoral poetry, coming back to those "verses of simple observation" that had brought him his first successes as a poet. The way in which he was looking at nature now was less that of a hunter than of a pastoralist. The poetic tension was not set on violence but on a richly patient and benevolent force.

The year before, he had edited two selections of Shakespeare's poems. One of them contained a selection of his sonnets illustrated by Leonard Baskin. A second broadcast of his play *The Wound* unleashed a volley of responses that were far from enthusiastic, but he knew the reproaches well and basically agreed with them, not to mention the fact that it was a relatively old text. For the time being, he was attempting to extract something that would be worthy of publication from the confused mass of *Orghast*, but with little hope of success. Above all he did not see the end of it. Moreover, the poems that he was writing at Moortown did not seem to have the same lasting quality as the *Crow* poems. Besides, he was not really writing with a view to publishing them. He was writing them for his own sake, to see if it would lead to something valuable in the end. But all the while, amid this uncertainty, the fear that his inspiration had run dry would sometimes take hold of him. He had vaguely hoped, when he had bought Moortown, that his brother Gerald would come back from Australia to work with him on the farm, but it was more and more certain that he would do nothing of the sort. It was now all too clear that he preferred to work in his airline company rather than come home and take up the old hunting trips with his brother. Ted found it hard to get over the disappointment. A rankling sense of loss was always there. And there was a pain in his throat. It would not go away. It had even grown worse. What was one to think? It would be cancer of course. If so, his days were counted. There was no time to lose. Ted Hughes hurried to make his will, and set about leaving everything in order before he finally made up his mind to see a doctor, who told him it was only a viral infection of the tonsils combined with a chronic inflammation of the sinuses. A new lease of life was given him. Immediately, he wrote to Luke Meyers for fishing implements that could not be found on this side of the Atlantic; rubber baits that used to be manufactured under the trademark Abou. He also found a let for Lumb Bank. The Arvon Foundation, a private establishment, wanted to open a second centre there proposing creative writing sessions to aspiring writers. Ted Hughes's photograph would appear on their brochure. He agreed to make certain improvements on the house for which he had to find extra funds. He would also have liked to find money to help Olwyn buy a house for herself, but he owed the American Treasury an astronomical sum in payment of the taxes due on the royalties of Sylvia Plath's novel. The success of Sylvia Plath's work was confirmed with each passing day. She was the object of a cult and had become an icon for the feminist movement. The consequence of this was that Ted Hughes was constantly vilified by her unconditional devotees who had rallied in a crowd ready for the lynching. On the basis of many of Sylvia Plath's poems, Ted Hughes was accused of having grossly abused her and, using some of her allegations to support their claim, some of his accusers came up with totally unfounded insinuations, claiming that he had Nazi inclinations: he often dressed in black and, in her poem "Daddy", Plath had portrayed a man with a *Mein Kampf* look who most obviously was Ted. One of these women, more dogged than the rest, called Robin Morgan, even went so far as to publish a grossly slanderous text, in which Hughes rhymed with "I accuse", making him explicitly responsible for the "murder of Sylvia Plath," in particularly indecent terms. He preferred to ignore the rumpus, which he considered both nonsensical and unbecoming. He remained silent in Devon, hibernating by his large fireplace, on sofas covered with animal skins that his brother Gerald kept sending him in exchange for old swords for his collection, inquiring as to the best way of getting a pedigree bull for breeding purposes. The personal attacks of which he was the butt left him with a strong distrust of the United States, and he obstinately declined the posts in American universities that continued to be offered him. But the female front of resentful ill-feelings was not unanimous, for he continued to receive numerous letters from women who had nothing particular to say, except that they hoped they might meet him some day.

The mounting wave of his fame was gaining force, and he could feel it rising around him like a fever. This was to be confirmed in 1974 when he was invited to Buckingham Palace to receive from the Queen herself a three-ounce gold medal, the *Queen's Medal for Poetry*, after being presented by her poet laureate, the venerable John Betjeman. Then he had a rather long conversation with Her Majesty, while Mrs. Carol Hughes had a very pleasant chat with the Lord Treasurer. Certain superficial minds might well have been surprised to see a very Christian and Protestant monarch reward a poet who made no secret of the poor opinion he had of Reformed Christianity. But very few indeed were those who risked a remark on the subject, so obvious did it seem to all that Her

Majesty's broad-mindedness could not fail to extend to a man whom every one of Her subjects regarded as the most brilliant poet of the kingdom. The same year, another collection of his poems appeared under the title *Season Songs*, linking him back to the bucolic vein of the great tradition of English poetry in which official poets had always excelled, at least since *The Faerie Queene* composed by Edmund Spenser in praise of the Virgin Queen Elizabeth I. The tradition had been masterfully pursued by William Wordsworth who, as people remembered, with the passing of years, had known how to temper the pantheistic paganism of his early works and gradually regain the Christian fold. In his new eclogues, Ted Hughes appeared as the poet of the English countryside, which he sang in a pacified mode tending towards the tone of children's literature. To compose these poems, he drew on the diary notes he had made in Moortown, nourishing a vein of inspiration that had been present in his work from the start. Ted Hughes's poetry was taking its place for good in the great English tradition of nature poetry, rich in poems that the English like to make their children learn by heart, as if the technological age were no more than a bad spell to be gone through.

He again consulted a lawyer specialised in the inheritance of intellectual as well as landed property in order to write out a will at his leisure, so as to make as much as possible of his property over to his children during his lifetime. He was pleased to learn, on that occasion, that the whole of his estate already amounted to half a million pounds. The discovery turned his mind towards finding means to further increase this figure. He hesitated: should he buy a larger farm or take up dealing in valuable antiques? Meanwhile, he bought a great red bull, weighing nearly a ton, which he never tired of admiring and of drawing, for he felt that, under his very eyes, he had a living specimen of the mythic animal that is so often represented in the art of ancient Greece. Besides, did he not aspire to be a classic himself? From all sides he was led to believe that his poetry would long outlast him, placing his name among the greats whose work deserved to survive. If further proof was needed he could find it in the fact that the Russian poet Yevgeny Yevtushenko, coming as a guest to his house that autumn, bore an official invitation for a reading tour of his poems in the USSR. Philip Larkin and himself were in fact the only two English poets whose work the Russian cultural authorities had judged worthy of possibly being translated into Russian. Ted Hughes did not have a good enough opinion of the regime which had made Yevtushenko its emissary to accept the proposal, but he was touched by the honour shown him, and the compliment that went with it confirmed him in the good opinion he allowed himself to entertain of his own work.

A more immediate reason for Ted Hughes not accepting Yevtushenko's invitation was his being engaged side by side with Daniel Weissbort in favour of dissident poets in Western Europe. At the time of the visit he was still working in tandem with János Csokits on the translation of the works of the Hungarian poet János Pilinsky. Moreover, Leonard Baskin, who happened to be at Moortown when Yevtushenko was there, had every historical and personal reason for having little sympathy with a regime whose attitude towards Jewish refuseniks he could not accept, let alone forgive. But Ted Hughes's disapproval went even deeper than that; it all harked back to the conviction that a rationalist materialism, in the broadest sense of the word, and the attitude of mind that was responsible for the extremely negative reception of his work on American campuses, were both tarred with the same brush. In his eyes, the biographical justifications with which it was cloaked vainly attempted to mask an ideological prejudice. There was indeed a strong relationship between a scientific technological outlook and the more recent developments of modern poetry, referred to as post-modernist; two attitudes against which the effort of his own poetry was directed. An important turning point in the history of Western poetry had been, he thought, the surrealist movement which had incidentally found almost no echo in Great Britain; Ted Hughes retained only its privileged association with Marxism and the Freudian theory. Although he had himself practiced a form of automatic writing in moments of personal distress, Surrealism as such seemed to him to pertain, in essentials, to an analytical attitude of mind; all things considered, such a mindset endorsed the purely rational spirit which, he was afraid, inevitably entailed the death of the world of spirits, in spite of an apparent romanticism which was, at bottom, all insincerity and acting. He felt instinctively that, on the whole, the trend of true poetry had always been opposed to that of Surrealism. The problem was that, in our modern age, when the weight of rational thought was so absolute, the true poet found himself in a position that was both comparable and radically opposed to that of the Renaissance humanists who had tried to think rationally in an age that was fighting a rear-guard action against them. Ted Hughes saw himself as a Giordano Bruno in reverse but whose thought went also against the mainstream of the times. He could therefore only be perceived as heretical, and was persecuted as such. The reproaches addressed to him as a man for his moral conduct were indistinguishable, in his mind, from the unfavourable critique of his works. But what he had to say to his contemporaries was of a piece with his sexual ethics and with the rules of conduct he had thought he shared with Sylvia Plath; it turned out, however, he had only been dictating it to her with an insistence that she was fustigating with equal force in her journal. He would have no end of pain to understand that Sylvia Plath had succeeded in finding her own freedom as a writer after violently breaking loose from him and from his influence. She had achieved this liberation, first, by revisiting the Freudian analysis of her adolescence and then, with some apparent contradiction, by turning to the Christian religion of her childhood, thus trying to adopt, successively, two paths to her own voice that were radically opposed to the approach of her husband to escape the paralysing influence of his fascinating genius. But Ted Hughes was a vatic ideologue who seemed only capable of perceiving the world through the coloured glass of his personal mythology, the truth of which he gauged in relation to the amount of psychological suffering that it had cost him to discover and elaborate it.

His responsibility in Sylvia Plath's suicide amounted to a tragic error, an error that entirely sufficed, he thought, to explain it. He had paid a high price for that in mental suffering and in the transformation of his deeper self. This error as well as the metamorphosis undertaken to redress it, he considered he had explained in the *Crow* poems, which bore witness to the slow and confused process of reconciliation between the masculine and the feminine principles in himself. But *Crow,* perhaps, had yet to be explained further. Perhaps it did not show clearly enough the link between the small pieces, the stark abstract myths, and certain changes that were taking place in the deeper levels of his being. He therefore undertook a sort of remake of the *Crow* poems that would at the same time be a rewrite with a sequel, to be published in a beautiful album entitled *Cave Birds*, with illustrations by Leonard Baskin on facing pages. These cave birds were metaphorical commentaries on the scenes of an alchemical drama once again drawing its inspiration from *The Chymical Wedding of Christian Rosencreutz*, but also from *The Egyptian Book of the Dead* which he had read alongside the Tibetan *Bardo Thödol*. The metamorphosis here was clearly defined as a metempsychosis. The poems told the story of the transformation of the soul of Socrates at his death, and his resurrection as a worshipper of Isis in ancient Egypt. It was as if Hughes was taking up the Nietzschean myth of Socrates as a musician, that is to say a philosopher whose over scientific and rational attitude was tempered by an artistic training that Socrates himself admitted was often recommended to him in his dreams. To Ted Hughes's mind, this reconciliation between the poet and the philosopher was roughly equivalent to a more harmonious deal between the male and female principles. The idea is made more explicit in the collection by the presence of a powerful nuptial poem entitled "Bride and Groom Lie Hidden for Three Days" in which man and woman are literally reassembling each other. The book ends with the figure of "The Risen", the emblem of individuation as defined by Jung, presenting the myth of a new human being miraculously transcending his present condition and achieving the alchemical union of reason and inspiration, masculine and feminine, but also matter and spirit. Once again, Ted Hughes was repeating a very personal vision of the world, yet presenting marked resemblances with existing theories.

He was also conscious that the metaphysical considerations, which his poetry constantly aspired towards, and which enabled it to take flight, had largely failed, so far, to filter through to his readers. The core of his message was being ignored. Either, as it so often happened in America, there were very negative reactions grounded on biographical reasons alone, for which no literary reasons were given or, as in England, the general attitude was one of adulation for a poet that the Queen herself seemed sometimes to want to canonise in his lifetime, remaining strangely deaf to certain problematical implications of his poetry. Ted Hughes himself, perhaps, was unable to control all the ghosts and demons that his rash opening of Pandora's box had let loose, and he was so impatient with the slightest reservation about his work that he would sometimes give the impression that he wanted to retire from the public scene and rely on posterity for a posthumous vindication of his work. His celebrity however increased. An exhibition dedicated to his work was organised by Keith Sagar at the Ilkley literature festival. He also took part, for instance, in the Cambridge poetry festival with his friends Miroslav Holub and Zbigniew Herbert, but also with two American poets, Robert Creeley, one of the key figures of the Black Mountain school whose ideas on poetry were not very different from those of Ted Hughes, and John Ashbery who wrote poetry much closer to that of the surrealists and of the modernist movement that Ted Hughes deemed aberrational. The room was packed and people listened to him reading the *Crow* poems in a religious silence that attested to the unquestionable veneration in which he was held at the time. Ted Hughes was in danger of becoming a sacred cow, and in England all criticism was immediately looked upon as being motivated by vulgar jealousy. Moreover, the mystery that gathered around his person was further increased by the fact that he categorically refused to appear on television, that he had not expressed himself on the radio for a long time and that he would not be photographed. Owing to a sort of superstitious queasiness, he seemed to mistrust any infringement upon anything too personal.

Had he made a mistake by authorising Aurelia Plath to publish the letters that Sylvia had written her? A certain Frances McCullough, who had been appointed to prepare an edition of these letters, wrote to him quite often to try to reach an understanding. She was trying to obtain a written agreement from Ted

Hughes along the lines that neither he nor his children would go to court over anything contained in the letters. But Hughes was worried by the blatant untruths they contained. He would call Aurelia Plath to witness over some of Sylvia's allegations that he had abandoned her without money, whereas he still had in his possession the chronological account of all the sums he had given her at the time. Among other very surprising details that he found most difficult to believe, there was the reference to an unfinished novel, said to have been entitled *Falcon Yard* and supposed to have been the story of their life together, from their first meeting at the *Saint Botolph's Review* launching party until their separation. Aurelia said that she had seen Sylvia burn the manuscript with her own eyes, but Hughes found it very difficult to believe.

More generally, Hughes was well aware that the publication of the letters was going to add substance to the fictional character that Plath had constructed, taking him as her model, and giving it his name, intricately entwining what was real and what was imaginary. What Hughes feared was to be judged in absentia, without any possibility of appeal, on the evidence of letters in which faithful memories were mixed with dangerous delusions. He would have to wage battle, he realised, with the ghost of Sylvia Plath. He intended to try his best to limit the damages that this spectre might cause to himself and to his family. The ghost, he thought, had already sufficiently avenged itself with Assia's and Shura's deaths, which had in their turn hastened the death of his own mother. In particular, he wished to erase all reference to Court Green from those letters destined for the public, lest the house should become a place of pilgrimage with Carol and himself as living attractions. He could not stop the tendency to turn him into a shady character in the legend of Sylvia Plath, but he thought that he could, in part, put some check on it, and it seemed to him a more desirable thing to do than to allow untrustworthy biographers, desperately casting about for spicy gossip with which to slander him shamelessly.

At this time, he was trying to fall back upon the position of the responsible head of the family. His main care was the important sums he had to pay in heavy taxes and for costly renovations at Lumb Bank amounting to thirty thousand pounds. His greatest regret was that it would prevent him from buying a few cows of the same breed as his pedigree bull, plus a few others of different breeds — Angus, Devon and Limousine — to improve the quality of his herd. Money was lacking just when he finally made up his mind about the breed of cattle that he wanted to raise. But graver issues were to be faced. He had to find a small cottage in North Tawton for his father, now eighty-four, where he could visit him every day, for it was sad to see that the old man did nothing all day but sit in front of his colour television set, abandoning himself to the anaesthesia of modern life that so grieved his younger son. *The Beacon*, his house in Yorkshire, was still unsold. Uncle Walt had been taken to hospital, but he had lost all will to live. These worries, and the long hours spent writing poems, made him neglect his work on the farm, and it annoyed him. Then his father-in-law, a patriarch and a last remnant of the old country life, fell ill with cancer and died in February 1976. Ted suddenly realised that with Jack Orchard's death his Moortown dream was coming to an end. The success of the farm relied on the experience and skills of the old man who had been so engrained in the timeless routine of the farm, year after year; Ted himself felt incapable of replacing him in his task. He started to sell his animals. He was even contemplating the sale of his land. In March, Uncle Walt finally succumbed; with his death a whole world passed away forever. The same year had seen the death of Henry Williamson, the author of *Tarka the*

Otter. In spite of his questionable beliefs, Ted had never ceased to like him; his death would confirm that the previous generation had had its day. Ted fell into a depression aggravated by physical suffering. Though he was clearly aware that his ailment was a classic case of psychosomatic illness, the knowledge could not relieve his pain. If he was not to sink with the apparent wreck of his pastoral dream, he must cling to poetry and dedicate himself entirely to it.

By March, he was flying to Australia with his father, where he would take part in the Adelaide literary festival. In the south of Australia, it was as an enthusiast reader of D.H. Lawrence that he enjoyed the subtle pleasure, known only to the well-read, of recognising the landscapes and the animals that he had described. But the public reading of his poems were disturbed by demonstrators who barged into the room chanting his name and brandishing posters accusing him of the murder of Sylvia Plath. He found a consolation of sorts by sleeping with the press attaché, Jill Barber, a thirty year old fast liver who, relying no doubt on the petty chronicle of the great man's foibles, had taken her chance with the help of a few bottles of Australian wine. As she had the project of settling in London, it was an ideal launching pad. Soon, while William Hughes was prolonging his first visit to Australia to spend some more time with his son Gerald, the two lovers were flying to England in different planes; they met again in London after Ted had called his Jillie to tell her that he loved her. This same year, they were seen together pretty often at various literary events or at dinner parties at the houses of some of Ted's friends. Once more he felt caught up in his past follies, and embarked on a new amorous adventure capable, he thought, of renewing his poetic inspiration. One day, he even called on Robert Graves, as a faithful proponent of his theory of the white goddess, to introduce his muse, as he called her, to the master. While Jill's new apartment was being done up, Ted Hughes would occasionally lend a hand with the wallpaper, and they spent some weekends at the houses of friends. She was cultivating the illusion that he was a widower, encouraged by the fact that he was speaking of marriage to her. But what he had in mind was rather a mystical union, without witnesses, at the summer solstice, in some magical place in his dear Devon, by the side of rocks charged with ancestral energy. For his gipsy girl, as he called her, the whole thing appeared a more prosaic affair, as she steered the mind of her impassioned lover to bring him to use his influence in favour of one of her friends seeking collaborators for her literary magazine. They smoked gauloises. It revived the mood of the fifties, in the good old days at Cambridge. Between two fishing trips, they paid an emotional visit to the tomb of Sylvia Plath. Jill was broad-minded: she had no objection, she said, to his seeing other women. A few months later, the muse from the Antipodes would put an end to the affair and take flight towards new adventures. Her amorous spree with Ted Hughes left her excellent memories. She would recount them at great length in the press, a few years after the poet's death.

At about the same time, he struck up a relationship with Emma Tennant, the daughter of Baron Glenconnor, whom he had seen, some time back, in the wake of Yevtushenko. Emma said that she fell in love with Ted's face because of its resemblance with those of the statues on Easter Island. She had called on him under the pretext of asking his help for the launching of *Bananas,* a literary journal that she wanted to get started. The publication would be in the surrealist style, long after Surrealism had gone out of fashion. In actual fact, it was a sort of *Titbits* or *Private Eye* for bluestockings, generously illustrated with mildly provocative pictures of female bodies. Of course,

Hughes's name and his social contacts doubtless proved useful to set the project going, but Ted Hughes would not take long to realise that what really fascinated her was the mystery surrounding the years during which he had lived with Sylvia Plath. She secretly hoped that, in the course of their pillow talks, she could bring him to confide to her such revelations as she might use to pander to the curiosity of the public. Indeed, she made no secret of it when, a few months after the poet's death, she came out with the full details of their affair. She did so without the least scruple, because she had always been perfectly clear as to her intentions with the man whose secret self she had thought she could bring to light. For a time he had gone as far as to talk, desultorily, of going to live with her in Scotland. At this moment of his life, Ted Hughes was still rather unguarded in his words and his behaviour, a surprising naivety, considering the fact that he cut such a figure. But there was every reason to suppose that he had not yet taken the full measure of his public stature.

However, the sudden collapse of the Moortown pastoral seriously rocked the idyll of his second marriage. His father had come back from Australia and had been staying some time in London with Olwyn. Then he came back to Court Green and had to be placed in a home for old people where he got up to mischief. Though Ted went often to see him, he no longer recognised his son. In spite of a rather trying family life, however, between an ageing father and adolescent children, Ted Hughes nonetheless resumed more regular literary activities. The same year, he received the visit of Dona Feuer, an American lady who had come to Europe with the Martha Graham's Dance Company. She had been impressed by Ted Hughes's introduction to his selection of Shakespeare's poetry, and she called to impart to him the reflections that this introduction had inspired in her. It was to be the beginning of a long correspondence. They would never meet again, but they would remain in contact for nearly twenty years, exchanging long letters, which gave Ted Hughes the opportunity of developing his ideas on the work of Shakespeare. From now on, he would more than ever pursue several projects in parallel, reviving an old ambition of his of simultaneously cultivating several poetic aliases. The children's poems that he continued to produce were gradually building up a universe of their own with its own special atmosphere. In *Moon Whales*, which was just coming out, there were imaginary animals living on the Moon described as the hidden face of our world, and he was preparing a sequel that would be called *Moon Bells*. He was using his diary in verse as a source for producing texts on country life that were on the borderline between poetry for children and for an English readership which was more and more urban, but which continued to feel a nostalgic attachment to nature.

In quite a different style he published in the spring a book of a peculiar sort under the title *Gaudete*: a Latin imperative, inviting readers to jubilations of a more particularly adult nature. It is a sort of small verse novel or a long narrative poem of rural gothic fantasies, recycling the old stereotype of the lecherous vicar. It tells the story of the Reverend Lumb, a village vicar assailed by mischievous evil spirits that replace him for a time by his infernal duplicate, while they take the priest himself into the underworld for a season in hell. The dissociation of personality is a favourite theme in English literature, brilliantly illustrated in the past by R.L. Stevenson's *Dr Jekyll & Mr Hyde* or by James Hogg in his very Calvinistic *Confessions of a Justified Sinner*. Hughes's Lumb is the satiric double of a vicar, who has decided on a literal application of the one Gospel imperative, "love thy neighbour", in a purely erotic register. To this end, he sets about getting all the women of the parish with child in the vain hope of siring a Messiah. A well-established medieval anti-clerical tradition came in support of an anti-Christian satire in the spirit of the author of the *Crow* poems. Hughes added piquancy to the dish with a dash of black magic, spiced it up with a few horror scenes, and moistened the whole with a large admixture of coarse humour. The farce culminates in a final roundup when all the participants disappear, without a trace of them being left, after an orgy of ritual rape and murder, in the blaze of the village church. The real vicar resurfaces at the end to celebrate, in a long epilogue, the female deity of whom he has become a devoted worshipper. This buffoonery, not in the best of taste, was diversely received in England, prompting Hughes to say that it had been blindly praised by one half of half-idiotic critics and slated by the other half. American readers, meanwhile, harmoniously conjoined in a universal contempt of the book, while at the same time the sales of Sylvia Plath's *Johnny Panic*, which was then coming out in an edition prepared by Ted Hughes, were reaching tens of thousands. All this was not really important, however, for Her Majesty Queen Elizabeth had not been shocked by Ted's bawdy tomfoolery; she had perhaps even been amused, for soon after its publication she made her favourite poet an Officer of the British Empire. This exceptional mark of honour was immediately to bring him an embarrassing display of excessive respect, which persisted for a long time; he did not quite know whether it made him feel more ill-at-ease than flattered in his vanity. Be that as it may, his greatest preoccupation was now to evade paying the exorbitant English taxes on his royalties by settling in Ireland, a thing that he ought to have done long ago, he thought, if he'd had the slightest grain of sense. Meanwhile, accompanied by his charming Jillie, he embarked on a promotional tour for *Gaudete* in the United-States. On the other side of the Atlantic the book was of course perceived as the work of a misogynist, which could but increase the vindictive anger of the "red guards" of Sylvia Plath who systematically organised happenings to disturb his public readings, chanting the title of Plath's emblematic poem — Daddy! Daddy! — and calling him a woman killer.

Back home, Ted Hughes found himself once again plunged in a domestic environment whose dull ordinariness was in jarring contrast to his high-soaring transcendental aspirations, which he could not bring himself to think were outdated, whatever everybody else might suggest. His daughter was now a healthy-looking young woman of Germanic appearance, preparing to join an art school, and who caused him futile worries by falling off her boy-friend's motorbike. His son was developing a passion for muscular exercises and competitive cycling, as if by way of opposing a father who had a visceral allergy to any Cartesian mechanisation of the human. Ted Hughes now liked to write in exercise books whose covers were decorated with photographs of picturesque country scenes. On one, a river flows under a bridge, bathed in autumn sunlight; on another one a bird brings a worm to his young in their nest. All the same, it was a precious consolation for him that his son had retained his passion for fishing and even dreamed of having a small boat to go on the river with his father. But the drought of 1978 made boating utterly impossible and he was even obliged to sell his remaining cows, which could not be fed on the farm. His father could no longer look after himself. To make things worse he had himself gone through two weeks of intense panic, which had left him mentally exhausted, when Jill had thought for a time that she was pregnant. It seemed to be written somewhere that he should never stop being beset with the miserable problems of his family lives, which looked all the more formidable to him as the tide of his inspiration had again reached its low watermark after the riotous excesses of *Gaudete*. He therefore took some poems from his *Moortown Elegies* to make a luxury book to be published by his sister Olwyn's Rainbow Press. It was a large-size book, bound in red morocco with a bull drawn by the poet stamped in gold on the cover. An edition of little less than two hundred copies was printed, all of them signed by the author, and put out for sale at the popular price of one hundred and seventy five pounds for each of the copies marked with a letter, and only one hundred and sixty for those in the numbered series. It was so profitable an operation that, the following year, Nicholas undertook to hand-print some of his father's poems that he sold to get pocket money and buy a fishing boat, at the price of five pounds a sheet, and fifteen pounds if there was a drawing. They sold like hot cakes. In the same positive spirit, Ted Hughes had Ralph Steadman's Steam Press print one hundred copies of a short story called *The Threshold*, to be sold at the price of one hundred and five pounds a copy. It was a sort of improvisation, halfway between the transcription of a dream and automatic writing, mixing a phantasy of easily acquired unlimited wealth with a rehash of the theme of *The Wound*. In a nightmare, multicoloured lizard women, not unlike Keats' Lamia, are tearing the narrator to pieces. The practice of literature had become a puerile but lucrative amusement, since the flimsiest things signed by the man whom England then regarded as the greatest of her living poets would immediately fetch exorbitant prices.

In March 1979, having bought a tail coat and a grey top-hat with waistcoat and matching bow tie, striped trousers and patent shoes, Ted went with Carol to lunch with the Queen at Her Majesty's invitation. The Queen indeed seemed to have a special affection for him, but a selective affinity existed between him and the Queen Mother who shared a passion for fly-fishing with him. That same spring, he would have the opportunity of catching two salmon in a stretch of the river Dee, which runs through the vast tracts of land around Balmoral Castle, where he had been invited to spend a week with Queen Mum, who resided for some time in Scotland every year in one or another of her numerous castles there, Glamis at Angus, or Mey in Caithness, or Brickhall at Balmoral. Ted Hughes, who was nearing fifty, had now grown more sedate, and he devoted more and more time to his favourite sport. Moreover, it was a pastime which enabled him to establish links of mutual trust with his son. They would spend long hours making artificial flies with feathers and coloured silk, choosing the best equipment and planning fishing trips. In April, they went fishing pike in some remote corners of Lough Mask in the west of Ireland. They dreamed of expeditions to distant countries, which would take them on the trail of migrating salmon and other noble fish, as far, perhaps, as Alaska, or else Mexico, Malawi or Africa. It seemed to him, sometimes, that he was reliving with his son some of the old joys he had so much missed when Gerald had left him for Australia; this same year, he was still writing to his brother to reproach him once more for having deserted him, leaving him orphaned, he said, when he went away and offered his whole life to Australia. Now, at last, it seemed that the pang of loss was less sharp, that he had retrieved the keenness of his desire for action. The tightening of bonds with his son happened around the time when Frieda, who was now eighteen, decided to get married, a hasty decision, coming sooner than her father would have expected. Olwyn, then fifty-one, broke off her marital relationship with Keith Gordon who ran *Modern Poetry in Translation* and the Rainbow Press; she had found a new companion who bore a strong resemblance to Ted Hughes, but who would soon prove a violent specimen of a man. Neither idyll would last long, but they modified the map of Ted's affections, who had taken them for granted for so long that it left him somewhat disoriented. He saw likewise with nostalgia that as the England of his youth passed away, Ireland, that paradise of ancestral rurality, was being invaded by Germans and Dutchmen buying all the beautiful houses, causing prices to rise so exorbitantly that Ted despaired of ever realising his dream of settling there.

However, a new poetic project was near completion. It consisted in writing poems to accompany photographs of the country of his youth taken by the photographer Fay Godwin. The book would draw its inspiration from the nostalgia evoked by the pictures of familiar childhood haunts that were so charged with emotion. He also aimed to satisfy the taste of the greater part of his readership, that is to say, of those who liked his poetry for the beautiful evocations of nature in which he excelled. It gave him an opportunity to do something in which he had achieved great mastery by concentrating on a mimetic observation of the outside world. Besides, for him photography had a magical power, for the representations of the world it offered were so faithful to the original that they had the awesome capability to create a phantom presence. Perhaps it was for this reason that he had such scruples about having his photograph taken, as if he literally felt, in front of the camera, like an animal fearing to be trapped. It was not that he disliked seeing photographs of himself, but he was averse to being taken for an object of minute observation, out of his proper context, like some freak at a fair. That may be why there are so few photographs of him, most of which were taken by relatives or friends and not by professional photographers. He was insistent that photographs of him should not come out without his approval. To give just one single instance, Bill

Brandt, after spending a few days in his company in order to know him better and be in the best possible conditions to take photographs of him, had been unlucky enough to produce images of Hughes that had called forth a violent reaction on the part of their subject. The poet, whose vanity was wounded, exclaimed that they looked like plaster casts of Frankenstein's creature taken to illustrate a catalogue of mechanical spare parts. Brandt had no choice but to offer to destroy the negatives to put an end to the crisis. Fay Godwin was luckier, perhaps because her way of looking at the world was closer to his. But she had not done portraits of him: her photographs were of picturesque landscapes, perfectly transparent, on which the eye of the photographer did not obtrude. The rare human figures were rustic characters whose time-weathered faces accorded well with their surroundings. Ted Hughes thought he had discovered that the Calder valley, where he spent his childhood, had been one of the last strongholds of Elmet, supposedly the last Celtic kingdom to have resisted the attacks of the Angles until the 7th century, when with the Saxons they crossed the North Sea to invade Britannia. For this reason he chose to call his collection *Remains of Elmet*. The archaeological vestiges depicted in the book were those of the textile industry, which had colonised the valley in the 18th century. The book exploited the vein of the sort of romantic ideology that puts a high premium on nature as against culture, and takes delight in the contemplation of ruins. Ted would later say that, while composing the texts, he had had the memory of his mother's voice in mind, to such an extent that he had had the feeling of intruding into the feelings of the deceased, and he had found this a rather upsetting experience. As these poems were of easy access, with no ambitious innovations, they were relatively well received. Some critics, however, pointed out that the language was too tense, the sound effects too brash, reminiscent of his first poems, with a tendency to force their effects upon the reader's ear, which sometimes bordered on caricature.

For some strange reason the composition of these poems left him exhausted, so much that he spent the rest of the year in bed, having severely sprained a muscle during a public reading of his poems. Indeed, on these occasions he would marshal all his strength, his two hands gripping the book open before him, arching his back so as to impart all the energy that he could muster into his performance. On this particular occasion, while summoning his strength, he had felt a strong pain in one buttock and when he left the room, he had been seen to limp. Intensive therapy had been necessary for him to overcome the cramp.

He had no doubt as to the existence of psychosomatic phenomena. He had endured the painful experience of their real nature in his own body. In the past, he had been able to observe them in his own mother, owing to the eloquent fluctuations of her health. It was one of the reasons that explained Ted Hughes's shamanistic vision of medicine. He could not be satisfied with the scientific approach that prevailed in the West. For this reason he placed a certain confidence in bonesetters and traditional healers. He had already had a painful experience, though, when he entrusted his spine to a confirmed quack, who had only succeeded in making it worse. In the early months of 1980, a rather surprising exchange of letters took place between Ted Hughes and Prince Philip who wrote to him from Buckingham Palace, in which they exchanged information on people who took an interest in paranormal phenomena. Neurosurgeons, journalists, healers of all descriptions: the prince and the poet exchanged addresses. A little later in the same year, Ted Hughes intervened to recommend the medicine man attached to Saint Bartholomew's Hospital in London and to the Royal Hospital of Devon and Exeter to His Royal Highness. It was a certain Ted Cornish of Okehampton, who claimed to be able to cure the heart deficiency of King Khalid of Saudi Arabia. Perhaps, Hughes suggested, the Prince would know a discreet diplomatic channel through which to convey the information to the Saudi royal family. Enclosed were the address and phone number of Ted Cornish and a letter from him.

For Ted Hughes, the end of the decade was a period of uncertainties, about his poetry as much as about other aspects of his life. Not that his intellectual curiosity had in the least abated, but it seemed to him that he was groping his way towards a new outlet, as if the violence that had dominated his youth had given way to a serene spirit of contemplation. Moreover, *Remains of Elmet* had demanded a greater effort of concentration than one might have guessed from the calm melancholy tone of the poems, for beneath their apparent simplicity lay a great inner tension. During those transitory periods when he was trying to recover his inspiration, or rather waiting for its return in utter helplessness, he would sometimes fall back into unfortunate enterprises, as prolific artists are often prone to do. He renewed his attempt to write for the theatre. Straining his talent once more, he allowed himself to be waylaid into writing the libretto of a musical comedy for children called *Pig Organ.* It was the story of a king who, being deprived of music, was condemned to be turned into a pig and was rescued from this plight by a pig organ, with a piglet at each of the pipes. The music was by Richard Blackford, but posterity has forgotten the name of the costume designer responsible for the pink rompers in which six adults and six children, grunting and snorting, wandered aimlessly on the stage with an air of boredom. Then came a poetry competition that Ted Hughes organised to try to levy funds for the benefit of the Arvon Foundation, the writers' school now established at Lumb

Bank. Apart from the poetry of Andrew Motion, who was eventually awarded the prize, Ted Hughes came across only one poem that he considered of any worth, although the name of the author did not stay in his mind very long. But the argument of the poem was much to his taste. It was an obscene love story between a woman and a baboon in a nightclub. Of the members of the jury, composed exclusively of friends, Seamus Heaney and Charles Causley also found the story very amusing. But if he had forgotten the name of the author Ted remembered the story well, because it occasioned a clash with Philip Larkin, who had not found it funny and had dug his heels in, declaring bluntly that if such a horror was considered as acceptable for the prize he would make his disagreement with the jury public.

But what did it all matter? Was it not time, anyway, to stop playing silly games? His old English teacher, John Fisher, who had believed in him since he was a schoolboy at Mexborough, had just died of lung cancer. Ted was sure that it was due to his having to spend his whole life breathing in air polluted by the coal power station near which he had been condemned to live. The boredom and depression engendered by modern life had done the rest by depriving him of all desire to live. It seemed more and more self-evident to him that, if it was to take a practical turn, his denunciation of modern society had to concern itself with ecology and the conservation of nature. The European Community was having damaging effects upon agriculture and, as far as he could see, it was going to bring conflicts among fishermen. It was fortunate that his son, who wanted to be a pisciculturalist, should have chosen a career that would keep him in contact with nature. Father and son, united by a common passion, went on a salmon fishing expedition in Alaska. They would never forget the long days spent tracking down fish in the river, standing waist deep in the powerful current, keeping a discreet but watchful eye on the bears that were fishing nearby without paying much attention to them. They had discovered a sort of luminous paradise. They slept in a tent, with the incessant sound of wind and water constantly in their ears, or else on the pebbles on the shore in the warmest hours of the afternoon. Clad in the habitual angler's garb — plaid shirt and check cap, fishing waistcoat bearing dozens of multi-coloured baits — Ted, round-stomached and round-eyed, posed good-humouredly for his son's camera holding up the most enormous fishes of his catch. Once back in England, they felt they could still hear the distant echo of the ceaseless motion of air and water and, when they closed their eyes, the vibrating light was still there, dancing behind their lids. Ah! If only Gerald could have seen that! But it was by the side of his father's bed, now in hospital and no longer able to recognise his son, that Ted wrote to his brother describing their fabulous fishing expedition in the great North. In June 1981 William Hughes passed away. To ease his last hours on earth, Ted read aloud to him from his latest collection of tales for children, *Under the North Star*.

VII

POET LAUREATE

During the period immediately following the death of his father Ted Hughes strove to overcome as best he could a dull state of depression. He sometimes had the feeling that he no longer belonged to a world that had grown too old too soon, and that he was becoming more and more barren. He was no longer very successful as an angler, and the thought recurred that the water in which he was casting his line was so poisoned with acids that fish could no longer live in it. As to poetry, he stuck to it as much as he could. He wrote in schoolboys' exercise books he had salvaged he did not exactly remember when or where, perhaps when he had been teaching for a while in Cambridge. Some of them still bore the name of the child to whom it had belonged, written in a painstaking hand: "Name: A. Williamson / Subject: English Composition". But all this was of little avail. Considering the time and effort that he was devoting to the task, the results were meagre indeed. The death of the people he had loved, all the memories of these dead people scattered along his path were weighing down his life. He would sometimes try to figure out what his life might have been like, if what had taken place in 1963 and 1969 had not happened. But it was impossible to imagine. He saw these tragic events of his life as steel doors that had closed upon him, cutting him off from just enough of his being for him to continue to live and leaving him, in the end, as a maimed person, shorn of many of his capacities. Perhaps, in such moments, grief spread insidiously like a poison into his system, leaving damage such as time could never cure.

In his moments of strongest depression, he sometimes had the strange impression that the state of the country was echoing the state of his mind. The pollution of rivers, the overexploitation of salmon and sea trout by British fishing boats, as well as foreign boats that EEC directives authorised to come and fish too close to that nook-shotten isle of Albion, were such that, in his eyes, resources for the future were sure to be jeopardised. He bought a 10-horsepower outboard motor for his 16-foot boat with which he intended to explore estuaries and make his way upstream on the rivers of Devon. He was involving himself more and more in the defence of the neighbourhood rivers which he knew so well. Being on visiting terms with the local gentry, he had fishing access to certain private stretches. He would obligingly lend his fame to help obtain a local TV station, or to support some other request in favour of a regional or parish organisation. But all these activities were diverting him from his true vocation. The time that he devoted to fishing or to his voluminous correspondence was lost for poetry. He sometimes felt that his life was flowing away into the channels of other people's lives, and that it was incumbent upon him to shut the door on importunate requests as soon as possible, to concentrate his creative energies entirely on the service of the muse, as he had always thought he should do. This feeling of a permanent haemorrhage slowly draining him of his vital reserves sometimes took very concrete forms. He could no longer find certain photographs of himself to which he was very much attached. One of them in particular, taken by his brother, when he was skinning a badger in the orchard with Frieda in the foreground with a rope bound tightly around her body: it must have been stolen, there was no doubt of it. If Gerald had kept the negative, could he have a print made for him? As if by magic, all sorts of documents did vanish from the house. Recently, the films had been removed from Carol's and Nicholas's cameras, probably by some guest who had taken great care to replace the reel and rewind it down to the same number in order to conceal his theft.

Fortunately, there was Ireland. Ted went there frequently to return the visits of his friend Seamus Heaney, in whom he recognised the greatest poetic voice to have appeared in Ireland since W.B. Yeats. That winter, he planned to go fishing to try to catch some of the large pikes in Lough Car. Alas, his old project to settle in Connemara would stay a pipe dream. But perhaps he could make his escape to Scotland. One thing was sure: he could feel clearly that he was not in good health. He started dieting again. Then, in the summer, he treated himself to a larger boat with a more powerful engine. While he sometimes wondered if there was still some poetry left in him to write, the volume of the collected poems of Sylvia Plath that he had published the year before was selling even better than the others. The money it brought in would bring back the nightmare of taxes. So he got rid of one part of the difficulty by selling all her archives to Smith College. The little money that was left when the taxes had been paid he wanted to give to Frieda, but she was jealous of her independence and was refusing presents. Finally, she let him buy a house for her, for what could be more natural than that a father should help his children build their nest?

In April 1982, Faber & Faber published *New Selected Poems 1957-1981*, which marked the conclusion of a second phase in his literary career. The first period had been similarly marked by the publication in 1972 of *Selected Poem 1957-1967*, which presented samples of his poetic production up to and including *Wodwo*. The new volume also took into account what he had written since *Crow* until *Remains of Elmet* and *Moortown,* a collection which Faber & Faber had republished in 1979 as *Moortown Elegies,* originally published by the Rainbow Press. Various other pieces had been added to the volume among which were the poems he had salvaged from the wreck of *Orghast*, lumped together under the title *Prometheus On His Crag*. The organisation went in terms of decades, as if the life and works of a poet must absolutely be compartmentalised in separate sections: 1972, 1982... When he turned his thoughts upon what his poetic factory might well turn out by 1992, he was both irritated and invaded by profound lassitude. Before setting his personal production line going again, he now devoted the greater part of his time to the publication of *Sylvia Plath's Journal* with Frances McCullough. His main concern was to cut out all that might be likely to do further damage to his already bad reputation and to disturb the tranquillity of his children. Besides, he was involved with Seamus Heaney in the compilation of a weighty poetry anthology that could interest as large a number of people as possible. It was by no means unpleasant, but it was a time-consuming job and left him little time for his own writing. The public readings of his poems also devoured much of his time and energy, and he would have liked to discontinue them. He had already decided to decline any offer of television broadcasts. On the other hand, his work had begun to be a subject of academic research. In 1981, two young academics from the North, Terry Gifford and Neil Roberts, published a *Critical Study* which came as the continuation of the process of scholarly reading of his work, started as early as 1975 by Keith Sagar in his book *The Art of Ted Hughes*, published by Manchester University Press. Moreover, Keith Sagar was preparing a second book in which he would publish the acts of a conference that he had organised in 1980. As if to confirm a process of canonisation already well on its way, the University of Exeter made him *Doctor Honoris Causa*, and he liked to say that rather unexpectedly he was "Dr Edward James Hughes, Master of Arts, Cantab., Order of the

British Empire." Wasn't that something to be proud of?

From time to time, the recluse felt the need to leave his hermitage. He went to Mexico with Carol for a holiday. Then he flew to Kenya and to the shores of Lake Victoria, near the sources of the Nile, to join his son Nicholas who was engaged with a scientific team from the University of Nairobi on a field study of *lates niloticus*, the perch of the Nile, a species of perch that is found nowhere else. Ted had feared a hostile reception on the part of the natives, but he was agreeably surprised to find the Kenyans friendly and welcoming. He would bring home memories of miraculous catches, for he had captured enormous specimens of the fish weighing from 80 to 100 lb. The fishermen's nets were regularly hauled in full of the enormous fish that were poured slithering onto the shore. At the sight, Ted Hughes was overcome with such a sense of wonder that he thought that he had not been so deeply moved since the birth of his children, so unbelievable did it seem and yet so unmistakably real, as if Lake Victoria was a compact mass made of a strange substance which, when it was spilt upon the shore, divided into these innumerable massive and wriggling particles. There was something biblical in such liberal abundance that was in painful contrast to the scarcity of fish in English rivers, a dearth that seemed to stem from the same source as his own incapacity to produce poems any more in which he could have faith. The state of his farm was also a saddening sight now that all the livestock had been sold; on a site once so fertile, where so many young had been brought forth at the lambing and calving seasons, there remained only one old pensioner, the red bull that had once been its pride. Ted, with a glint of anticlerical humour, had called him Sexton, uniting in the same word the church hand with the heavyweight sex toiler. But today, Sexton was dragging himself along lumberingly, nonchalantly chewing the cud, too old even to be sold. At the time, the Hugheses seriously thought of taking up farming again; their idea was to fatten bullocks or else to raise a flock of sheep, for they missed the presence of animals on the farm.

Ted was writing a lot, but the certainty that what he was writing was not the best that he could produce gnawed away at him ceaselessly. He felt a sort of guilt, he had a sense of duty left undone, for he was convinced that what he wrote did not correspond to what he had to say, and that he was nothing near to bridging the gap. Moreover, he felt that the literary climate was not favourable to him. The prevailing ideology was the same as that which he had fought in his youth. It had set in and had even acquired a greater force. Here was an interesting field of research for a sociologist or a historian of ideas. He would have liked to attempt a detailed analysis of this situation some day. But for a poet, for a poet like him, the atmosphere was asphyxiating and gave him no lift. At times, he would feel close to despair, he felt there was no hope of being heard, let alone understood by his contemporaries. Any attempt at conversing directly with the dominant ideology was doomed to failure; they were not on the same wavelength. All that was left for him to do, perhaps, was to speak to the walls of his room, shut up in his retreat of Devon, as if in a prison, exiled within himself from the world around him, seen as an old fool whom nobody would listen to any more.

The reviews of his new poems had been far from enthusiastic, as was to be expected, for they contained nothing new, but it nourished his doubts and his melancholy. Some critics, however, were more perceptive than others, as for instance Christopher Reid who, in an article entitled "The Two Voices of Ted Hughes" unearthed the dual character of his poetic voice with great clarity, a fracture that some years back Ted

Hughes had confided to his sister Olwyn as one would an intimate secret. In these selected poems, Reid said, two Hugheses could be heard who were difficult to reconcile but who coexisted harmoniously in his poems. Hughes I was a nature poet, perfectly at ease in this well-established English tradition. But Hughes II was a metaphysician and a moralist whose obtrusive Manichaean vision of the world very often gained the upper hand. Reid went as far as to point out a rigid ideological turn of mind, that was not un-connected with the fanatical attitude that Sylvia Plath had once blamed him for. One could detect, he said, a lopsided routine at work, which tended to drag him into the rut of a discourse that was too predictable and apt to churn out a particular type of bad poem that went on hammering at the same wearisome figures of speech, showily flexing their muscles. In conclusion, the critic wished for more poems in the style of Hughes I, who knew how to express himself clearly without abating anything of his passion for truth.

There was every reason to believe that Ted Hughes heard the criticism and decided to act upon it. He immediately tried to get back into the good graces of his contemporaries, taking care to avoid preaching at them ponderously, and he gave them only beautiful evocations of nature, pleasant and glossy. He drew upon his fishing memories and the profound, ecstatic feeling that he derived from his pastime. His new collection would be called *River*. In external appearance, it was a well-produced book of large size in the style of *Remains of Elmet*, which had been a commercial success. The poems were illustrated with photographs by Peter Keen, whose anecdotal aestheticism of the glossy magazine illustration type had a soothing effect. *River* is one of those books one finds upon sitting-room tables, the ideal thing for a gift. It partakes of an attempt to make poetry a luxury commodity to be savoured at leisure after a day's toil by readers rendered avid for images by television. The poems, made up of very short lines in free verse, are distilled with distinguished sparsity on large white pages containing very little text so as not to repel a modern public. This creates a calm and serene atmosphere with an artistic hint of discreet orientalism.

Indeed, Ted Hughes had for some time been fascinated by a certain traditional Japanese aesthetic style, in particular that of the Noh and of the Kabuki, the spirit of which he had allowed to seep into his own texts. He had imbibed a peculiar lightness of touch from the haikus, those short Japanese poems that in their three lines encapsulate a whole philosophy of existence. Ted Hughes had not properly speaking submitted himself to the discipline of the haiku, but he had written his poems in a style that based its effects on suggestion and evocation, inchoate gestures and silent abandonment to the beauty of Creation. The poet had allowed a discreet place for himself in the poems under the guise of an old sage, an adept of the angler's ascetic art of fly-fishing, whittling an ample and pure gesture out of the hundred of preliminary casts to place the fly just right at the end of a line whose flourish in the air had a spellbinding grace. Fly-fishing presented itself as a British analogue of Tai Chi Chuan, the ritual dance invented, or so they said, in the 12th century by the monk Chang San-Feng who, as he observed a snake defending itself against the attack of a crane, had discovered that the secret of victory lay in defeat, or how to win by yielding to one's adversary. Developed at first as a martial art, Tai Chi Chuan had now become in fact a way and a view of life. But was it not also the secret that Ted Hughes had discovered at the end of the adventure of *Orghast* and of *Prometheus on his Crag*? For Sogis had managed to succeed where Agoluz had failed once he had understood that to achieve true victory one must stop fighting. This formless energy, this vital liquescence tumbling and rolling in the river, was it not precisely the tao, the basic principle of which Lao Tse spoke in his *Tao Te Ching*? The violence of the themes, the powerful machismo of the language that had been so characteristic of Ted Hughes's first manner, had at last found a harmonious resolution in *River*. It was the placid celebration of a vitality in which powerfulness had now joined up with innocence, force with weakness and motion with immobility. In the past, the angler's line had been the metaphor of the writing of a predatory poet who wanted to ravish the secret of the other world and carry off its spoils. Now, this same line was no longer an aggressive cast, but a long continuous thread weaving a harmonious link with the world by its meditative and contemplative to-and-fro movement, grasping nothing, refusing nothing, on and on, indefinitely. Metaphysics was not absent from these poems but, at last, Hughes had ceased to address his readers in the strident accents of the Methodist preacher; he was now content with a sort of contemplative religiosity. In the primeval soup of the river, the disappearance of individual lives counted for nothing faced with the millions of births that were taking place there. This mythical and yet quite real place, where life and death seemed to conjoin, was what was being celebrated in these poems which went so far as to propose the river as the locus of a new alliance between man and his natural milieu. But the ideology did not go much further; it remained a soft version of the re-enchantment of nature, picking up a well-established trend that had been going on for several hundred years, and whose return to favour was, in essentials, quite the going thing.

He did not need to read what the critics said (it was something that he refused to do anyway) to know that he had tapped a rich vein. The short moments during which he had been worried were no more than the habitual spells of doubt between two books. By a striking coincidence, Frieda had finally decided to divorce and to make a new start; she had become a new person. She had taken up painting again and was about to publish a book for children of which her father thought very highly. Many signs showed that the poet was getting his breath back. He was again ready to accept invitations to festivals. He had attended St Magnus' festival in the Orkney Islands, and on this occasion he had not forgotten to take his fishing rod with him. He would also make a round of schools in the North to encourage children to love and practice poetry. He resumed public readings of his poems to raise funds for the NSPCC, the National Society for the Prevention of Cruelty to Children. Sotheby's was organising an auction sale of some of his manuscripts to raise funds for the Arvon Foundation. He was also lending his name in support of a campaign for the protection and preservation of the environment in Devon. A matter of grave urgency was to save the river Torridge from imminent destruction because of the filthy waste and irresponsible exploitation of its fish stock. All in all, he had every reason for regaining confidence in his capacities. His personal creativeness was in such stark contrast, he thought, to the sterility of the English civilisation of his time that it confirmed him in the belief that he was right. He thus went on working with renewed conviction and the same year published a farm fable for the young illustrated with engravings by R.J. Lloyd, entitled *What is the Truth?* For he still tended to be very didactic, plodding on in the direction of Platonic unveiling, according to which Truth must always be found behind the veil of appearances.

That summer, the drought had again rendered the rivers mute, but it did not stop the flow of his personal production. He indulged the pleasure of writing till the end of the year. He had learnt of the death of Bet-

jeman, but had not paid much attention to the specula-
tions in the press about who was going to replace him
in his royal function. A few days before Christmas,
the Queen had appointed his successor. Ted Hughes
was the new Poet Laureate of the British Crown.
Since the Queen appointed him, it was necessarily a
good choice. Yet, if the choice was utterly unques-
tioned, at the back of some people's minds there remained the idea that the post was generally not occupied by the most brilliant poet of his generation; this
was perhaps because it is difficult to distinguish oneself by composing poems for court and national occasions, but also because of the romantic idea that great
poetry cannot be a commissioned performance. Alfred
Alvarez, however, took his stand and spoke plainly.
Availing himself of the opportunity thus offered to
make up for certain ill-advised pages that he had imprudently risked in the past, he declared that it was the
first time since Tennyson that the post of poet laureate
would be occupied by the best living English poet.
The adjective "living" had particular overtones in the
case of Ted Hughes, who had often been blamed for
the death of Sylvia Plath, but it was also to resonate
with particular irony in an era when it seemed that, as
had been said in other circumstances of Americans
Indians, a good poet could only be a dead poet. Be
that as it may, it was a purely honorific title, the al-
lowance attached to the post was only of £70 per
annum with a 42-gallon tierce of Canary wine. It
could not have been jealousy that prompted Philip
Larkin to say that, of course, in a sane world, Ted
would not be Poet Laureate, he'd be the Village Idiot.
The witticism was greeted by apparently embarrassed
laughs, which so often in England are the conventional mask of an all too sincere feeling of glee. Ted
Hughes would later say that Philip Larkin could not
have been Poet Laureate himself in fact, because politically he inclined too much to the right.

Ted Hughes had known what to expect when he had accepted the Laureateship. He was sure that it would not be long before he was burnt in effigy, for everyone knows, he said, that honours are only the prelude to insults. He was right, and did not have to wait long to see his saying confirmed. The satirical magazine *Punch* had already published a cartoon: on a bridge, a young schoolmistress called Druscilla tells her friend Jeanet of her great concern about the growing illiteracy that one can observe in the country. Under the bridge, they discover the tramp Ted Hughes in a huff, who there and then reads to them two of his own poems, announcing his sponsors at the end of each one. "Alas! Jeanet exclaims, I'm afraid you're right, Druscilla!" It was the price to pay for celebrity. But Ted Hughes did not care. He was reading more voraciously, if that was possible, than he had ever done. He had set about reading the standard classics: Homer, Virgil and Ovid, and certain great novelists like Melville and Dostoyevsky. It seemed to him that it was indispensable that he should tend towards a spare style, such as he had already begun to develop in *River*, if he was to produce poetry that could stand the test of time. He was convinced that chance had had but little part in his appointment, which was rather an acknowledgement of the fact that he was exactly fitted for the function of official poet of the English nation. He saw that there was a link between his role and that of the sovereign. Ted Hughes, after all, was a convinced monarchist. He would say in a famous short poem that the nation was a soul and this soul a wheel of which the crown was a hub to keep it whole. To have the title of Poet Laureate conferred on him was to accede to a position that was equivalent to that of a shaman in certain primitive societies. His mission, he believed, was to intervene, on the suggestive plane of myth, to take care of the collective unconscious of his contemporaries and, if possible, to influence it through his poems.

This new function immediately increased the number of readers who wrote telling him what they thought he should do to write good poetry. These well-meaning counsels, offered with an assurance that was all the greater because it came from people who had never written the first line of poetry, began getting on his nerves so much that it was impeding his writing faculties. He gradually stopped opening his mail. It had in any case become so abundant that it would have required a full-time secretary to deal with it. So he left it unanswered, and even came to ignore it altogether. Instead, he admired Carol's green fingers as she made a wonderful job of the garden. People around him would sometimes remark that his eyes were becoming more and more asymmetrical: his left eye being very often mischievous and full of irony, whereas the right eye had become cold and melancholy, and could even at times take on a nearly cruel expression. The difference seemed to extend to the whole face. His lock of by now greying hair still fell obstinately down over his eyes. He still had the same nonchalant gait, but his gaunt stooping figure had grown a little more round-shouldered, as if the increase in fame had imposed upon him a more modest posture. In his dreams, an image of paradise insistently recurred, very much resembling faraway Alaska, where bears hibernate or hunt for migratory salmon in winter amid the thrilling sound of running water and the rapturous overflow of northern light.

In February 1985, he composed *Rain-Charm for the Duchy,* in which he had imagined, from the dead of winter, a summer storm breaking on the Duchy of Cornwall to celebrate the baptism of Prince Harry. Prince Charles and Princess Diana had sent him a letter to say how much they had loved the poem. Then *What is the Truth?* was awarded the *Guardian* prize.

But once again the past and its petty sequels were to catch up with him. Lynda Wagner-Martin, who had been approached about writing the official biography of Sylvia Plath was finally rejected by Olwyn. Ann Stevenson was contacted in her place, and Olwyn managed to convince her, owing to a substantial advance from the publisher, to write a biography of Sylvia under the control of the estate, that is to say of Ted and herself. There was, it seemed, no means of escaping the unrewarding business which, of course, would give people an opportunity to accuse him of manipulating Ann Stevenson so that she should not write anything in his disfavour. He was, indeed, wasting an important part of his life trying to exercise a right of inspection over the way in which it was going to be written. It was time squandered, because human lives, he felt sure, were under the control of occult powers which poetry alone was able to reach. It was therefore beyond the power of a simple prose text to fully account for them. He himself did not know the truth about those years of his life that he had shared with Sylvia Plath. Without running the risk of going wrong, who could honestly speak of the complex skein of circumstances and of the obscure reasons that had made a tragedy of it? In his eyes, it did not matter much to know whether or not Sylvia had been mad, and at what precise moment of her life, whether it was right or wrong to classify her as a schizophrenic, or again if he found it unpardonable that she should have burnt some of his manuscripts. In any case, does the life of a person not have a sacred character that it is indecent to profane, even when that person is a prominent personality? As to the question of knowing what, really, had taken place, in all probability, nobody would ever come to the crux of the affair. He himself was doing his best to understand what had happened, using all the resources of the very act of writing, which enables the writer to become aware of what he would never have discovered otherwise. If there were keys to these enigmas, no doubt, they would be found in poetry; for this reason, and in great secret, he was writing poems not intended for publication, which were his personal search for truth about Sylvia and about himself.

He sincerely believed in the existence of occult forces, which could have beneficent or baneful influences on our lives. Poets and seers intuitively perceived their existence. His mother had also been able to do so in her time, and now he thought he had inherited her gift as a spirit medium. Traditional healers also worked on this intuition. Ted Cornish, a well-known healer, had contacted him some time before, because he thought that Ted was the only person who sympathised enough with his beliefs to consent, perhaps, to write the story of his life. Would Ted Hughes become Ted Cornish's biographer? In a manner that was not entirely unlike a shaman's experience, Ted Cornish had discovered his vocation when another healer had told him that he would be able to conquer his handicap only if he could turn his energy towards healing other people. The prediction had been fulfilled and Ted Cornish had become a widely known healer whose capacities had been partly acknowledged by certain great medical authorities of the country. Ted Hughes set about getting information; he witnessed some of his cures and was treated himself with a certain success, apparently. During the whole summer of 1985, he hesitated whether to recommend him to Philip Larkin who was, he knew, suffering from cancer. At last, in November, on an impulse and prompted by his good heart alone, he took up his pen to write to him and give him the address of the healer in the hope that perhaps he could do something for him. But Monica, Larkin's faithful companion, answered saying that he was dead. Ted Hughes felt deeply mortified by the painful blunder. If only he had known that Philip was so near the end he could have avoided inflicting such a cruel indelicacy on Monica. It was, he said, a great part of our consciousness of the world that was gone with him. He had lived with the thought that he would always be there, because he had reached a point where his poetry seemed to retain infinite possibilities. At the funeral service in Westminster Abbey, Ted Hughes must have appreciated the ludicrousness of being asked to read a passage from the Bible at the burial of such a confirmed unbeliever; he fulfilled his task to the sound of jazz, a style of music that he found ridiculous but that Larkin had loved so much

The sad truth of death had made a traumatic intrusion into the mental world of Ted Hughes who, once again, was going through an experience that constituted one of the central tenets of his theory. There is a poem in the epilogue of *Gaudete,* in which he says that truth always makes itself known through an event that cuts through the illusory skin of ordinary life. Taking up, in fact, a point that had already been made by Aristotle, he explains that this revelation can happen in two different ways: either truth is revealed slowly, or it falls upon one suddenly, out of the blue as it were. In other words, either truth comes to us in the form of insidious gossip that is eventually accepted as undisputed truth, or it strikes home with the sudden illumination of a flash of lightning. Now, the death of Philip Larkin had penetrated his consciousness through a combination of these two revelatory manners. He indeed had long had the intuitive perception of it before experiencing the shock of its revelation, which destroyed once and for all the efforts he had made to try to persuade himself to the contrary. In the fishing process, which had a central place in *River*, the attack of the fish upon the lure, at the other end of the line, provides an excellent metaphor of such an encounter with truth. The time-friendly activity of fishing, viewed as a sort of contemplative dance, or as a particular form of meditation, was one way of conducting one's courtship with the truth of the world which, nonetheless, when it visits one with indubitable certainty, always manifests itself in an unforeseen and brutal manner. This was a particular aspect of his theory of revelation, which he had not really invented, but he had set his mind on expressing his views on the subject to his readers, to signal to them that it was imprudent to put blind trust in one's idea of truth: a thing is not true because everyone believes in it. He thought that it was necessary to repeat this trite and obvious truism, for it was a way of discreetly and obliquely suggesting that the purely materialistic vision of the world held by modern society might possibly be wrong, in which case the risk of a brutal awakening was not so very unlikely. In *Remains of Elmet* he had suggested that the industrial revolutions of the 18th and 19th centuries had proved to be dead ends. In *River*, he pleaded for a way of looking at the world that would rely less on the common habitual assumptions which, however abusively, underlie our Western vision of the world, always too sure of being in the right and never questioning its basic premises. A similar way of thinking also found expression in his books for children. In *The Iron Man* Hughes had tried to show that it was not a good idea to systematically refuse to welcome what was alien to our culture. These themes returned as the subject matter of a new book, whose title was perfectly clear as far as his preoccupations were concerned: *Ffang the Vampire Bat and the Kiss of Truth.*

During this same year 1986, he also published *Flowers and Insects*, another fine slim book of attractive aspect, illustrated with paintings by Leonard Baskin. Continuing to exploit his contemporaries' taste for nature poetry, Ted Hughes gave full rein to his talent for observation, but bending the apparent naturalism of his descriptions in a patently anthropomorphic direction, lending his subjects the sort of feelings you would expect in their observer. Nothing but ecstasies, displays of courtship, gaping corollas, to such an extent that the critic on *The Times,* after a surfeit of exclamation marks, humorously entitled his review "Porn among Plants". In fact it was not limited to plants, but it extended to insects, and birds, and even spiders. One poem dwells complacently on the coital mores of Epeira, a small spider that has the fascinating habit of devouring her male partner when she has no more use for it. But in fact, the fascination described by Hughes in the poems rested less on sexual satisfaction than on the thrill of the supposedly ecstatic moment of a birth, or the blooming moment when a metamorphosis is being accomplished. He felt enraptured by the beautiful instant of creation when a flower, or an insect, comes into existence, detaching itself from the great One, for a brief moment of sexed existence before returning to the womb of Mother Earth. On the whole, however, these innovative aspects of *Flowers and Insects*, which were developments along the lines of the breakthroughs initiated by *River,* fell short of fulfilling the hopes that they had raised. It may well be, too, that the tastes of the majority of his readers were encouraging the poet to produce poems that were easy to read, poems that would not challenge their certainties too directly.

As for Ted Hughes, he continued to be dissatisfied with the images of himself that professional photographers, at the request of the publicity department of his publishing house, kept proposing to him. The last to date had shown him a photograph on which he looked, he said, as if he had just woken with a terrible hangover, giving him an idea of his death mask before his time. It depressed him so much that he enjoined the photographer to send him a written promise never to use the photograph. The result was that his head did not appear on the dust jackets of his books as was the fashion. As a result, Ted Hughes was more a name than an image in the minds of people. On a symbolic plane, his public figure was slowly becoming an institution, for he was now also president of the Poetry Book Society, an association founded by T.S. Eliot to promote contemporary English poetry. The same year, Cambridge made him Doctor Honoris Causa and he received an honorary fellowship from Pembroke College, where he had been a student. Whether it was due to a sincere admiration for his poems, or in recognition of the importance of his status as Poet Laureate, or for reasons that had to do with his active involvement in the protection of the environment, the Prime Minister Mrs. Thatcher and Mr. Dennis Thatcher sometimes requested the honour of Mr. and Mrs. Hughes's company at receptions they gave at 10 Downing Street.

At the same time, and in comic contrast, Ted Hughes was required to appear in court in a libel case against him and a dozen other people following a film that had come out in 1979 based on Sylvia Plath's novel. The script-writer, apparently in need of sensationalism, had imagined a female character who harboured a homosexual passion for Sylvia Plath, and he had added a sequence in which mention was made of a project of suicide in common between the two girls. The additions were of course pure fantasy, but on the strength of a vague resemblance with this fictional character, a woman who had known Sylvia Plath at the time when she was a student of Smith College was suing various people, among whom Ted Hughes, claiming several million pounds in damages. The adventure ended with an acquittal, but only after he had been exposed to the indignity of standing in the dock on the other side of the Atlantic. He had occasion to speak with the plaintiff, who struck him as slightly deranged. The incident, when he looked at it calmly, was of little consequence; it was nevertheless exactly the sort of event which would make him fight shy of the folly of men, and reinforce his tendency to isolate himself, causing him to become as reserved and quiet as a shrinking violet. For the moment, he thought that he would be more useful helping to preserve nature, rather than wasting his time in such futile arguments. Between a visit to the fisheries on the Isle of Lewis in the Hebrides and a reading session of his poems at Victoria on Vancouver Island, he was doing his best to protect the otter in the rivers of England polluted by dieldrine, a pesticide that had until recently been used by sheep farmers. But if the fight to save the otter was successful, he would still have to defend its habitat from a tourist association that wanted to set up signposts to mark out the scene of the adventures of Tarka the Otter, so as to guide the numerous admirers of the famous book by Henry Williamson on the spot. He was also doing all he could to block the creation of an amusement park on the banks of the river at Knaresborough, arguing that it would be pure vandalism and would only end up defacing the beauty of the site which today fostered the idea of this self-defeating project. The true friends of nature had no need of signposts and amusement parks, and it was the height of absurdity to have to fight so that they should not be forced upon them. It seemed to him just as important to be active in defence of his local environment as to be able to refuse to pledge his support to literary enterprises that were meant to promote poetry in conditions of which he did not approve. He refused, for instance, to sign a petition asking for a plaque to be fixed in memory of Ezra Pound, because he did not want to forget that Pound had compromised himself with fascism in Italy. English newspapers would have been in their right, he maintained, had they entitled their article "Memorial Plaque for a Traitor" and poured forth a spate of insults upon the committee which had taken such a step. In short, it would have been more urgent, he thought, to start by examining whether a case could possibly be made in favour of Ezra Pound.

Experience had taught him that, in the life of a poet, it needed much less than what Ezra Pound had dared to do to sully a reputation and compromise the future of his work. The story of his own life, as written much against his will by Sylvia Plath's biographers, who had too often considered that a good way of promoting her was to run him down, had resulted in his work being practically never studied in the United States. He often reflected that he had been wrong to suppress the passages in Sylvia's writings which had seemed liable to harm his children and himself for, in so doing, he had given the impression that he had something to hide, which might pass for a tacit recognition of guilt. Similarly, the fact that he had systematically opposed the negative judgments being passed on Sylvia, and the way in which he had supported Aurelia when she had tried to evade her responsibility by promoting the shield of Sylvia as a model daughter, had done nothing but contribute to the image of himself as the only villain of the story. The result of that was that several generations of American students would be brought to consider as real historical facts the verdict of guilt passed on him by biographers who were not entirely scrupulous or unprejudiced in setting up their assumptions. Just as he could not be indifferent to the critical reception of his work by the public, so he ought not to have remained absolutely silent, as he did, on the chapter of his life with Sylvia Plath, for by so doing he had let the story of his own life slip out of his hands. One day, no doubt, he would have to take up his pen and give his personal version of what had happened.

He would explain to Janos Csokits, the Hungarian poet with whom he continued to correspond since the already far-off days when they were translating Pilinski's poems together, that the biography of Sylvia Plath that was to be written by Ann Stevenson, under his sister's and his own supervision, had inevitably given rise to a quarrel between the two women. He had tried not to get mixed up in the fray, but he could not but see that echoes of it had already leaked out to the press. The long and the short of it was that his dearest wish was to get rid of the millstone round his neck by selling off Sylvia Plath's manuscripts, and entrusting the care of her legacy to a lawyer. He was busy collecting information to know how it could be done. But he also solicited Csokits's advice about a critical text that he had first had the idea of writing during the trial, in which he attempted to draw a sort of map of Sylvia Plath's psychological make-up and of her set of personal symbols which could be found, he thought, in her literary works as well as in her most intimate writings. The life of Sylvia Plath could be visualised on this map through the different steps and movements of her evolution choreographed by a very particular family drama. It was for this reason that he hesitated to publish the text during Aurelia's lifetime, but it was at least a sincere attempt to express in his own words how he understood Sylvia's life.

But he was also receiving letters of encouragement. In March 1988, for instance, Stephen Spender wrote to congratulate him on the courage with which he continued to live and write in spite of the difficult conditions of his life. If many of his contemporaries did not scruple to cry with the pack, others were quite aware that he was being faced with a sort of lynching. It was due, of course, to the question of how much responsibility he undeniably had in Sylvia's suicide, but it was nonetheless clear that the aggressiveness of their attacks stemmed from the very heart of his poetic discourse, which gave vent to his impassioned feelings against the prevailing ideology of his time.

There was something of a poète maudit in Ted Hughes, at a time when the tyranny of conformist political correctness wanted to pass for the avant-garde. However, if his first-rate poetry was somewhat coldly received in some intellectual quarters, his children's literature went largely unnoticed by these severe watchdogs in the service of conformity, perhaps because it was not commonly regarded as great poetry. This part of his work, however, despite its lesser pretensions, had constantly met with frank unflagging success. He continued valiantly to shoulder the load for the perfectly legitimate reason that it provided him with a regular source of income, but also because he was convinced that the leaven of poetry could work on these young minds, at an age when their innocence guaranteed that they would be very susceptive to its influence. In June 1988 his *Tales of the Early World* appeared. Immediately after their publication, he took a plane to Alaska with his son Nicholas for a well-deserved three-week fishing trip.

Until the autumn of the following year, Ted Hughes pondered over and perfected another collection of poems that would demonstrate that he had at last found and mastered the new voice, which he had already tentatively explored in *Remains of Elmet* and *River* — *Wolfwatching* was probably his finest book since *Lupercal*. Seventy-five copies of the title poem had already been printed on Nicholas's small Albion hand-press seven years before. The title was an allusion to bird-watching, but *Wolfwatching* proposes quite a different way of looking at the world and its inhabitants. Through the power of empathy that is a characteristic mark of Hughes's nature poems, the contemplation of the wolf finally leads to seeing the world through the eyes of the animal. In a way, one could say that the poet was revisiting one of his first poems in which the penetrating look of the fox literally projected itself into his own. But the wolf, like the jaguar of some years before, is shut in a cage at the zoo. It is, perhaps, one of those which sympathised with his grief as he lay sleepless, nailed to his bed by a pain in the shoulder, like a Prometheus deprived of light, in the apartment at 23 Fitzroy Road, after Sylvia's death. But what spirits of handsome savagery could still linger behind the pale eyes of this captive animal? Just as in the past Ted had imagined that Sylvia's mental spaces resembled some Sahara, he now sees that the eyes of his wolf are like empty doorframes in the middle of nowhere. Is it the end of metaphysics? The unthinkable envisaged at last? Or could it be that the spirits don't wait till death's last step to leave a captive wolf? In other poems the same anxious thought recurs of a gaze piercing through appearances, but in vain. In particular, there is a diptych, a poem built on the model of a painting on two hinged panels, entitled "Two Astrological Conundrums". The first part of the poem describes a shaman's flight, journeying through the entrails of a tigress that has devoured him. In the second part, the character of William Tell suddenly appears. This hesitant archer, a variant of the Taoist fisherman, is the younger Ted and his steel bow, the one he used to shoot in the archery contests of his youth. The new voice that can be heard is that of a poet who dares, at last, to speak of himself and of those who are close to him with sincerity and authenticity, a voice that finally declares its presence in accents that disarm the criticism of hostile and angry readers. He evokes memories of the past, of the old people he has known, to whom old age, coming on apace, brings him nearer — his father William, his uncle Walt, with their memories of the First World War. And also a woman and mother figure — is it Sylvia? Is it Edith? The recollection of her slides into images of the textile industry, like the sewing needle whose chamfer is exactly like the groove of a pine needle. There is an evocation of reservation Natives, the memory of Edith's dark hair, and the ingrained class consciousness of Ted who liked to say that the fate of the English working-class was comparable to that of Native Americans. That was, he said, the unexploded bomb in British society. And there were also those terrible texts, like "Take What You Want But Pay For It"; it is the poem of a man who cannot believe in Christian resurrection, and who sees in the pieta the only possible representation of a salvation of sorts, insofar as a son, at his death, can be said to be restored to the body of his mother. In "Us He Devours," he confines his belief to a Holy Gargoyle and its gaping mouth, since in his eyes the only force through which a god, perhaps, is shaping the world is Hunger. But the blissful hatchings of *Flowers and Insects* find an echo in the last poem when the dove welcomes death's embrace, happily surrendering its finite being in the totality of the world.

Hughes was looking back to his past to effect a new mutation of his poetic voice, one that was rich in new inflections, displaying the full range of its tones with consummate art in a book of telling brevity. The same year, he also published *Moortown Diary,* which contained approximately the same texts that had already been published ten years before in *Moortown Elegies*. In more ways than one, he was thus confirming a retrospective movement which rounded off a new phase of his intellectual adventure. After working long and devotedly to advance the cause of poetry, perhaps, his poetic vocation, was on the point of being recognised, since His Royal Highness Prince Philip was inviting him to Buckingham Palace to discuss, among other things, the benefits there would be in promoting theatre for children, by organising competitions on themes that would at the same time alert the young to the necessity of preserving the environment. But it must have been written somewhere that certain zealous avengers would not let him pursue such futile enterprises. Triggered into action, perhaps, by Ann Stevenson's book on Sylvia Plath, which Alvarez reviewed, saying that he had never read a biography whose author so much disliked his subject, a petition was drawn up, under the pretext of the alleged existence of a divorce agreement between Ted and Sylvia, claiming that he had no right to inscribe his name — Hughes — on her tomb. The signatories saw it, they said, not only as his failure to honour the memory of Sylvia Plath, but also as a crying disregard for literary history. They demanded, moreover, that a signpost should be erected to guide tourists more conveniently towards this place of literary pilgrimage. Hughes, who was in a good position to know whether such a document existed, decided, as usual, to treat the new offence with scorn. When Sylvia's tomb in Heptonstal graveyard was profaned for the fourth time by anonymous hands intent on chiselling out the name of Hughes from the tombstone, he ordered a new one to be erected. But to make the task more difficult for the vandals this time, he asked the stone-cutter to carve the letters of his name deeper into the hard granite.

VIII

WINTER POLLEN

Ted Hughes, as he advanced in years, was becoming a more and more controversial figure. This was due, partly, to the persistent hatred that some of the admirers of Sylvia Plath harboured against him. It was also due to his exacerbated anti-modernism which, often taking a militant turn, made him an easy target for the zealous supporters of current post-modernism. Soft ideology is hardly mild for its detractors. Ted Hughes was the very type of the vestigial romantic, and a grumpy old fogy, to boot, who in the eyes of the crowd of right-thinking trend-setters had all the qualities required of a nearly perfect scapegoat. Was he a pro-environmentalist? It had to be for bad reasons, since he shared his convictions with some members of the royal family. There was, as everybody knew, a rather dubious vein of ecology, defended by hard-boiled conservatives and fierce supporters of hunting and fishing and other such regrettable traditions. It was a very questionable type of romantic pastoralism, which too often went hand in hand with a mulish refusal to subscribe to the basic notion that metaphysics, and a host of other superstitions, was dead. His being Poet Laureate of the Crown confirmed his detractors in these opinions, since it would have been hard to imagine a more archaic and stuffy function. Poetry itself was a literary genre that history would certainly confine to oblivion, and which would probably not survive the post-metaphysical era into which humanity seemed to have irreversibly entered. In such a context, the radical decision that Ted Hughes had taken to be a poet in the absolute sense of the word and to devote his life entirely to poetry was tantamount to a social battle or to an ideological struggle.

Proof of it was, he thought, the sustained aggressiveness that his life and work constantly prompted. For really, if he had been just one of those second-rate poets, with whom every period of history abounds, if what he had to say had had no bearing on what was happening to his contemporaries, they would probably have treated him with the same indifference that they showed to those other poets. Instead of which, he had to take infinite precautions every time he ventured out of hiding, which inclined him more and more to cloister himself in his beloved Devon. As soon as he emerged from his foxhole, like some modern Orpheus from Hades, he was seen as some sacred monster, attended everywhere he went with the stunned respect of those who used to savage him in the press. His long dishevelled hair, his shaggy white temples, his bushy eyebrows, still reinforced the supernal and Miltonic impression that he produced on privileged audiences, all the more so as it was a rare spectacle.

One thing, presenting a double-sided issue, really worried him: it was that he had not been understood either in his life or in his work. For this reason, discounting the second-rank activities that he was constantly saddled with, he always had two centres of interest. First, he pursued the poetic task that he had begun with *Wolfwatching,* in a resolutely autobiographical style, which would perhaps enable him some day to make known his own version of his life with Sylvia Plath. It was a work of long standing, which perhaps would never be published in his lifetime, but he laboured at it conscientiously, as a sort of spiritual exercise through which he was seeking dialogue with the spirit of Sylvia Plath, undertaken with great sincerity, as one prays. And second, he felt that he must also leave behind him an explanation of what poetry had meant for him. It would have to be done through a wide-ranging reflection upon English literature. There was this exchange of letters with Dona

Feuer, which had been going on for years. The reflections had given rise to voluminous reading notes that would have to be organised into a theoretical whole. But this could not be done overnight; long years of assiduous work would be necessary. For the time being, he was preparing a re-edition of his choice of poems by Shakespeare, the same as those in the 1971 edition. Also in the domain of anthologies, his publisher, who was also Seamus Heaney's, asked them to make a new selection of poems. It would be called *The Kit Bag*; Ted described it to Seamus in terms of a spiritual survival kit, a package of spiritual necessities to help people weather the wars and famines that the next century held in store, a sort of shield or a vaccine.

At the same time, the Universities of Ulster and of Aberdeen were jostling for the honour of conferring upon him the title of Doctor Honoris Causa. As he could not be in Ireland and Scotland at the same time, he had to make the necessary arrangements to smooth things out. There was also Bill Merwin, the American friend from Boston who wrote from Lacan de Loubressac urging him to involve himself actively in the defence of the rain forests of Hawai. At about that time, he was also writing to John Major who had just succeeded Margaret Thatcher, to press him to look upon the ongoing ecological disaster as a war to be waged, that is to say as a high priority. Later, he would be pleasantly surprised when he discovered that the English people were quite willing to make sacrifices for this cause. But to everyone's sad disappointment, the government was much too passive on such environmental issues. In the texts that children wrote for literary competitions, he could see that they themselves were sorely preoccupied by the state of their natural environment. He wrote to Prince Philip, the Duke of Edinburgh, to ask his help to collect funds for the preservation of the steelhead trout of

British Columbia. He sent well-informed letters to Michael Heseltine, the Minister of Agriculture, in order to acquaint him with the unforeseen consequences of the proliferation of drift nets on the northeast coast of Scotland — namely the disastrous state of the region's hotel trade which depended on fishing tourism, and had already thrown four hundred people out of work. He pleaded in favour of cooperation between the Ministry of Agriculture and the National River Agency in order to limit and eventually to forbid the use of drift nets. Michael could easily win many votes by this means. But he did not just use his influence to call the attention of men in a position of power to the importance of these issues, he also became involved himself in concrete actions. A good instance is the support he gave to Mr. Ian Cook, the proprietor of river banks and fishing rights in Exeter, in the action he brought against the South West Water Company about the pollution of rivers in Devon. On this occasion, Ted Hughes publicly expressed satisfaction that Mr. Cook had won his case and obtained substantial damages, with the water company also donating a considerable sum to the Institute of Freshwater Ecology. The court also declared that his right to clear water was valid and guaranteed by the Magna Carta of 1215. The Poet Laureate, on this occasion, requested leave to speak and declared that the victory of an individual over the corporate juggernaut was of great importance for the ecological cause, but also that the decision of the court would be an important landmark paving the way to a revival of Common Law, the system of law based on judges' decisions and customs which guarantees an individual's rights and liberties in England.

However, there was another front on which Hughes particularly wanted to be active — education. He wrote to John Major insisting on the need to reform the education program, insisting, among other things, on the importance of rehabilitating the practice of exercises aiming at developing memory in primary school pupils, but also of promoting an effort of reflection upon technical training methods, for he complained that schools too often confined themselves to pumping learning and skills into pupils, an indispensable thing to do, but that ought not to be done to the detriment of the time that should be devoted to the development of creativity and of mental capacities of invention. One does not educate a child properly by exposing him all day long to television programs, but rather by encouraging him to imagine and make one himself. More generally, he regretted that in education, as well as in art, it was considered enough to imitate the outside world and to reproduce its external appearance rather than strive to imagine and reinvent it. To his brother Gerald, who patiently applied himself to painting, he said that it was a waste of time to strive after the representation of the outside world; one should forget Rembrandt and Constable and study Michelangelo and El Greco. It was clear that his conceptions had undergone a radical change since the days back, in the sixties, when he recommended beginners in poetry should start with "verses of simple observation". He was also writing to the chairman of the Northern Examinations and Assessment Board to protest about the optional essay in the newly-devised A level for English Literature being dropped. Admittedly, creative-writing study groups had perhaps produced undesirable consequences, but it was because they were not well conceived; to bring about positive changes, a vigorous effort had to be made to give schoolteachers adequate training. These subjects were of paramount importance for him, because he was convinced that, by orienting teaching activities away from the development of children's creativity, the English educational system was committing a grave mistake that would atrophy the brain resources of the younger generation. The discontent of Western civilisation, he was sure, was linked to a long standing phenomenon, many centuries old, derived from the overly narrow humanistic principles on which education was based, dating back to the Reformation at least, which had caused people in the West to stay exiled from an important part of themselves and to become paralysed by rational thinking; people who refused, in short, to know themselves. He did his share, modestly, for the defence of his ideas in the debate on education, by organising writing contests and by publishing with Faber & Faber a collection of texts written by children whose ages ranged from four to twelve, letting himself be guided in his choice by his sense of the pleasure their authors must have taken in writing. Ted was only too aware that creation was a source of great joy. But he also thought that the problem of education had the same origins as the environmental disaster that he was doing his best to help tackle, for they both stemmed from the same cause, which was our objective manner of looking at the world. In both cases the problem was the unbearable assumption at all levels of human existence that the world was a mere collection of objects, without any relation to those who perceive it. Ecology, in the broadest sense of the word, was our way of inhabiting the world, as one says that the soul inhabits the body, for he was convinced that we are intimately connected to the world by a relation of mutual creation. It was the old romantic discourse, that of Wordsworth who, two centuries before, had declared that he did not need any other tutor than nature for his guidance, adding that we half create the natural world and half perceive it through the senses. It was a typical modern error to presume that the latest ideas are necessarily deemed the best. In those years, Ted Hughes found ideas very similar to his own in the French poet Yves

Bonnefoy, while he was also reading Éluard and Baudelaire.

Public opinion, in its apparent fluctuations from one day to the next, struck him as being not so much a mirror of the circumstances of the moment as obscurely responsible for them. He saw an illustration of this fact in the change of mood that seemed to have accompanied the coming to power of the new Prime Minister, for England under John Major seemed suddenly to regret the frantic social competition which it had approved under Margaret Thatcher only a few weeks before. It was, perhaps, not of primordial importance in itself but, more generally speaking, the mental life of the English nation seemed to be governed in part by ancient and obscure forces which were perhaps all the greater because their existence was denied. It was, no doubt, what Jung had called the collective unconscious and, precisely, as he was re-reading Shakespeare for the umpteenth time, it seemed to him that he was now better able to understand some essential workings of its machinery. He had more than once made the observation that the state of his health was closely linked to the thoughts that took possession of him at certain periods, so that it had always seemed to him that, in some way, he was composing his poems with his whole body. In March 1991, as he was studying *King Lear*, he meditated on the fact that Gloucester, once his eyes had been plucked out, nonetheless kept an intuitive vision of the way in which the world and men went on, while King Lear, though not blind, was on the contrary sorely deprived of vision. To his great astonishment, Hughes was suddenly affected by shingles, which forced him to keep to his bed and rendered him half blind — even totally blind some days — with a shooting pain in his right eye. Every night, the solution of problems that Shakespeare was posing him came to him in his sleep, so that he was composing in his dreams new chapters of his book, whose ideas and themes, it appeared to him, were strangely in unison with the multiple variations of his pain.

By the end of March the disease had gone, and he was able to resume work with a new pair of spectacles and a reduced keenness of sight in his right eye. In April, he finished writing what he called his *Shakespeare*. Owing to a steady, continuous effort he had composed the book from his notes and his correspondence. He now had a typescript of five hundred pages ready for publication. In May, he left for Scotland, to spend a week, as he did now every year, with the Queen Mother whose zest for life enchanted him. She had a never-failing optimism and took an interest in everything. She seemed to have made a rule of always looking on the bright side of things, making her a person of very congenial temper, who was always surrounded by friends. The years seemed to glide over her and she had the vivaciousness of a young woman. Ted Hughes, having recovered his calmness of mind in her delightful company, prolonged his visit to Scotland by another two weeks of well-deserved holiday, so as to rest while fishing and enjoy the beauty of Scotland. He went to Glen Strathfarrar, to the north of Loch Ness, a few miles downstream, west of Inverness, in order to go up the valley from the natural reserve there. He liked the wild-looking river, winding through the old Caledonian forest where a great number of deer were still to be found. He had heard Uncle Walt say that the Farrars owed their family name to this region, Farrar being the name of the river because Strath had approximately the same meaning as Glen, so Strathfarrar meant in fact the valley of the Farrar, which had given its name to the whole region around Inverness: *varar* meant to meander slowly. It might just be possible, also, that his mother's ancestors had been farriers, but the two explanations were not necessarily exclusive. Ted Hughes was thus abandoning

himself to a reverie in which language was inseparable from place, both having an ancestral depth that
he called dialect, and which intimately permeated the
language and the work of Shakespeare, as if the bard
had possessed an intuitive knowledge of this sort of
spiritual substance that was the soul of Britain. In
Scotland — in North Britain, a name that could not be
used without difficulty here, since the Act of Union
had conferred political unity upon the British Isle at
the beginning of the 18th century — there came to him
poems rich in irony and humorous detachment, such
as his poetry had never known before. He let the spirit
of the popular folk tales seep into him in a comic
mood that played with exaggeration, verbal dexterity,
and the supernatural, to produce a sort of literature
that takes delight in its myths without quite believing
in them.

Ted Hughes was one of those people who are not
superstitious but who believe in ghosts because they
have seen them. Myths for him were quite real, although they existed on a very different plane from
that of ordinary reality. That was also how he practised astrology — without really believing in it. It was
for him merely a sort of divinatory exercise, an activity he liked to call pseudoscientific, but which had
in common with poetry a roundabout way of looking
at the world. Poets, after all, do not write in verse for
aesthetic reasons, or to make it easier for children to
commit their poems to memory, but because he who
is attentive to rhythm and rhyme is obliged to look at
what he wants to say out of the corner of his eye, letting meanings come to him that the fixed stare of science would frighten away. Myths are not to be confused with factual language, they are filters or prisms
destined to render apparent what, without them,
would remain invisible. The pictures they produce,
taken as a positive statement, are always erroneous
and cannot be corrected: their value lies in the fact

that they emerge into existence with us. Ted Hughes was a seer. In his world, myths and ghosts rubbed shoulders with the objects and beings of ordinary life, and he did not always clearly distinguish the ones from the others. Among these mythical presences, for instance, it seemed that he had no doubt that an English lion really existed. The fact that practically nobody believed in it did not weaken his certainty of the mysterious existence in Britain of a species of mountain lion, a sort of large black wildcat, a little like a jaguar, which he thought was even fairly widespread in Britain. He knew several persons who had seen it. Carol had even found herself within a hundred yards of one, and had been able to watch it for several minutes. Recently, three of these animals had been killed in Scotland, but scientists refused to admit that they were native to the place and preferred to say that they had escaped from some zoo. Yet, these wild animals regularly killed sheep and deer. They were more like the Loch Ness monster, they supplied food for ridiculous legends in which nobody could or would believe, so incongruous did they seem in Britain. But for Ted Hughes, they inevitably brought to his mind the thought of the jaguar that had visited him in his dreams, and that he had drawn on the walls of his rooms at Cambridge.

The thought sometimes came to him that the place that he occupied in the literary world was somehow comparable to the place the animal had in the context of modern England. His poetry remained largely misunderstood by his contemporaries because he had neglected to supply the necessary theoretical aid that would have made it less obscure and more easily acceptable. He was confident that his book on Shakespeare would provide his work with the critical instrument necessary to its comprehension, for it exposed his personal vision of the world, developing his thoughts on what literature ought to be and on the history of ideas. His project had consisted in studying the works of Shakespeare in their entirety, his poems as well as his plays, to try to reach an organic synthesis of the founding myths underneath. What was at stake in Shakespeare's work was intimately linked to the destiny and the genius of England. The Bard had grasped and untangled their intricate and arcane relationships perfectly, at a very crucial moment in the history of the nation, between the Reformation and the Enlightenment. At the centre of Shakespeare's work, Hughes detected a Tragic Equation whose early beginnings he traced back to the tragic incomprehension between Venus and Adonis. The myth dealt with the same problem that he had touched upon in his *Crow* poems and later in *Orghast* and in his other metaphysical poems. A battle was engaged between two deities that set the masculine principle of the Logos God, rational, classifying, authoritarian, against the feminine principle of the primordial Goddess, the embodiment of the unlimited reproductive energies of nature.

For this reason Hughes entitled his book *Shakespeare and the Goddess of Complete Being*. The title, of course, implicitly referred to Robert Graves's *White Goddess* and asserted its link to the school of thought inspired by the work of Carl Gustav Jung. But Hughes's huge display of erudition and eclecticism, which was extremely wide-ranging, would disconcert some of his readers. He traced in the work of Shakespeare a marked tendency towards the resolution of the Tragic Equation which bore a striking resemblance to the analytic procedure via which Jung intended to resolve the crisis that Freud had identified in his book *Civilisation and its Discontents*. Hughes saw in *The Tempest*, one of the late plays, the solving point of his equation, the vanishing point where the parallel lines of the Logos God and of the Goddess of Complete Being finally converge, where Caliban meets Sycorax, where Adonis meets Venus who, in the poem, seeing her love repulsed by Adonis, is tragically changed by her lust into a devilish boar. The book was as much the work of a poet as of a scholar and, though written in prose, it has to be read as a hybrid and innovative discourse that courageously accepts the ambitious challenge of taking in hand problems that were raised by several first-rate authors before him.

Hughes's intentions were quite well understood by numerous intelligent readers. The great Irish critic Seamus Deane, for instance, perhaps because he came from an Irish academic tradition upon which Jung had had a greater influence, seized the meaning of the book marvellously well. But elsewhere the book was literally savaged by a cohort of critics. Some of them, knowing no bounds, gave the Poet Laureate a regular thrashing, an enjoyable activity apparently, which seemed to have become the favourite sport of the tribe. One conceited clown, who did not understand Hughes's analysis of the boar in *Venus and Adonis*, found it hilarious to claim that the Poet Laureate maintained that Shakespeare had been obsessed with pigs. Another one, trying to be smart, declared that it was apparently an academic dissertation, but that the footnotes were missing as well as the index and the bibliography. Yet another called him "a cultural peasant in search of a miracle". *The Financial Times* published a cartoon of Ted Hughes reading a volume of Shakespeare's works upside down. Once more, it was the deplorable spectacle described by Baudelaire in his *Albatross*. If things had gone no further, Ted Hughes would no doubt have proved sufficiently hard-skinned to bear it with relative indifference, but then came an article by John Carey, an Oxford don, who had waxed indignant that so famous a poet should have presumed to encroach so massively — and indiscreetly — upon what he considered, no doubt, as his private hunting ground. He read Ted Hughes's book like a provincial politician boiling with impatience while listening to the speech of his contender in a municipal election. Taking up his pen, he composed a review for *The Times*, going into malignant hysterics and laying into Ted Hughes with unbridled venom, calling him a donkey-eared vandal, achieving, if nothing else, a perfect demonstration of his own loutish manners. Some time later, cut to the quick by the attack, and feeling perhaps that the status of the don obliged him to react to his base insults, Ted Hughes stooped as far as to enter into a tussle with him. In a letter to *The Times* he set the critic in the category of class-room gladiators who are wont to knock together crude effigies of dead poets to make a mishmash of them in front of easily impressionable students. But, he added, these knackers, on coming out of their yard, should be kept in quarantine before they are allowed further abroad to cut up and slander the living. The trouble with critics, he remarked elsewhere, was that with them the rule of the game was that the bullfighter must live but the bull must die.

That being said, however, he was quite well aware that the reactions that his book provoked came from the fact that it painfully revealed the slumbering sense of the sacredness of the world, a still sensitive nerve in English culture, which had obviously not yet been desensitised, in spite of it apparent secularisation. He identified his adversaries as the henchmen of this logical positivism whose centre was at Oxford University and which resulted in an allergic rejection of everything relating to myth, or what they considered as pure irrationalism. In his eyes, it was still the same fraudulent God, the Logos God, that was expressing himself through the rancorous pen of Carey. His book had been characteristically well received among writers and playwrights but had been slated by academics and regnant critics. Since his student days, he had old scores to settle with the University and this attack was now, to his annoyance, reviving unpleasant memories. Nothing had changed since that time, and his poetry was still running counter to academic discourse, sticking in the throats of academic pundits. He had not learnt, like his friend Seamus Heaney, for instance, to be wary of a hostile critical reception, because his success had so far dispensed him with having to take it into account. But when he tried to intervene in the theoretical discourse of his time in order to influence, if he possibly could, the way in which he was being read, he saw the ideological hard core of his work rebound upon him with a force that was proportional to the polemical intransigence with which he had expressed his convictions. He was quite ready to admit that what his book brought, if indeed it brought anything, to the body of criticism on Shakespeare's work, was of rather secondary importance. What mattered most was that his *Shakespeare* was providing a philosophical context for a full appreciation of his own poetry. And it was in fact a very detailed exposition of his way of thinking, of his convictions and preferences, even if another book of explanations, perhaps, would have been necessary to complete that understanding. He ought to have used as an epigraph for his book, he said, the quotation from Wittgenstein: "if a lion could talk, we would not be able to understand him".

But the old lion was running out of patience with so-called common sense, though it was a virtue so eminently English. He thought that its pronouncements were at best dubious and more often erroneous. Not that, in his eyes, English society was decadent, but it had in fact reached the lowest stage of its spiritual decline and had to start again from scratch. Ted Hughes spoke of "psychic cleansing" to designate the totalitarian violence that was exerted against poets and against the imagination; he looked upon this violence as the logical unfolding of an ideological warfare, the same that Blake had already denounced more than two centuries before, and against which he had conceived his poetry as an act of resistance, as a spiritual fight. The program that Hughes had assigned to his poetry was thus to be the alchemy that would operate the rebirth of inspiration. He was soon to meet with some signs of this revival, as for instance when he received a copy of the first collection of poems by Simon Armitage, then a young poet of twenty-nine, and from Yorkshire too, who enclosed a letter with his book, care of Faber & Faber, saying that he meant it as a gift to acquit himself of a sort of debt. For he owed him, he said, his first poetic breath of fresh air, since Hughes's poetry had been his oxygen during all those years of his youth when he had been like a drowning man, hoping to rise to the surface one day.

Ted Hughes had belatedly come to the conclusion that if his work was undoubtedly admired by poets and poetry lovers, if it was already exerting a considerable influence on English poetry that time would probably confirm, its critical reception had suffered in the absence of a theoretical work that might have facilitated its comprehension. Perhaps he had relied too much on his poems' capacity to live their own independent life without his having to look after them. In a culture that had forgotten its poetry as it had forgotten its dialect, or its Latin, it was necessary to look after one's poems as one should one's children. It was not enough to bring them forth into this hostile world, one still had the obligation to help them survive in it. The poems that he had published since *Crow* had undeniably met all too often with incomprehension. The fault had been partly his, admittedly, because he had ignored all criticism and had neglected to enter the lists against the more or less anonymous reviewers, whose insolence was on a par with their incompetence. He saw, therefore, that he would have to build what he called a habitat for his poems, that is to say a structural boundary that would map out and define a song area for them, but also that he would have to provide a body of more immediately comprehensible explanatory texts, that would act as a stronghold and shield off attacks from intruding barbarians. There is nothing, after all, more vulnerable than a poem. There is nothing easier for your average philistine than to find apparently irrefutable arguments to sneer at a work of art, however great the genius of its author; the more original the work and the more attention it requires from the reader, so the more efficient will be the onslaughts.

Ted Hughes therefore decided to commit another book to the purpose of defending his poems with theoretical ramparts. He followed up the publication of *Shakespeare and the Goddess of Complete Being* that had come out in April, with a volume entitled *A Dancer to God; Homage to T.S. Eliot,* in September 1992. It was a collection of speeches that he had given on various occasions, such as the official unveiling of a memorial plaque in London, in front of the place where Thomas Stearns Eliot had lived with his wife Valerie, at 3 Kensington Court Gardens. In this work, he was seeking to establish the existence of a political and ideological filiation between himself and the poet who, thirty years before, had officially welcomed him on the threshold of his career as a full member of the poetic community. Ted Hughes had at least one thing in common with the venerated author of *The Waste Land*: it was the vision of modern England as a distressful spiritual wasteland. Of course, Eliot was avowedly a Christian who had embraced the Anglican rites when he became a British citizen, but he was also a confirmed royalist. He had, furthermore, defined himself with forthrightness as an Anglican in religion, a royalist in politics and in literature a classicist, which meant that he wanted to fit creatively into the literary tradition and not break with the past. He had written a famous article on "Tradition and the Individual Talent," in which he explained that each artist operated a sort of chemical transformation on the poets of the past without whom he could not have existed as a poet, but who after him would no longer be the same. Ted Hughes, who endorsed this theory, was thereby declaring his ambition to take his place among the greatest poets of the nation. But the most important thing was elsewhere. Eliot's dynamic conception of tradition was not so far removed from the notion of a "spirit" of the nation with which the poet was seeking to dialogue or to negotiate, so to speak. The resemblance enabled Ted Hughes to quote Eliot as an example of the great poets that he identified with shamans, of whom Shakespeare was of course the archetype.

Moreover, T.S. Eliot had propounded another theory, which was just as famous as his reflections on tradition, that drew on an interpretation of the history of ideas that was very similar to that of Ted Hughes. Eliot had indeed suggested that English civilisation was characterised by what he had called a "dissociation of sensibility," a sort of historical accident that had affected the "mind of England" in the 17th century, at about the time of Shakespeare's death, when the spirit of the Reformation had tilted towards a humanistic empiricism that would later become the driving spirit of the Enlightenment. Eliot defined this change very simply as the divorce between thought and feeling which would give rise to the development of scientific understanding, to the detriment of poetry and more generally of those creative forces of the human spirit that were not purely rational. In T.S. Eliot's critical essays, this dissociation of sensibility was a mere hypothesis to which he would return on several occasions but, to a certain extent, Hughes claimed to have deepened and systematised the notion. He traced the first signs of this dissociation back to this Republic from which Plato wanted to exclude poets, and Hughes stigmatised what he called the "Socratic spirit" that inspired such an exclusion. The metamorphosis of the soul evoked in Hughes's most metaphysical poems was a reform of this Socratic spirit, destined to perfect his philosophy by the acquisition of poetic and musical skills. The romantic poets, in England as well as in Germany, had shared the same programme at a time in the history of European ideas when the ideal of pure reason seemed to have reached its limits. Eliot himself claimed to have traced signs announcing a reunification of sensibility in the late poems of Shelley and Keats, which would ideally mean a reconciliation between thought and feeling, reason and passion, and even poetry and philosophy. This would make the modern age, from Shakespeare to the present day, into a long parenthesis that the 20th century was called upon to close. The metamorphosis, the reconciliation, the transmutation of the soul through the poetic alchemy of language that Ted Hughes dreamt of, celebrated this unification. He aspired to be the English poet who would realise the unification of sensibility.

The dissociated sensibility seeking reunification was another way of expressing the problem that in his *Shakespeare* he had sought to investigate in terms of what he had called a Tragic Equation. Besides, he had found very similar ideas and also a certain number of images in the work of Nietzsche, among which that of Socrates as a musician. The author of *Orghast* shared with the author of *Thus Spake Zarathustra* the idea that the Reformation had been the semi-paralysis of reason, which meant that Protestantism had opened the way to rationalism, but had stopped halfway. Hughes, who said that Socrates was the ass that had brought us Christ, would not have disavowed the theses developed in the *Antichrist*. It was clear that the spiritual filiation between Hughes and Nietzsche was mainly via Jung, since the Swiss psychologist was known to be a committed disciple of the German philosopher. The kind of evolution of human nature that Hughes was looking forward to, as well as the ideal of "individuation" — that specific growth stage towards which Jung's psychology was directed — both drew their inspiration from Nietzsche's super-man, the myth of the ideal superior man of the future.

The respect that the venerable figure of Eliot continued to impose on the critical pundits probably explains the relatively moderate tone of most of the reviews of the book. However, inflammatory outbreaks were not completely over. *The Times Educational Supplement* published a humorous cartoon showing the two poets under jumbled traits: Hughes with Eliot's impeccably parted hair on one side and Eliot with Hughes's dishevelled head of hair. In *The Spectator*, however, that venerable institution in the English quality press, the poet Stephen Spender who, with T.S. Eliot himself, had helped launch Hughes's career thirty years before, seized the opportunity of a review of his previous work to analyse the continuity between the two books and he declared, without hesitation, that *Shakespeare and the Goddess* was "a work of genius on the nature of poetic genius".

Whereas at the beginning of his career, after a few years of obscurity, Hughes had met with frank and massive success, he now felt that it would be an uphill struggle to ensure it would survive, despite so many early promises that it was destined to do so. perhaps he had been ill-advised in some of his initiatives. Perhaps he should not have published *Gaudete*. But the present state of affairs was also the result of the evolution of prevailing ideas in England at the time. It appeared to him that the fight in which he was engaged for the survival of his own poetry was also in favour of Poetry itself. That was why it was so important to continue to write and to publish. In June, under the title *Rain-Charm for the Duchy*, he published poems composed for special occasions as Poet Laureate. He was also preparing a volume of contextual texts that he had been writing along the years in various circumstances: notes upon the books he had read, interviews and other miscellaneous articles. It was one more effort to remedy the lack of theoretical buttressing from which his work might suffer in the future. To be sure, Keith Sagar, to whom he had briefly shown his explanations of Coleridge's poems, was soon to publish the acts of a second conference. Moreover, these changes in the scholarly environment of his work induced new outposts for the study of his work, gradually cropping up here and there, with Keith Sagar, Terry Gifford and Neil Roberts in Britain, Ann Skea in Australia, Leonard Scigaj in the United States. They wrote to check with him if their theories were plausible or to ask his permission to quote from his work. But it would be better still if the new generations were given the possibility of reading what he himself had had to say on the literary production of other authors as well as on his own. Yet, as it seemed increasingly clear that time must do its work before his ideas could gain ground, he found an optimistic title that looked with confidence to the future for his next collection of articles: he would call it *Winter Pollen*, having in mind less Shakespeare's Richard III, playing the villain throughout the winter of his discontent, than Shelley's hope when, in his *Ode to the West Wind* he wants to scatter his words to the wind of the future. For if winter comes, can spring be far behind?

But for the moment he had to weather mighty storms born of trivial things, in particular the epic contest that had arisen over the choice by the Kent school authorities of a tale for children entitled *How the Polar Bear Became* for the Eleven Plus competitive examination. Hughes said that he had conceived the fable as a satire on vanity. It tells the story of a bear who is very proud of his white coat, which in warm climates enabled him to win all the beauty contests. But the bear thought it wise to emigrate to the North Pole so as not to sully his immaculate fur, and in this polar region where whiteness is the most common thing there is, its unnoticeable beauty was eclipsed by that of a brown mouse. Alas, the choice of this text was severely condemned in *The Daily Telegraph* as being very politically incorrect — if not downright racist — by a member of the Kent County Council, Mr. Dai Liyanage, who happened to be an Asian. He argued that in a multicultural society, such a text ought not to have been proposed as a subject in a competitive examination. Ted Hughes answered by philosophically quoting Hamlet: "there is nothing either good or bad, but thinking makes it so". Then he published an admonitory article in *The Times Educational Supplement* to call the public's attention to the fact that his fables had been composed with a moral but since the moral lesson of one of them had been called into question, on the occasion of a serious disagreement between a school inspector and a single County Councillor, full responsibility for their interpretation rested henceforth with the readers. The fact remained, nevertheless, that Ted Hughes was a little like Gulliver in Lilliput: the volley of arrows that were shot at him were trying to make up for their puny size by their number. Again he had to face the reproach in *The Sunday Times* of not having written anything for the fortieth anniversary of Queen Elizabeth II's accession to the throne. The newspaper went on to issue a general invitation to all the poets of the nation to do the task of the defaulting Poet Laureate. Several poets answered the invitation the following week with great elegance, their witty contributions poking fun not at the "PL" but at the week-end journalists who had been so grossly ill-mannered as to launch a mean attack over a trifle. Ted Hughes judged it necessary to remind people that the Poet Laureate was under no obligation to write poems, that his function did not expressly require that he should write poetry. He did, however, satisfy the pressing need to read his verses that seemed to have been expressed by publishing in *The Independent* — a very good choice to help drive his point home — a poem in which the Queen was mentioned only once. As one good lesson deserves another, it was said that nobody understood a single word of the poem. What! Ted Hughes feigned to be surprised and, rendered slightly more disdainful by this thrashing, he said that the poem was no more difficult than ordinary crosswords puzzles published in newspapers, adding that he could not have imagined that his countrymen would have had the slightest difficulty in identifying such essentially English symbols as the lion and the unicorn, or that they had never heard of Falstaff, Prospero, Ariel or the Faerie Queene.

As he was correcting the proofs of his collection of articles called *Winter Pollen* he remembered that he had thought for a while of calling it, somewhat nonsensically, "Burnt Foxes" for he felt, at times, overcome by fatigue like some wild animal at bay. Doubtless the part that was foisted on him in the legend of Sylvia Plath had much to do with his difficulties, as much because of the warping influence it brought to bear on the sound evaluation of his work, as because of the heavy toll that this burden of cares was taking on his consciousness of the world, and on the state of his soul. In his mind's eye, he pictured the consequences upon his life of Sylvia Plath's suicide as a blizzard ceaselessly returning to impose wintry conditions upon his existence, and periodically freezing up his inspiration. As soon as Sylvia's letters appeared, edited by Aurelia Plath, he immediately regretted having allowed the publication of such things. Reading them over, he did not doubt that they would deliver the final blow to his reputation in America. As he thought of the irreparable wrong that had been done to it, he nearly gave way to despair. Surely, the truth of his relations with Sylvia was much more complex than what was coming out of these letters. It would have been necessary to publish the correspondence of his first wife in its entirety, in particular the letters from her mother and from her analyst Ruth Beuscher, who had both advised her to break with him. When he had discovered these letters, after Sylvia's death, he had mused over the fact that these women had not wanted to leave the slightest chance of their being reconciled; and he had seen Sylvia's curious hesitations during their last meetings in a rather different light. But these letters, curiously enough, were among those that had disappeared from his archives, though they must certainly be somewhere. There were other letters too, and if the whole truth must be known, it would be better to have them all published. All things considered, when he had chosen to drape himself in silence, and to treat calumny with scorn, he had perhaps done himself more wrong than if he had tried to defend himself. And again, when he had cut out whole passages in Sylvia Plath's journals before publication, giving the impression he had something to hide, he had thought at the time that he was protecting his children, but now Nicholas and Frieda were themselves asking him why these journals could not be published in England too. After all, the rights were his only for another twenty years, and then it would be published anyway. He thought, moreover, that if readers were given the possibility of seeing with their own eyes how Sylvia expressed herself in her journals, light would be thrown on much of the phantasmal stuff on which her legend was made. There were, however, entire pages in her journals in which she accused him of the worst things imaginable, things which *he* knew existed only in her imagination. But here the problem was perhaps insoluble. Besides, he also felt guilty of having allowed the publication of texts in which people other than himself were smeared, such as the American poetess Adrienne Rich to whom he wrote to tell her how disgusted he was with himself for having allowed the publication of things which he himself felt ashamed of for the sake of others.

With the passage of time, however, the resentment that had filled him in the seventies, when the posthumous glory of Sylvia Plath was being erected on the ruin of his character, was slowly dying away. He regretted now the sudden bout of paranoia that had made him cancel his son's American citizenship. Nicholas now worked and lived in Alaska, he had even studied there at the University, and it seemed that his career would depend in great part on his being an American citizen. Acting upon the advice of the specialised lawyer that he had engaged, he therefore contacted Janet Malcolm, one of Sylvia Plath's biographers with whom he was on friendly terms, to ask her to write a letter that would help him to plead his cause. It is not pleasant to admit having made mistakes. It seemed that he would never cease to pay the penalty. Regrets still clung to him. He was quite aware that the humiliating terms that had been repeatedly forced upon him, on both sides of the Atlantic, had slowly sapped his confidence. Whenever he tried to write, the thought of the public was constantly in his mind and he could not imagine it other than sneering and hostile. He was becoming paranoid, as he knew quite well, but he could not help it. This was one of the reasons why he had sought refuge in writing for children, because they remained blissfully ignorant of such problems. Another trick that he found useful to loosen the icy grip in which the critical blizzard had locked his inspiration, was to pretend that he was writing for another public, in another period of history, that would be untouched by the petty prejudices of his contemporaries, and that would judge his work with impartiality, according to its worth. He knew perfectly well that he also had readers who were wholly in sympathy with his person and his ideas, but it was only by pushing them forward into some ideal future that he managed to imagine them with a force that was sufficient to make him want to write again.

It seemed this year that winter would never end. A few events also darkened his humour. In February, his sister-in-law died after an eighteen-month illness during which Carol had nursed her. Then a woman in a restaurant into whose eyes he had looked had told him yes, she was dying of cancer. She was thirty-five, in the prime of life. The rain did not let up. The wind was icy cold. At some turning, in one of those narrow, hedge-lined lanes of Exmoor, he crashed his Volvo and broke the headlights: seven hundred pounds' damages. The sale of a few manuscripts, through the agency of the esteemed Roy Davids, would help pay for this unforeseen complication. A local hunt met at the farm, they lost track of the fox, an incident that was frequent enough, not far from the place where Carol, a few years before, had seen the black beast, the mysterious leopard. A matter of pure coincidence of course, but *The Times Educational Supplement* published a cartoon representing Ted Hughes as a sort of centaur with the body of a tiger. In what secret corner, he wondered, could God be hiding his store of extra days?

For the time being, Ted Hughes had plenty of humdrum tasks to see to; it was, he said, as if he had stumbled onto a conveyor belt. He had, for instance, to write a letter of recommendation for the young Irish poet Paul Muldoon, to attend to a project aiming to erect a monument on the tomb of Robert Graves, to send a courteous letter to a Member of Parliament who had sent him some remarkable poems by a handicapped child, to Peter Brook, who had insisted on showing him the poems of an autistic woman, to the Minister of Agriculture who, to solve the anglers' problems, had found nothing more intelligent than to propose a reduction of the number of anglers authorised to fish in the Taw and the Torridge. Nevertheless, there were still occasions for rejoicing. He had, for instance, sold his house in Yorkshire for two hundred thousand pounds, which he remembered having bought for only six thousand. He gave one half of the sum to each of his children, so that his daughter now had a house at Perth, Australia, and a flat in London, while his son, for his part, preferred to hoard his money. Then Seamus Heaney invited him for a change to participate in his latest lecture on poetry at Oxford, in the splendid Sheltonian amphitheatre where he was given a warm welcome. He also went to the Sturga Poetry Festival in Macedonia to receive a gold medal; then he went to give a lecture at the Arvon Foundation at Totleigh Barton, then again to London for a public reading of poems with Simon Armitage. The impression he had of not being loved by his contemporaries might, after all, not be so well-founded as all that, and could simply be due to a flitting spell of dejection: he was constantly being asked to take part in various projects. He responded enthusiastically to a collective project, concerning forty-two authors, to write a fine collection of *New Metamorphoses* in the style of Ovid. The idea was indeed quite in the pastoral spirit that was so dear to him and, on the other hand, the notion of metamorphosis was such an essential characteristic of his Goddess of Complete Being that the very existence of the project was like a ray of light. He plunged into it with such gusto, avidly re-reading his Ovid for the occasion, that he soon produced a collection of *Tales from Ovid* that composed a volume thicker than any of his preceding poetry books.

There was no doubting the fact that Ted Hughes's inspiration came in cycles, like the seasons, and poems came to him like leaves to the trees: periodically. The sole publisher he had ever had, who had always supported him, Faber & Faber, was asking him to compile a new edition of his *New Collected Poems* as a follow-up to the two earlier ones of 1972 and 1982. His short stories would be published separately, together with a few others that had never been published before, in a volume entitled *Difficulties of a Bridegroom*, together with his radio play of 1963. He was also preparing a new collection of tales for children, *Dreamfighter*, that would regroup stories about the creation of the world. But above all, there was the project, which had fermented over many years, of publishing his own version of his life with Sylvia Plath. Was it because the style of Sylvia Plath, who had drawn her inspiration from the events of her life and from her most intimate feelings was strangely contagious, Ted Hughes, in an interview with the *Paris Review,* explained that he felt a curious confessional urge to speak of himself and to tell the story of his life. He had already written a fair amount of such autobiographical poems, but he still hesitated to publish them. By way of justification for constantly postponing their publication, he told himself that it was of the utmost importance, in this matter, to consult the stars before deciding upon a date, in order to secure the best possible chances of success. Besides, he had so many other things to do, for he had plunged headlong into a profusion of literary projects, among which were a whole series of translations of theatre plays that he had begun, as an implicit acknowledgement of regret, perhaps, for not having sufficiently left his mark in this department of letters. He was translating several plays for the London stage: Euripides' *Alcestis* was his favourite on account of king Admetus, a healer and therefore a shaman, Racine's *Phaedra* and also *The Awakening of Spring,* a juvenile tragedy by Frank Wedekind which had been banned from the English stage until the sixties, because of its bold evocations of adolescent sexuality and of its denunciations of the repression of all forms of sexuality by the moral diktats of an "idiotic religion". He was also translating the play by Frederico Garcia Lorca, *The Blood Wedding.* He did not spare himself, recording T.S. Eliot's *Four Quartets* for the BBC, giving many public readings during which he exerted a magnetic spell over his audiences by his physical presence and his thunderous voice that lent his poems a monumental quality. The look on his face had been altered a little by the translucent tortoiseshell-rimmed glasses that he now wore; he seemed deliberately to avoid looking people in the face, giving the impression that he wanted to elude their curiosity, visibly doing nothing to court favour with them, never smiling, always firmly planted on his feet, set slightly apart, as if preparing for some physical work, sometimes providing a few explanations between the poems, moving the while his right hand horizontally in front of him and holding his book solidly gripped in the other. He read his poems slowly; imparting to them an electric vibration, as if alive with the shock of a sudden discovery.

He had now decided that the time was ripe to accept the most advantageous offer for his manuscripts among those that were made to him by American Universities keen to increase their collections. He turned first to Keith Sagar and Ann Skea, two academics in whom he had complete confidence, to put his archives in good order, but he soon realised that it was a task that he alone would be able to perform, so he settled down to an undertaking that would take him several months to see through, and that reminded him of many minute details of his existence. There were one hundred cardboard boxes or so in which he had carefully stored all his writings, letters and notebooks, never throwing away anything but the sheets of scribbled paper that he would sometimes crumple up into a ball and let drop onto the floor. As he scanned each sheet patiently, his eyes would sometimes fall upon something he could not imagine coming tomorrow into everybody's knowledge. Wouldn't an unscrupulous biographer, or a scandal-monger, be tempted to make bad use of such intimate revelations? He saw more and more clearly that some sorting out would have to be done. He therefore set aside documents that were too private in character in order to place them out of reach of the curiosity of voyeurs, for he had to protect himself but, above all, to preserve the privacy of his children and of his second wife.

The question of his inheritance was rather complex. It would have been simpler, in a way, to leave everything to Carol. It was a subject that they often discussed between themselves. For a brief while, Green Court resounded with quarrels like those that had occurred there many years before, when his sister Olwyn, who often came to discuss problems with him that arose about his translation of Racine — for she knew French better than he did — had overheard a conversation that had led her to think that she would be excluded from his inheritance. But such would not be the case. She would inherit, along with his children, a comfortable part of the royalties appertaining to Sylvia Plath's legacy. Anyway, it seemed normal that a wife should inherit her husband's property. But he was also troubled with much more trivial cares. What was he to do, for instance, with the barrel of Canary wine that he received every year in consideration of his function as Poet Laureate? He would have been hard put to drink these 42 gallons every year, not to mention a special gift from Spain to the Poet Laureate of 108 gallons of sherry. He had the rich idea of putting it up for sale at £4 a bottle under the appellation of Laureate's Choice. He even designed a fine stick-on label decorated with a hoopoe, that he had drawn himself, accompanied with his signature. There would certainly be enough wine connoisseurs to clear all the stock. Finally, he thought better of it, fearing that it might again set people gossiping about his behaviour. Yet was it not his unimpeachable right to sell what belonged to him?

But what did it matter after all? It could well continue to be stored in his cellar, he had more important things to attend to than bother his head about selling wine. The defence of rivers and of angling more than ever required all his efforts. In support of this action Ted Hughes helped the West Rivers Society to set up a relief fund in order to put up the necessary money for lawsuits arising from gaps in the legislation of the National Rivers Authority. Angling and fish, he wrote in a local newspaper, was only one aspect of the larger issue concerning clear water, for people had to realise that all the filth that was dumped in the river Exe would be found, sooner or later, in the cups of tea of the inhabitants of Exeter. One could also learn, in the *Manchester Evening News* for instance, that Ted Hughes had founded a Theatre and Environment Society destined to encourage the creation of a repertoire of plays on environmental themes for the young, by means of a £500 grant awarded to each play that would reach the stage of publication. One might well wonder, indeed, how he could find the time and energy to have so many tasks in hand at the same time. But the Poet Laureate seemed now to have set his heart on taking his function very seriously. Among other examples of this extensive activity, the very popular *Sunday Telegraph* reported that the Royal British Legion had asked Ted Hughes to propose a new version of the hymn *Eternal Father Strong to Save* for the seventy-fifth anniversary of the Legion;

the hymn had been composed in 1860, at a time when English forces consisted essentially of the Navy, but it was now considered necessary to find some way of including the Army and the Air Force as well. Several attempts had already been made to that effect, but which had not been judged satisfactory, and the Legion had turned to the Poet Laureate a little as a last resort. He alone, however, found a solution that the Legion was happy with. The problem was as follows: the sailors have to face the perils of the sea, it can also be said that the air force are facing the perils of the air, but what could be said of the army? It could not be said that they were facing up to perils of the land, for it was precisely the land itself that was in danger, and besides, it was of course unthinkable to envisage, albeit implicitly, that one should ever have to fight on English soil. Ted Hughes's solution was to write a third stanza evoking the perils of the sky, all that the unlucky stars and the contrary winds hold in store, sweeping the combatants along without distinction on sea and land. The hymn in this new version, recorded and broadcast by the BBC, was played for the first time at the Abbey of Sherborne in Dorset, on Remembrance Day, the Sunday nearest to November 11th which, in the year 1996, was the next day. It was, for Ted Hughes, the occasion of coming to terms with the memory of the two wars of the century that had always been painfully sensitive for him. For the first time he wore the poppy that he had long refused to wear in his youth.

Soon, he would have the confirmation that what he had feared for some time was definitely true: he was suffering from cancer, and his friend Ted Cornish could do nothing for him. In January, already, he was on chemotherapy, which left him very sick, and modified his physical aspect considerably. On some days, he was barely able to hold his fountain pen. He resolved not to tell people anything about his illness as long as it was possible. He continued to do all the tasks that he had always thought it behoved him to do. With Macmillan he was publishing an anthology of poems and stories composed by children below sixteen years of age, the product of a competition that he had organised with the W.H. Smith bookshops. He wrote a letter to say that he was in full agreement with the decision taken by the Environment Agency to ban the use of hoop and trammel nets in the Taw and Torridge estuaries, which reduced the number of salmon upriver where they used to be caught for sport, thus providing jobs for numerous people in hotels and in various fishing related tourist activities, and he proved his point by adding a list of all the establishments in his region that had been forced to close on account of the decline in the number of salmon.

In March, his archive set out from Green Court, under the personal supervision of the librarian Stephen Enniss, for the United States where it would be housed in the special collections department of the Woodruff Library of Emory University in Atlanta. The treasure trove comprised no less that one hundred thousand items and various documents, stored in eighty boxes weighing a total of two and a half tons, to say nothing of a secret trunk that was to be kept closed for twenty-five years, or as long as Mrs. Carol Hughes was alive. In September, he had sold his farm after the death of his bull Sexton. Then he began to take steps for the publication of his autobiographical poems that he had composed on purpose to give his own version of his life with Sylvia Plath. The rare friends to whom he had talked of his project, like Keith Sagar and Tom Gunn, were encouraging him to go ahead, but he asked them to keep the matter secret for fear that hostile measures might be taken with a view to savaging the book as soon as it came out, so great was his feeling of having bared his heart and laid himself defenceless for his readers to do with him as they pleased. He hesitated, uncertain about when would be the most auspicious moment to launch the book onto its public career; he said that he wanted to study the stars at his leisure to choose the most favourable date for its publication. In November, he offered a dozen of these poems to *The Times* to be serialised and commented on by Erika Wagner, one of the biographers of Sylvia Plath. In January, the whole collection was published by Faber & Faber under the title *Birthday Letters.* Nearly one hundred thousand copies had been ordered before they were actually printed and put up for sale. None of these poems were dated but some of them had already appeared among the hitherto unpublished poems in the last edition of his *New Selected Poems*. They were mostly written in the second person, since they were letters addressed to Sylvia Plath. Some of them evoked the memory of Assia. This he had already done at greater length in another collection of poems called *Capriccio*, a limited edition of fifty copies, sold at a prohibitive price, and published by Leonard Baskin's Gehenna Press. A sort of respectful reserve attended the publication of these poems. Ted Hughes said to those who were close to him that he felt as much relieved as king Midas's barber for publishing these secrets that had harassed him for thirty-five years. During the same month his *Tales from Ovid* were awarded the Whitbread prize; then in March, the *Birthday Letters* were awarded the *W.H. Smith* prize, and Queen Elizabeth decorated Ted Hughes with the medal of the Order of Merit. He also wrote a letter to John Carey with whom he had once bandied words about his *Shakespeare*. He had said many times, in private — but to what extent was this intuition of his to be trusted? — that it had been a fatal mistake for him to write too much in prose and to have too long neglected poetry. He thought that he had thus opened his guard and weakened his immune system, like those shamans who were said to fall ill and die as soon as they ceased to shamanise. In October, he was also granted the Forward prize for poetry, but he was by then too ill to receive it personally. On 28 October 1998, Ted Hughes died of heart failure while he was being treated for cancer of the colon at the private clinic of the London Bridge Hospital. The funeral service was held in the church of North Tawton, near his home, in his village of Devon, by the Reverend Terence McCaughley, an old Cambridge fellow student, now a Presbyterian minister and Emeritus Professor of Gaelic at Trinity College, Dublin, with whom he had liked to sing when they used to meet at *The Anchor*. A bat flitted about in the church, above the coffin, while Seamus Heaney read a poem by Ted Hughes. Then the friends wandered for a time in the village while the closest members of the family accompanied the poet to Exeter to attend the cremation. His ashes were scattered over the heath of Dartmoor, in the heart of Devon where he had so much liked to live.

In January of the following year, Ted Hughes was posthumously awarded the T.S. Eliot prize for *Birthday Letters.* Then on May 13th, 1999, on the anniversary of his mother's death, a thanksgiving ceremony was held in Westminster Abbey. *God Save the Queen* resounded when the Queen Mother, dressed in black, made her entrance with the Prince of Wales to take her place in the nave. After an oration in praise of the great man, some of his poems were read and sung. A memorial tablet would soon be placed in Poets' Corner where his name now figures among those of the great English poets.

EPILOGUE

When one leaves the village of Belstone in Dartmoor, going south, a path runs out across the fields, goes through a gate then continues over the moor towards the Taw marshes that fill the cirque dominated on its west side by the denuded mass of Steeperton Tor. It then follows the meandering course of the river which, so close to its source, is here no more than a brook, once one has passed the ancient mines of Knack, after crossing the river many times, now on this side now on that, it finally disappears. Still pushing on in the direction of the source, farther to the south, one comes upon a grassy knoll on top of which lies a flat stone whose granite is not quite the same as that which is found in that part of Devon. The stone was placed at the request of the Prince of Wales to whom this part of the land belongs, serving as practice ground for the British Army. Apart from this thoughtful gesture, the Prince had also, it was said, ordered a stained glass window for his private chapel, to commemorate his friendship with the Poet Laureate. Five years passed before the public discovered this long massive stone in the secluded place near the sources of the Taw, the Teign, the Dart and the East Okement. The poet had asked that only his name, his dates and the initials of the Order of Merit, his most cherished title, should be engraved on it: Ted Hughes OM 1930-1998.

CHRONOLOGY

1930 - 17 August, Mytholmroyd (West Yorks.), birth of James Edward Hughes, 3rd and last child of William Henry Hughes and Edith Farrar Hughes.

1938 - The Hughes move to Mexborough (North Yorks.)

1943-49 - Mexborough Grammar School.

1946-50 - Publishes poems in the school journal *Don & Dearn*.

1948 - Wins Open Exhibition scholarship to Cambridge University.

1949 - Joins the RAF for two years.

1951 - Goes up to Cambridge, Pembroke College.

1954 - Graduates from Cambridge in social anthropology.

1956 - Published four poems in the one and only number of the *St. Botolph's Review*. On 26 Fébruary, meets Sylvia Plath, American student in Newnham College. Marries Sylvia Plath on 16 June (Bloomsday), honeymoon in Benidorm, Spain.

1957 - Teaches English in a secondary school near Cambridge while Sylvia Plath finishes her MA. Poems published in *Poetry*, the *Spectator, Nation, Harper's*, the *TLS*, the *New Yorker*, the *London Magazine*, the *New Statesman*. On 14 April, first BBC broadcast. June: embarks for the USA with Sylvia Plath. 18 September, publication of his first collection of poems *The Hawk in the Rain*.

1958 - Teaches "creative writing" at the University of Massachusetts, campus of Amherst. April: poetry reading in Harvard. Meets Leonard Baskin.

1959 - Autumn: Yaddo (Saratoga Springs), starts working for an oratorio on the *Bardo Thödol* or *Tibetan Book of the Dead* for Chinese composer Chou Wen Chung. December: back to England with Sylvia Plath.

1960 - *Lupercal.* 1st April: birth of daughter Frieda Rebecca Hughes.

1961 - *Meet my Folks!* 31st August, the Hugheses settle in Court Green, Devon.

1962 - 17 January, birth of son Nicholas Farrar Hughes. 18 May, the Hugheses welcome David Wevill, with his wife Assia Gutman Wevill. Late September: separation, Ted Hughes goes to London.

1963 - 11 February, Sylvia Plath commits suicide.

1964 - *Nessie the Mannerless Monster.*

1965 - Collaboration to *Modern Poetry in Translation* with Daniel Weissbort.

1966 - January to May, lives in Ireland with Assia and his children, then comes back to Devon.

1967 - *Wodwo* and *Poetry in the Making.*

1968 - 19 March, first performance of *Seneca's Œdipus. The Iron Man. A Choice of Emily Dickinson's Verse.*

1969 - March, Assia Gutman Wevill commits suicide killing her daughter Shura. 13 May, death of mother, Edith Farrar Hughes. Buys Lumb Bank house, later to rent it to the Arvon Foundation.

1970 - Marries Carol Orchard. *Crow* and *The Coming of the King and Other Plays.*

1971 - Writes the script of *Orghast* for Peter Brook in Teheran. *With Fairest Flowers while Summer Lasts. A Choice of Shakespeare's Verse.*

1972 - *Selected Poems 1957-1967.* Buys Moortown farm, in Devon, and works as farmer with father-in-law Jack Orchard.

1974 - Queen's Medal for Poetry.

1975 - *Season Songs.* Ilkley Poetry Festival.

1976 - *Moon-Whales and Other Moon Poems*. Death of Jack Orchard.

1977 - *Gaudete.* Sylvia Plath : *Johnny Panic and the Bible of Dreams*. Order of the British Empire.

1978 - *Moon-Bells and Other Poems. Cave Birds.*

1979 - *Remains of Elmet. Moortown.*

1981 - *Under the North Star. Collected Poems* of Sylvia Plath. February: death of father, William Henry Hughes.

1982 - *Selected Poems 1957-1981. Journals of Sylvia Plath* with Frances McCullough. *The Rattle Bag* with Seamus Heaney.

1983 - *River.*

1984 - *What Is the Truth?*

1986 - *Ffangs the Vampire Bat and the Kiss of Truth. Flowers and Insects*. President of the Poetry Book Society.

1988 - *Tales of the Early World.*

1989 - *Wolfwatching*. Arvon Foundation buys Lumb Bank. *Moortown Diary.*

1992 - *Rain-Charm for the Duchy and Other Laureate Poems - Shakespeare and the Goddess of Complete Being - A Dancer to God; Tributes to T.S. Eliot.*

1994 - Poems for *After Ovid, New Metamorphoses.*

1995 - *New Selected Poems 1957-1994 - Difficulties of a Bridegroom.*

1997 - *Tales from Ovid*

1998 - *Birthday Letters*. 28 October, death of Ted Hughes, aged 68.

SELECT BIBLIOGRAPHY

WORKS BY TED HUGHES
Published by Faber & Faber unless otherwise specified.

POETRY

A Choice of Shakespeare's Verse. 1971; 2nd ed. 1991.
A Primer of Birds. Gehenna Press. 1981.
Birthday Letters. 1998.
Blood Wedding. 1996.
Capriccio. Gehenna Press, 1990.
Cave Birds. 1978.
Collected Animal Poems. 4 vol. 1995.
Collected Poems. Paul Keegan, ed. 2003.
Crow. 1970.
Elmet. 1994.
Flowers and Insects. 1986.
Gaudete. 1977.
Lupercal. 1960.
Moortown. 1979.
Moortown Diary. 1989.
New Selected Poems 1957-1994. 1995.
Orts. Rainbow Press, 1978.
Rain-Charm for the Duchy. 1992.
Recklings. Turret Books, 1966.
Remains of Elmet. 1979.
River. 1983.
Season Songs. 1976.
Selected Poems 1957-1981. 1982.
Wodwo. 1967.
Wolfwatching. 1989.

POETRY & TALES FOR CHILDREN

By Heart. 1997.
Collected Plays for Children. 2001.
Earth-Moon. Rainbow Press, 1976.

Ffangs the Vampire Bat and the Kiss of Truth. 1986.
How the Whale Became. 1963.
Howls and Whispers. Gehenna Press, 1998.
Meet My Folks. Faber & Faber, 1961.
Moon-Bells and Other Poems. Chatto & Windus, 1978.
Moon-Whales and Other Moon Poems. Viking, 1988.
Nessie the Mannerless Monster. 1964.
Tales of the Early World. 1988.
The Cat and the Cuckoo. Sunstone Press, 1987.
The Coming of the Kings. Faber & Faber, 1970.
The Dreamfighter and Other Creation Tales, 1995.
The Earth-Owl and Other Moon People. 1963.
The Iron Man. 1968.
The Iron Woman. 1993.
The Mermaid's Purse. Sunstone Press, 1993.
Timmy the Tug. Thames and Hudson, 2009.
Under the North Star. 1981.
What is the Truth? 1984.

PROSE

Difficulties of a Bridegroom. 1995.
Letters of Ted Hughes. 2007.
Poetry in the Making. 1967.
A Dancer to God; Tributes to T.S. Eliot. 1992.
Shakespeare & the Goddess of Complete Being. 1992.
Winter Pollen. 1994.

TRANSLATIONS

Alcestis. 1999.
Phèdre. 1998.
Selected Translations. 2006.
Seneca's Oedipus. 1969.
Spring Awakening. 1995.
Tales from Ovid. 1997.
The Oresteia. 1999.

BIOGRAPHICAL SOURCES

Alvarez, Alfred. *Where Did It All Go Right?* Bloomsbury, 1999.

Feinstein, Elaine. *Ted Hughes; the Life of a Poet.* Norton, 2001.

Hughes, Gerald. *Ted and I.* London: Robson Press, 2012.

Huws, Daniel. *Memories of Ted Hughes 1952-1963.* Five Leaves Publications, 2010.

Koren, Yehuda and Eilat Negev. *A Lover of Unreason: The Life and Tragic Death of Assia Wevill.* Robson Books, 2006.

Myers, Lucas. *Crow Steered, Bergs appeared.* Proctor's Hall Press, 2001.

Middlebrook, Diane. *Her Husband; Hughes and Plath—A Marriage.* Viking, 2003.

Plath, Sylvia. *The Journals of Sylvia Plath.* 2000.

——. Letters Home; Correspondence 1950-1963. 1979.

Roberts, Neil. *Ted Hughes: A Literary Life.* Palgrave Macmillan, 2006.

Stephenson, Anne. *Bitter Fame: A Life of Sylvia Plath.* Viking, 1989.

Tennant, Emma. *Burnt Diaries.* Canongate, 1999.

Weissbort, Daniel. *Letters to Ted.* Anvil, 2002.

Woodruff Library Archives, Emory University, Atlanta, USA.

STUDIES

Bassnett, Susan. *Ted Hughes.* Northcote House, 2009.

Bentley, Paul. *The Poetry of Ted Hughes.* Longman, 1998.

Bishop, Nicholas. *Re-Making Poetry; Ted Hughes and a New Critical Psychology.* Harvester Wheatsheaf, 1991.

Boyanowsky, Ehor. *Savage Gods: in the wild with Ted Hughes.* Vancouver: Douglas & McIntyre, 2009.

Byrne, Sandie. *The Poetry of Ted Hughes: A readers' guide to essential criticism.* Icon Books, 2000.

Faas, Ekbert. *Ted Hughes: the Unaccommodated Universe.* Black Sparrow Press, 1980.

Gammage, Nick, ed. *The Epic Poise: A Celebration of Ted Hughes.* Faber & Faber, 1999.

Gifford, Terry. *Ted Hughes.* Routledge, 2009.

Gifford, Terry, ed. *The Cambridge Companion to Ted Hughes.* Cambridge University Press, 2011.

Gifford, Terry, ed. *New Casebook: Ted Hughes.* Palgrave Macmillan, 2014.

Gifford, Terry, & Neil Roberts. *Ted Hughes: a Critical Study.* 1981.

Groszewski, Gillian. *Hughes and America.* Palgrave Macmillan, 2016.

Hadley, Edward. *The Elegies of Ted Hughes.* Palgrave Macmillan, 2010.

Hirschberg, Stuart. *Myth in the Poetry of Ted Hughes: a Guide to the Poems.* Barnes & Noble, 1981.

Moulin, Joanny. *Ted Hughes, la langue rémunérée.* L'Harmattan, 1999.

———. *Ted Hughes, New Selected Poems.* Didier Érudition, 1999.

Moulin, Joanny, ed. *Lire Ted Hughes.* Éditions du Temps, 1999.

———. ed. *Ted Hughes, Alternative Horizons.* Routledge, 2004.

Rees, Roger. (ed.) *Ted Hughes and the Classics.* Oxford University Press, 2008.

Robinson, Craig. *Ted Hughes as Shepherd of Being.* MacMillan, 1989.

Sagar, Keith. *The Art of Ted Hughes.* Cambridge University Press, 1978.

Sagar, Keith. *Poet and Critic: The Letters of Ted Hughes and Keith Sagar.* The British Library, 2012.

Sagar, Keith, ed. *The Achievement of Ted Hughes.* Manchester University Press, 1983.

———. *The Challenge of Ted Hughes.* Manchester University Press, 1994.

Sagar, Keith. *The laughter of Foxes. A Study of Ted Hughes.* Liverpool University Press, 2000.

Sagar, Keith & Stephen Tabor. *Ted Hughes: A Bibliography 1946-1995*. Mansell, 1998.

Schuchard, Ronald ed. *Fixed Stars Govern a Life*. Academic Exchange, Emory University, 2006.

Scigaj, Leonard. *Ted Hughes*. Twayne, 1992.

———. *The Poetry of Ted Hughes, Form and Imagination*. University of Iowa Press, 1986.

Scigaj, Leonard, ed. *Critical Essays on Ted Hughes*. Macmillan, 1993.

Skea, Ann. *Ted Hughes: The Poetic Quest*. University of New England Press. 1994.

Smith, A. C. H. *Orghast at Persepolis*. Eyre Methuen, 1972.

Usha V.T. *The Real and the Imagined: The Poetic World of Ted Hughes*. Mangal Deep, 1998.

West, Thomas. *Ted Hughes*. Methuen, 1985.

Wormald, Mark, Neil Roberts and Terry Gifford, eds. *Ted Hughes: From Cambridge to Collected*. Palgrave Macmillan, 2013.

Xerri, Daniel. *Ted Hughes's Art of Healing: Into Time and Other People*. Academia Press, 2009.

Printed in Great Britain
by Amazon